UNDERSTANDING CRIMINAL LAW

C.M.V. Clarkson is a Professor of Law
at the University of Leicester

D1585803

UNDERSTANDING LAW
Series Editor: J.A.G. Griffith

Understanding Contract Law
John Adams and Roger Brownsword

Understanding Law
John Adams and Roger Brownsword

Understanding Criminal Law
C.M.V. Clarkson

Understanding Public Law
Gabriele Ganz

Understanding Equity and Trusts
Jeffrey Hackney

Understanding Tort Law
Carol Harlow

Understanding Property Law
W.T. Murphy and Simon Roberts

C.M.V. Clarkson

UNDERSTANDING CRIMINAL LAW

Third Edition

LONDON
SWEET & MAXWELL
2001

Published by Sweet & Maxwell Ltd
of 100 Avenue Road, Swiss Cottage, London NW3 3PF
(*http://www.sweetandmaxwell.co.uk*)

Copyright © C.M.V. Clarkson, 1987, 1995, 2001

C.M.V. Clarkson has asserted the moral right to be
identified as the authors of this work

ISBN 0–421–71750 5

Typeset by LBJ Typesetting Ltd of Kingsclere

Printed and bound by Clays Ltd, St Ives plc

CONTENTS

ACKNOWLEDGEMENTS

The author would like to thank the University of Leicester for granting him study leave which enabled this book to be written. He would also like to thank the Law Faculties of the University of Cape Town and the University of Port Elizabeth for receiving him as a Visitor during this period. But, most of all, his thanks are to his wife, Barbara, to whom this book is dedicated.

EDITOR'S PREFACE

This series is directed primarily at two groups of readers: the general reader who wishes to understand what it is that lawyers are talking about, and the law student who is told that he is about to study a subject called tort, or contract, or criminal law, or property, or trusts and equity, or public law. These titles convey little that is clear about the nature of their subjects, and the extra-legal meanings that attach to some—such as contract or criminal law—may be misleading.

Each book in this series seeks to explain what the subject is about, what are the special kinds of problems it seeks to solve, and why it has developed as it has. The books are not all meant to be summaries of their subjects, each of which covers a complicated area of human activity.

The law student will, in his or her course, be expected to read much longer and fuller texts on the subjects, to attend lectures and tutorials. The books in this series seek to provide introductions to be read early in the course or before it begins. It is hoped that these introductions will enable the student to grasp the essentials before coming to grips with the details. So also, the general reader who wishes to pursue the subject more fully will have to read the more detailed texts.

Although these books are intended to be introductions, they are not meant to be simplifications. These are not "easy" books, however clearly they are written. Understanding law is not an easy matter. This is not, as is often said, primarily because lawyers use words with special meanings. It is because law has to deal with the complications, both personal and commercial, that people become involved in. We are all busy as ants, more purposeful and sometimes less efficient. Law tries to regularise these complications and so cannot avoid being itself complicated.

The intention of the series will be achieved if the books give the reader a broad perspective and a general understanding of the legal principles on which these different subjects are based.

John Griffith

1

INTRODUCTION

This book is primarily concerned with the substantive criminal law. Its main focus is on the general principles of criminal liability and the structure of the various criminal offences. Such a study can be meaningful only if one knows what is the purpose of the criminal law and if one examines its rules in that context. This functional approach makes it possible to understand the rationale of the various offences and their relationship to each other; one is in a position to evaluate and criticise the substantive law and, if necessary, to suggest reforms.

Accordingly, this book starts with an introduction to the nature and development of the criminal law, including a brief mention of the purposes of punishment. The second and major section examines the main elements in the construction of criminal liability and the leading criminal offences. The emphasis throughout this section is on the purpose of the criminal law and the rationale of its various rules so that the relationship between the various concepts and offences can understood. Finally, armed with this understanding of the substantive law, the final section is devoted to a more detailed exploration of the theme running through the whole book, namely, the function of the criminal law.

1. THE NATURE AND DEVELOPMENT OF CRIMINAL LAW

The criminal law is a body of rules listing the various criminal offences, identifying the ingredients thereof (including common elements such as general defences) and specifying the potential punishment. For instance, the criminal law tells us that, amongst others, rape and theft are crimes; it tells us exactly what the elements of these offences are and what potential punishments they carry.

The list of crimes (in the sense of wrongdoing punished by the community) in early law was extremely short, and included as major offences witchcraft and incest (Diamond, 1950). For offences such as homicide, wounding, rape, theft, etc., the only remedy in primitive law was self-help. As society developed, self-help was replaced by a system of enforced payment of compensation. The harmed victim, or his or her kin, was entitled to compensation from the wrongdoer. Such offences were thus not perceived as public wrongs affecting society as a whole. Only the victim or his or her kindred had sustained a loss and was entitled to have this loss made good.

The community at large did however have some interest in such forms of wrongdoing. Even in Anglo-Saxon times severe punishments were meted out against offenders who were unwilling or unable to compensate. By the end of the twelfth century it had been realised that such wrongdoing had implications beyond the simple harm sustained by the victim. First the wider community and then the king began to assume responsibility for criminal justice. Those who had broken the "king's peace" were brought before the king's judges who were itinerant justices. The charges were laid on behalf of the community by a "grand jury". Punishments were imposed that did not involve compensation to the victim. In short, the criminal law began to assume one of its most distinctive features, namely, that it is concerned with public wrongs.

A crime is a public wrong in the sense that the public at large is affected by it. The community is threatened or offended by the crime. For example, the crime of rape does more than harm the victim. Society is threatened and made less secure by the rape: the rapist could strike again. Accordingly, society is not prepared to leave the matter to the victim to seek compensation. Rape is made a crime and society attempts to apprehend the rapist and secure his punishment. The extent to which this model of crime as an "offence against society" is still true today is explored in the final section of this book.

Two related features dominated the early criminal law. First, most offences were extremely broad, covering a wide range of wrongdoing. For instance, there was only one homicide offence, the present distinction between murder and manslaughter coming into existence only in the fifteenth century. Secondly, until the end of the twelfth century it appears that the criminal law was primarily interested in the amount of harm done. People were punished not because they were blameworthy but because they were instruments of harm. Such thinking led some primitive laws to punish all instruments of harm. Thus animals could be executed and axes burned. They, and the person who used them, were tainted with evil. Such thinking is still with us today to a certain extent. For instance, if a carving knife were used in a murder we would all regard as distinctly odd (to put it mildly) the person who knowingly used that knife to carve a Sunday roast.

Naturally, this emphasis on the results of action as opposed to the culpability with which the offender acted was an important reason for the breadth of criminal offences. If a victim was killed, that death alone was critical in defining the offence and so it was not surprising that there was only one broad homicide offence. (Even accidental or justifiable killings such as those in self-defence were embraced within the offence; in such cases, however, a pardon would often be granted by the king, exercising his royal prerogative of mercy.) The present distinction between murder and manslaughter is based very largely on the different degrees of blame attached to the defendant and could hardly have existed in a system of law that did not draw such distinctions.

Towards the end of the twelfth century an important shift in emphasis began to occur and people came to be regarded as moral agents who could be held responsible for their actions. This changed attitude was probably due to a combination of two strong forces: the growing importance of canon law with its emphasis on moral guilt, and the revived Roman law with its stress on the psychical element of blame in criminal liability (Sayre, 1932). It became important to judge the quality of people's actions in the sense of exploring their motivations and the circumstances surrounding their actions. People, being responsible moral agents, could be judged in terms of praise and blame in a way in which one would not judge an animal or an axe. A proper judgment of their moral guilt necessitated an exploration of their state of mind. Emphasis began to be placed on the mental element in crime. The concept of *mens rea* (guilty mind) began to develop in English criminal law. (For a fuller discussion of the concepts of responsibility and *mens rea*, see pp. 54–55.)

Of course, once the concept of blame or culpability was established in the law it was inevitable that sooner or later the broad offences would be subdivided so as to reflect the different degrees of blame involved. So when, at the end of the fifteenth century, homicide was divided into two main categories, the division soon came to be based primarily on the presence or absence of "malice aforethought"—an indicator of a special degree of blame. Such thinking has continued to inform the structure of the main criminal offences up to the present time. Thus the paradigmatic crime is regarded as one where the offender has intentionally caused the prohibited harm, for example, intentionally causing death is murder. However, while this model, involving the conjunction of the twin concepts of blame and harm, is still central to the construction of the core crimes of violence and dishonesty, the profile of the criminal law has changed radically over the past century, and particularly over the past few decades. One of the most striking changes is the marked proliferation of criminal offences into territories not traditionally associated with crime such as consumer protection (Consumer Protection Act 1987), nursing (Nurses, Midwives and Health Visitors Act 1997) and copyright (Copyright, Designs and Patents Act 1988). Even in the areas more traditionally associated with crime (injury to persons, public order, etc.), the political mood in the United Kingdom has changed sharply with an ever-increasing belief that the panacea for all social evils is the creation of criminal offences. The wisdom of this approach will be challenged later (pp. 244–256) but, for now, what is important to note is that with this vast increase in the number of criminal offences, there have been several (mostly) related trends that have pushed a majority of criminal offences away from the classic model.

First, there has been a sharp rise in the number of strict liability offences: crimes that require no blame or culpability on the part of the offender. There are more than 8,000 offences in English law (Ashworth, 2000a) with more than half of them being strict liability offences (see p. 135). Linked to this is the increasing trend towards the creation of regulatory crime. Many fields of activity are now regulated by statutory schemes and enforced by regulatory authorities such as the Environment Agency, the Health and Safety Executive and H.M. Customs and Excise. While these schemes create vast numbers of criminal offences (mostly involving strict liability), the regulatory authorities enforcing the scheme do not regard the prosecution of offenders as their main task, preferring to adopt a compliance strategy of advice and assistance to persons and companies involved in those activities. Thirdly, there has been an increasing trend away from the paradigmatic crime towards the criminalisation of specific dangerous activities which involve risks of harm even though no actual harm has been caused. Examples of such risk-creation offences include those relating to possession of firearms, careless and dangerous driving and failing to ensure the health, safety and welfare at work of employees. Finally, there has been an increasing recognition that the structure of criminal offences can sometimes be dictated by the context in which the crime is committed. For instance, causing death by dangerous driving is a quite separate offence (with separate penalties) from causing death by other dangerous activities.

This changed profile of the criminal law raises many challenging questions. Are strict liability offences justifiable? Is it acceptable that a shoplifter be prosecuted by the police while a company whose actions might have caused extensive harm is dealt with by advice or administrative sanctions? To what extent is it justifiable to criminalise dangerous activities where no harm has resulted? Most of these and other questions relate to whether (or, to what extent) it is justifiable to depart from the paradigmatic crime, and what the consequences of such a departure should be. Accordingly, it is crucial to assess what weight should be attached today to the twin peaks of classic crime: blame and harm—and, of course, to examine their precise meanings. Such an assessment, along with a consideration of the implications of a departure from the paradigm, is one of the main tasks of this book.

Another important challenge facing the criminal law has come with the enactment of the Human Rights Act 1998 incorporating the European Convention of Human Rights into English law. This Convention guarantees various rights which could force a reshaping of some of the substantive rules of the criminal law. For example, Article 2 (right to life) has a strong potential for impacting on the rules of killing in self-defence. Article 8 (right to respect for private life) has clear implications for certain sexual offences, particularly those committed in private. Section 6 of the Human Rights Act 1998 mandates all public authorities (which includes courts) to comply with the Convention so far as it is possible to do so and section 4 gives appellate courts a power to make declarations of incompatibility. The importance of these developments cannot be over-emphasised and their impact on English criminal law will be considered, where appropriate, throughout the book.

An important, albeit self-evident, feature of the criminal law is that the commission of a crime can be followed by criminal proceedings. Criminal offences were originally divided into felonies and misdemeanours, which was broadly a distinction between serious and lesser offences. This distinction was abolished by section 1 of the Criminal Law Act 1967. Today two sets of distinctions are drawn. First, there is a distinction between serious arrestable, arrestable and non-arrestable offences (Police and Criminal Evidence Act 1984). This distinction refers to the powers given to the police to arrest offenders without a warrant and to powers to detain them for an extended period of time. Secondly, crimes are also classified as being summary offences, indictable offences or offences triable either way (Criminal Law Act 1977). A summary offence is one that must be tried by a magistrates' court; there is no jury in such courts. An indictable offence is one that must be tried in the Crown Court where the trial is by jury. An offence triable either way is one that allows magistrates to try the case if they feel that is appropriate and if the defendant agrees.

Apart from the different courts involved, criminal proceedings differ in several respects from civil proceedings. While any citizen can bring a criminal prosecution, it is normally handled by the police and the Crown Prosecution Service, although it should be emphasised that increasingly prosecutions are brought by government departments such as the Inland Revenue or by inspectorates such as the Health and Safety Executive. Generally there is no time limit for criminal proceedings. And finally, the procedure, rules of evidence and rights of appeal are very different from civil proceedings.

2. PUNISHMENT AND SENTENCING

The real distinctive hallmark of the criminal law, however, is that convicted offenders become liable to censure and stigmatic punishment. Damages in civil actions, particularly exemplary damages, can seem similar to punishment. Their purpose, however, is to compensate a person for loss. The purposes of criminal punishment, on the other hand, are more varied and controversial. While this issue will be canvassed at greater length in the final section, it is important at this stage to list the four most commonly stated purposes of punishment. These are retribution, deterrence, incapacitation and rehabilitation. Whichever of these aims is invoked, the purpose is a public one (as opposed to a private, compensatory purpose). It is the State that is exacting retribution or incapacitating a dangerous criminal and so on. In doing this the State is publicly condemning and censuring the defendant's actions. This results in a special stigma not attaching to defendants in civil actions—hence the phrase "stigmatic punishment".

In the early development of the criminal law punishments were crude, Draconian and indiscriminate (in the sense that a wide variety of crimes all carried the same potential penalty). Punishments varied greatly over the centuries: for instance, before 1285 the punishment for rape was castration and blinding. However, generalising somewhat, the punishment for misdemeanours was in the discretion of the itinerant justices, fines and whippings being the most common punishment; felonies were generally punishable by death so that a wide array of offences such as murder, rape and theft all carried the same penalty.

The position today is completely reversed, in that a wide variety of punishments are now available. These range from imprisonment, various community sentences, fines, compensation orders right down to conditional and absolute discharges. Broadly speaking, the sentence imposed should be proportionate to the seriousness of the crime. For the most trivial offences a discharge can be ordered. For slightly more serious offences, particularly strict liability, road traffic and lesser property offences, the fine is the most extensively used sentence being imposed in 84 per cent of summary non-motoring cases and in 35 per cent of indictable cases (Barclay, 1993). For more serious offences a community order becomes appropriate and for the most serious crimes, a sentence of imprisonment can be imposed. Some of the other orders, particularly compensation orders which are extensively used, are usually imposed in addition to another order.

Having selected the type of sentence, the sentencing judge also has considerable discretion as to the length or severity of that sentence. Statutes specifying terms of imprisonment are laying down maxima. Theft, for instance, is punishable by a maximum of seven years' imprisonment. The judge can impose any period of imprisonment up to this maximum (or, of course, any other type of sentence). It ought to be borne in mind that all offenders serving sentences of imprisonment will obtain an early release (formerly called parole) from prison after serving half of their sentence or, if sentenced to more than four years' imprisonment, after serving anything between half and two-thirds of their sentence at the discretion of the Parole Board.

It is thus clear that tremendous discretionary power is vested in the sentencing judge. Which sentence is chosen, and its length, depends very much on what the sentencer sees the purposes of punishment and the criminal law to be. It is to this issue that the final section of this book will be primarily devoted.

Finally, it is crucial to stress (and it is very much a theme of this book) that not only judges are influenced by the purposes of punishment and the criminal law when sentencing convicted defendants. These concerns have also been of prime importance in the shaping of the substantive criminal law. The rules of the criminal law (the "substantive" law) and the punishment of offenders are two sides of the same coin. A whole range of substantive issues, for example whether offences of strict liability are justifiable or how the boundaries of the law of attempt or conspiracy should be drawn, are, in reality, issues about whether punishment is justified in such cases and would help achieve the purposes of the criminal law. It is to these substantive issues that we now turn.

2

CONSTRUCTING CRIMINAL LIABILITY

1. INTRODUCTION

(i) Values

The criminal law sets standards that largely reflect community values of what is wrong and harmful. For instance, few would disagree that murder, rape and theft are such wrongs. By setting these standards and punishing those who do not conform to them, lawmakers hope to strengthen respect for the standards and to encourage people to comply with them.

In laying down such standards the criminal law has to address the issue of what community values are so important that they need to be enforced by the criminal law (as opposed to other mechanisms of social control, such as education, morality or religion). For example, is sniffing glue or selling pornographic books the sort of activity we want to punish using the criminal law, or should we simply try to educate people into not participating in such activities? Discussion of this point will be reserved until later when the broader issue of the function of the criminal law is examined.

(ii) Communicating the values: fair labelling

It is not enough simply to lay down these standards. They must be communicated to the public and potential wrongdoers. This communication must be in a language and in a form that is accessible and comprehensible to such persons. This raises the issue of how precise this communication must be. One can imagine two possible extremes. On the one hand, Robinson (1997) has proposed that the criminal law be subdivided into two codes. The Code of Conduct, addressed to the general public, would declare in broad terms that certain conduct was prohibited: for example, "You may not cause bodily injury or death to another person". This, he claims, is all that the public and potential wrongdoers need to know in order to adjust their conduct to avoid the prohibition. The Code of Adjudication, addressed to the personnel of the criminal justice system, would contain the technical rules governing the precise boundaries of criminal liability (for instance, whether a defendant was at fault in causing bodily injury or has a defence such as duress). This latter code would also grade the seriousness of the offence and lay down the appropriate level of punishment.

Such an "idiot-proof" Code of Conduct provides no guidance to the general public and prospective wrongdoers of the relative seriousness of differing wrongs. It fails to mark distinctions fundamental to our morality such as that it is worse to kill someone deliberately than to injure them accidentally. Such basic moral messages should not be hidden away in the Code of Adjudication for the eyes and ears of experts only. The law, in addressing the public, should convey these distinctions by labelling and grading offences appropriately.

The principle of fair labelling is widely accepted as one of the guiding principles that should underpin the criminal law. Criminal offences should be categorised and labelled to capture the essence of the law-breaking involved and to convey the level of rejection of the activity involved. For example, the wrongdoing in robbery (involving an attack upon a person which can induce fear, risk of injury, further violence and so on) is qualitatively different from that in theft. The public intuitively understands that these are very different forms of lawbreaking, which should be marked by the existence of separate offences, and, to emphasise that it is a more serious offence, robbery carries a much higher maximum penalty.

While the prime function of fair labelling is communication with the general public, it is equally important that wrongdoers understand the allegations against them so as to be in a position to respond to them (Duff, 1998). To achieve this the law must label and reflect wrongdoing in legal categories which resonate with ordinary understandings.

It follows that offences should be defined with sufficient specificity to capture what is morally significant about them. But how much specificity is required in order to mark moral distinctions? One could go to the opposite extreme from Robinson's Code of Conduct and label and grade all offences with such precision that all relevant moral characteristics are marked. In the United States there has been some movement in this direction with many offences being divided into different degrees. The problem with this approach is that can lead to over-specificity and a bewildering array of offences. For instance, the Twentieth Century Task Fund Force (1976) examined the crime of armed robbery and concluded that it would be necessary to divide the crime into six degrees, each with its own penalty. Such an approach goes too far. The criminal law is a communicative enterprise and offences should be labelled and structured in a manner that assists, rather than obscures, communication. Having too many offences differing only in detail will not facilitate this communicative endeavour.

Accordingly, what is needed is a compromise between the above two extremes avoiding the pitfalls of both over-generalisation and over-specificity. In short, something of a broad-brush approach is called for where significant differences between wrongdoings can be marked. Less significant differences can be dealt with at the sentencing stage. This raises the central issue: what counts as a sufficiently significant difference as to warrant separate crime status?

Traditionally, offences have been grouped into broad categories or "families of offences" (Gardner, 1998). The main criterion used in this broad categorisation is the harm caused. So we have homicide offences, non-fatal offences against the person, sexual offences, property offences, offences against the administration of justice, public order offences and so on. Each family of offences comprises various specific offences, the criteria for the subdivision being threefold: harm, culpability and wrongdoing. For instance, with homicide offences the harm (death) is always present but the culpability of the defendant (for example, whether he or she killed intentionally or recklessly) is thought to be sufficiently significant to warrant distinguishing intentional killings (murder) from reckless killings (manslaughter). With the non-fatal offences against the person both the harm caused and the culpability of the defendant can differ: one can cause serious bodily harm or actual bodily harm and it can have been caused intentionally or recklessly. With such offences fair labelling must do more than capture the essence of the lawbreaking; it must communicate the level of seriousness of the activity concerned. So, intentionally causing grievous bodily harm is a more serious offence, carrying a higher maximum penalty, than causing actual bodily harm.

Within other families of offences, it is the essence of the wrong involved that justifies separate labelling of offences. "Wrongdoing" is a loose term that, amongst other things, can signify the way in which the harm is brought about (see p. 184). For instance with property offences, property deprivation could have occurred by theft, deception, blackmail or through damage. In terms of accurate labelling what matters here is not the extent of the harm. What seems to have a greater resonance with our common understandings is the different form of wrong involved in these examples of property deprivation. Very often crimes are best described with reference to their paradigms: the clearest and most obvious example of the crime. On this basis the paradigmatic theft differs so materially from the paradigmatic deception (see p. 239) as to warrant the existence of two separate offences. It should be stressed that the notion of a "wrong" can encompass factors other than the way in which the crime was brought about. The essence of the "wrong" can sometimes be determined by the context in which the offence is committed. For instance, it can be argued (p. 211) that the context in which certain killings occur (such as, driving a vehicle on a road dangerously) might be sufficiently significant to warrant separate crime status. (This argument can be taken further to suggest that the context can be so significant as bring the crime within a separate family of offences. So, causing death by dangerous driving could be regarded as belonging to the family of driving offences rather than the family of homicide offences.)

Where the factors justifying separate labelling are the harm and culpability of the defendant, an important function of fair labelling is communicating the degree of rejection of the activity involved and these offences should be ranked in a hierarchy of seriousness. However, in other families of offences where crimes are differentiated by the distinct wrongdoings involved (and not by the level of harm or culpability), offences need not be structured in a hierarchy of seriousness. Theft and obtaining property by deception are markedly different wrongs but, as the harm and culpability can be similar, the one is not necessarily worse than the other. The function of fair labelling in this instance is simply to distinguish the two offences clearly.

2. GENERAL PRINCIPLES OF CRIMINAL LIABILITY

Having decided on the degree of offence-specificity that is appropriate, the law must define each proscribed activity (crime) with some precision. It must be clear and specific about the standards it is laying down. The European Convention on Human Rights has been interpreted to require that offences must be defined to sufficient precision to meet a standard of certainty. To say that murder is, and ought to be, a crime, and that it should be quite distinct from manslaughter, begs the question: in what circumstances is killing to be treated as murder? The surgeon who performs a dangerous operation on a patient might well "kill" that patient (that is, the operation could be the cause of the patient's death), but if the operation were performed under proper conditions by a surgeon trying to save the life of the patient, one would clearly not wish to punish the surgeon. Or, putting it another way, the law must define murder (and other homicide offences) in such a manner as to exclude the surgeon from its ambit. Having decided that there should be a crime of rape distinct from that of indecent assault, it is necessary to define the precise circumstances in which a rape is committed. Should this crime cover the man who genuinely believes the woman is consenting to sexual inter-course when in fact she is not? Should it encompass the man who has intercourse with a woman who is so drunk she is unaware of what is happening? And should it be rape to persist in intercourse with a woman who initially consented to penetra-tion but, mid-way through the intercourse, changes her mind?

The problem is one of defining the circumstances in which a particular crime is committed. Every crime raises its own particular problems of definition. For instance, issues relating to vaginal or anal penetration are unique to the crime of rape. Nevertheless, most crimes do raise broadly the same general issues. Should it be criminal to cause a harm if one genuinely thinks one is not causing any harm (say, because one has made a mistake and thinks one's "victim" is consenting)? Should it be criminal to try to commit a crime, or simply to plan a crime, when no ultimate harm occurs? Should it be criminal to cause a harm deliberately if one thinks it is necessary to do so to save one's own life? In what circumstances can someone be said to have "caused" a harm? The answers to these and other similar fundamental questions are often called "the general principles of criminal liability"—the basic rules for constructing criminal liability.

Traditionally, the basic rule has been expressed in the Latin maxim: *actus non facit reum nisi mens sit rea* ("an act does not make a man guilty of a crime unless his mind is also guilty"— per Lord Hailsham in *Haughton v. Smith*, 1975). So, before criminal liability can be imposed, the law generally insists upon proof of two elements:

1. *Actus reus*: certain conduct by the defendant. This conduct can be simply forbidden in itself (for example, possessing a firearm contrary to section 1 of the Firearms Act 1968). Such crimes are known as "conduct crimes". But more usually, particularly with serious crimes, the conduct must cause a forbidden consequence (for example, pulling the trigger of a loaded gun and thereby killing the victim). Such crimes are known as "result crimes".
2. *Mens rea*: a blameworthy or culpable state of mind (for example, intending to kill the victim when discharging the gun).

These two elements must coincide in time. The defendant must have the necessary *mens rea* at the moment he or she commits the *actus reus*; it is not sufficient that he or she had *mens rea* before or after the *actus reus*. So if a defendant accidentally discharges a gun, killing the victim, there is no *mens rea* at the time of the *actus reus*. If that defendant, not realising that he has already killed the victim, then decides to murder her and shoots the corpse, there can be no liability for murder. The *mens rea* (intending to kill) did not coincide with the *actus reus* (killing the victim). The law is, however, prepared to adopt a flexible approach in this regard by holding that in certain cases there can be a "continuing *actus reus*" and all that is necessary is that *mens rea* exist at any stage during this extended *actus reus*. In *Meli v. Thabo* (1954) the defendants, in accordance with a prearranged plan, struck their victim over the head in a hut. Believing him to be dead, they took his body to a cliff and rolled it over. In fact the man was not dead, but died of exposure while unconscious at the foot of the cliff. It was argued that the *actus reus* (the act that caused death) was rolling the body over the cliff and at that time the defendants had no *mens rea* as they thought they were disposing of a corpse. This argument was rejected, on the ground that what had occurred was "one series of acts" and that as the defendants had *mens rea* at some stage during this series of acts (when they struck their victim in the hut) the necessary coincidence of *actus reus* and *mens rea* had been established; the defendants were guilty of murder.

Another way of explaining this decision is that the original attack (which was accompanied by *mens rea*) was still an operating cause of death (albeit not the only cause) and, because the action of rolling the body over the cliff was part of the same broad criminal venture, it did not break the causal chain. In *Le Brun* (1992) a man hit his wife on the chin knocking her unconscious. While trying to drag her body away he dropped her causing her death. It was indicated that the purpose behind his dragging her away was critical in determining whether the chain of causation was broken. If his actions had been designed to help her, the changed motivation would constitute a completely different type of action and so causation would not be established. But if he were trying to dispose of what he believed was her corpse, such action within the same broad criminal enterprise would not break the chain of causation.

It is commonly stated that the *mens rea* must correspond with the *actus reus*. There must be *mens rea* (intention or recklessness) in relation to each element of the *actus reus*. This is known as the *principle of correspondence*. So, if the *actus reus* of the offence is "causing injury", the *mens rea* should be intention or recklessness as to "causing injury". The idea is that a person is only culpable in respect of harms he or she chose to bring about or risk.

English law is not totally committed to this principle of correspondence and in some instances holds persons liable for offences even when they do not have full *mens rea* in relation to the *actus reus*. These are known as crimes involving *constructive liability*. For example, part of the *actus reus* of section 20 of the Offences against the Person Act 1861 is "inflicting grievous bodily harm". The principle of correspondence would require the *mens rea* of this offence to be "intentionally or recklessly inflicting grievous bodily harm". Instead, it is a crime of constructive liability as the only *mens rea* required is intention or recklessness as to the infliction of some bodily harm.

Proponents of the principle of correspondence reject constructive liability on the basis that it turns the criminal law into a lottery with the level of liability being determined by luck. For example, the defendant strikes his victim only foreseeing some harm. The victim falls backwards, hits her head on a sharp object and suffers grievous bodily harm. The defendant should not be responsible for such fortuitous consequences lying outside his control. There is, however, another emerging school of thought that rejects strict adherence to the principle of correspondence and supports some instances of constructive crime (Horder, 1995, Clarkson, 2000). The gist of this view is that a defendant, by embarking on criminal activity (say, an attack), has crossed a moral threshold; he is engaging in a morally different course of action compared to those who act lawfully. Any results that flow from this criminal activity are not "pure luck". By choosing to attack the victim the defendant made his own luck and is responsible for any result flowing from that attack. The arguments for and against constructive liability will be considered later (pp. 162, 208).

These two general prerequisites, *actus reus* and *mens rea*, are not required for every crime. In particular, many crimes can be committed without *mens rea*, namely the so-called crimes of strict liability. Further, and this point must be stressed at this stage, these two prerequisites vary greatly from crime to crime in the precise form they take. For the crime of attempt, for instance, it must be proved that the defendant acted with intent to commit the full offence whereas for other crimes, such as criminal damage, it is sufficient to establish that she acted recklessly. In other words, both the *actus reus* and *mens rea* requirements have a chameleon-like quality in that they change their colours from crime to crime. Particularised fine-tuning with regard to their precise meanings is necessary in relation to each particular offence.

These Latin terms, *actus reus* and *mens rea*, have been condemned by Lord Diplock in the House of Lords in *Miller* (1983) as being unhelpful and confusing terminology. Indeed, they are more than this: they are positively misleading for two main reasons. First, the Latin maxim suggests that if the forbidden harm is produced by a defendant acting with a specified state of mind, criminal liability will inevitably ensue. This is clearly not always the case. For instance, a defendant might intentionally kill another but escape all criminal liability because he has a defence, such as self-defence. Or, despite having the requisite *mens rea* for murder, he might instead be convicted of the lesser offence of manslaughter because he has a partial defence, such as provocation. Such defences cannot naturally be accommodated within the language of *actus reus* and *mens rea*. Consequently, divergent interpretations have emerged as to how the constituent elements of a crime should be defined employing the orthodox terminology. One view is that there are, in reality, three ingredients of a crime: *actus reus, mens rea* and the absence of a valid defence. On the other hand, it can be argued that there are only the two basic components of a crime, *actus reus* and *mens rea*, but that the existence of a defence negates either the *actus reus* or the *mens rea*. However, the problem with all these interpretations is that they tend to obscure the real issue which is simply one of determining who *ought* to be brought within the ambit of the criminal law, and at what level (for example, murder or manslaughter). While it is often useful to analyse crimes in terms of *actus reus* and *mens rea*, the true construction of criminal liability cannot be made dependant on any artificial and rigid classification.

The second reason for doubting the traditional analysis is that the terms *actus reus* and *mens rea* have, over the years, so changed their meaning that these original descriptions do not accurately reflect the reality of the law. For instance, the orthodox view is that *mens rea* denotes a mental element. We shall see that English law sometimes deems a defendant to have *mens rea* if she fails to consider an obvious and serious risk. It is somewhat artificial (although possible) to describe the absence of a state of mind (failing to consider the risk) as a state of mind.

An alternative way of constructing criminal liability involves escaping from the technical constraints of the *actus reus* and *mens rea* concepts and viewing the criminal law as generally seeking to punish those who are *blameworthy in causing or risking harm*. The level of punishment meted out will reflect the degree of blame or fault to be attached to their conduct as well as reflecting the extent of the harm they have caused. In many cases, of course, the reason why we blame someone for their conduct is because of their state of mind at the time of that conduct. Thus we blame a defendant who deliberately strikes his victim and knocks her down a flight of stairs. If that defendant had instead tripped on a badly fitted carpet on the stairs and accidentally fallen into the victim knocking her down the same stairs, our moral assessment of the event would be quite different. We would not blame this latter defendant, and, accordingly, would generally not seek to punish him. So, in many cases, the presence or absence of a particular state of mind (*mens rea*) in the defendant can indicate whether or not we blame him for his actions. But traditional *mens rea* is no more than an *indicator* of blame. We can sometimes blame a person who does not act with *mens rea*. If our hypothetical defendant had consumed an excessive amount of alcohol or drugs and, while staggering drunkenly down the stairs, had unwittingly knocked the victim down, our response might be: he ought to have noticed the victim; he ought not to have rendered himself so intoxicated that he became unaware of his surroundings and his actions; we blame him for getting so intoxicated that he caused harm to the victim.

Further, we do not blame all persons who act with *mens rea*. A defendant might intentionally cause a harm yet not be blamed because he had a valid justification or an excuse for his actions. For instance, if the "victim" on the stairs had been about to stab our defendant, we would regard the latter as being free from blame when he took defensive action and deliberately pushed the "victim" down the stairs.

A good illustration of these two different approaches to the construction of criminal liability can be seen in the case of *Kingston* (1995). In this case the defendant's drink was laced with drugs. In a state of intoxication he indecently assaulted a fifteen-year-old boy. He did know what he was doing (*i.e.* he did have *mens rea*) but claimed the only reason he did it was because of the drugs. In a controversial decision the Court of Appeal (Criminal Division) in *Kingston* (1993) held that there would be no liability in such a case. If surreptitiously administered drink or drugs cause a person to "form an intent which he would not otherwise have formed" the defendant should escape liability. Many persons might have secret urges to do criminal acts but they cannot be blamed if they exercise control and restraint and refrain from the activity. On the other hand, if they voluntarily drink or take drugs and then give in to their urges they can be blamed for "dropping their guard". But if the only reason their inhibitions are removed is because someone else has secretly laced their drinks, they can be regarded as blameless and should be free from criminal liability and punishment. The Court of Appeal approach demonstrates dramatically that criminal liability ought not to be based simply on a conjunction of *actus reus* and *mens rea* but rather on there being harmful conduct committed by a *blameworthy* actor. Kingston intentionally sexually abused the boy, but was blameless and so should escape criminal liability.

The House of Lords in *Kingston* (1995), however, rejected this reasoning and adopted the more formal and traditional approach that because Kingston committed the *actus reus* with the necessary *mens rea* he should be liable. Their Lordships expressly rejected the "argument which treats the absence of moral fault on the part of the appellant as sufficient in itself to negative the necessary mental element of the offence". This House of Lords approach is representative of most of English criminal law. While the criminal law generally seeks to punish

the blameworthy, the element of moral blame is usually incorporated into the definition of the *actus reus* and *mens rea* of the
crime; there is no specific extra requirement that blameworthiness be established. One (very important) exception to this is the
crime of theft and other property offences that require proof of
dishonesty. As we shall see (pp. 226–229) establishment of
dishonesty involves the fact-finder (magistrate or jury) making a
moral evaluation of the defendant's conduct to establish
whether it is blameworthy.

As we shall see (p. 228), many condemn this exceptional
approach and the Law Commission (1999) is highly critical of
this additional requirement of blameworthiness in the form of
dishonesty having to be established. On the other hand, it is
very difficult to justify the imposition of criminal liability and
punishment in cases where "the intent itself arose out of
circumstances for which he bears no blame" (*Kingston* (CA)
1993). The criminal law is an institution of blame and censure
and this blatant severance between blameworthiness and criminal liability seems inappropriate. However, the problem is that
the concept of "blameworthiness" is too vague and nebulous to
be an effective tool in the construction of criminal liability in real
cases. Fearful of commencing on the slippery slope of moral
evaluations leading to uncertain results, other recent English
decisions have also distanced themselves from the view that
mens rea (in the sense of mental awareness) is but an indicator of
blameworthiness: "*mens rea* does not however involve
blameworthiness" (*Dodman*, 1998). Such an approach is unfortunate. To avoid the danger of vagueness and uncertainty, one of
two approaches could be adopted. First, blame could be defined
as including *mens rea*, lack of defence, becomingly dangerously
intoxicated and so on. For instance, in South Africa (whose
system of criminal law is based on Roman Law and more akin
to the Continental European legal systems which tend to favour
this "normative theory of culpability") there has been a recognition of the dangers of culpability being solely in "the judge's
head" and not in "the head of the accused" (Snyman, 1995).
Accordingly, in order to control the bases upon which evaluations of culpability are made, it has been suggested that blame
be based on four presuppositions: (i) awareness or capacity for
awareness of unlawfulness; (ii) capacity to act in accordance
with the law; (iii) decision to act (*mens rea*); (iv) in circumstances
under which the law could have expected him to act differently
(Snyman, 1995). Alternatively, if such proposals were perceived

as too radical, one could stick with the traditional terminology of a crime involving an *actus reus* and a *mens rea* and a lack of defence but insist that the interpretation of these concepts be shaped by the criterion of blame. On this latter basis, the defendant in *Kingston* (1995) did have *mens rea* but his lack of blameworthiness should have permitted the development of a defence (irresistible impulse) to persons in his situation.

The approach adopted in this book is that, especially with the House of Lords' rejection of any "normative theory of culpability", a familiarity with the orthodox terminology is essential and is therefore preserved in much of this book. Nevertheless, in order to gain a true understanding of the criminal law and how its rules came to be shaped, an attempt will be made to explain the construction of criminal liability in terms that (mostly) reflect the reality of the thinking underlying the development of the law—at least for the paradigmatic crimes presently under discussion. Viewed in this way the criminal law generally constructs its rules so as to punish those people who are blameworthy or culpable in committing their wrongful acts or in causing or risking harmful, prohibited results.

We are now in a position to examine the various elements involved in the construction of criminal liability and to expose the precise meaning of these concepts and to explain when and how they apply in the criminal law.

3. CONDUCT

(i) Necessity for conduct

Criminal liability cannot be imposed on a defendant unless she has "acted"—unless there is conduct. English law does not punish for "thought-crime". No matter how evil a person's thoughts and intentions, the law insists on a physical manifestation of such intention before it will intervene. There are several reasons for this insistence on conduct as a prerequisite of criminal liability. In evidential terms, it would be extremely difficult to base criminal liability purely on a defendant's evil intentions. Without conduct as corroboration, how could one ever prove that such evil thoughts existed? How could one differentiate between daydreams and fixed intentions? Also, evil intentions, by themselves, are not regarded as sufficiently dangerous to justify the intervention of the law; the mental decision might be too irresolute ever to be translated into action. Mere mental decisions to commit crimes pose no threat in themselves to society; they do not infringe other people's rights to security and so no identifiable harm exists for the criminal law to punish. And finally, it would be an intolerable invasion of liberty and privacy for the law to try to punish mere thoughts. Only when those thoughts are converted into action is the law justified in intervening. The requirement of conduct helps preserve the liberty of the individual by limiting criminal liability as much as possible.

(ii) Extent of conduct

The exact type and amount of conduct required varies from crime to crime. For most crimes there must be sufficient conduct to constitute the prohibited wrong (for example, actually possessing controlled drugs which is an offence contrary to the Misuse of Drugs Act 1971), or sufficient conduct to cause the harmful result (for example, for murder the defendant must do those acts necessary to be a cause of the death of the victim).

However, for certain other crimes, the law is satisfied by a lesser physical manifestation of the defendant's criminal intention. Let us consider how much conduct is required in four areas of criminal law: attempt; conspiracy; incitement; and aiding, abetting, counselling and procuring.

(a) Attempt

With an attempt to commit a crime, the defendant has not produced the forbidden harm, but must have tried to do so. For instance, with attempted murder the victim has not been killed but the defendant must have made an effort to murder her. It is not enough that he has decided to commit the crime. The law, as explained, insists upon conduct—a physical manifestation of a decision. The problem is to establish how much conduct is necessary before it can be said there has been an attempt to commit the crime.

Take, for instance, the case of *Campbell* (1991) where the defendant, who planned to rob a sub-post office, drove his motorbike to near the post office, parked it and approached the post office, wearing a crash helmet as disguise. He was carrying (hidden) an imitation gun and a threatening note that he planned to pass to the cashier in the post office. He was about one yard from the post office door when the police, who had been tipped off, arrested him. On appeal against a conviction for attempted robbery it was held that he had not done enough towards the crime. Section 1(1) of the Criminal Attempts Act 1981 provides that in order to be guilty of an attempt to commit an offence a person must have done "an act which is more than merely preparatory to the commission of the offence". All the acts done by Campbell amounted to no more than "mere preparation" for the crime. So, not only will the law allow one to plan crimes in the privacy of one's own head, but it will also permit one to merely prepare for the commission of that crime. Only when a defendant has proceeded beyond the stage of mere preparation will the law seek to intervene.

We have examined why the law demands some conduct. But why does it insist on so much conduct? Why does the law not punish purely preparatory acts? After all, when a person has started preparing for his crime we are able to overcome the evidential problem of not being able to prove "mere intentions"; his actions now demonstrate some firmness of purpose; arguments concerning invasion of liberty and privacy become less plausible when a person has actually committed physical actions directed towards the commission of a crime; and, of course, imposing liability for preparatory acts would allow the police to intervene at an earlier stage to prevent the commission of crimes. Such reasoning led the Law Commission (1973) to propose that liability for attempt should be imposed at a much earlier stage when the defendant had only taken a "substantial step" towards the commission of the crime. For example, a person "reconnoitring the place contemplated for the commission of the intended offence", as Campbell had done earlier, would be liable for attempt under this proposal.

Such thinking reflects what can be described as a "subjectivist" approach to the law of attempt. This approach, while insisting on some conduct as corroboration of the defendant's purpose, nevertheless stresses the mental element of the defendant. He intended to commit a crime; he is dangerous and needs restraining; he also needs rehabilitation and punishment in order to deter him and others from attempting to commit crimes. Criminal liability can thus justifiably be imposed at a much earlier stage.

However, while English law has embraced a subjectivist approach in many other areas of the criminal law (including impossible attempts: see pp. 165–170), it has here preferred the view that liability in such cases would involve too serious an invasion of personal liberty; it would open the door to the possibility of abuse by the police and "goes much too far in making guilty intention overshadow guilty conduct" (Law Commission, 1980). Also, the mere preparer is regarded as relatively non-dangerous. Only when he has got sufficiently near to committing the crime that he can be said to have "broken through the psychological barrier to crime" (Williams, 1978), or to have "crossed the Rubicon and burnt his boats" (*Stonehouse*, 1978) can he be regarded as sufficiently dangerous to warrant restraining. In short, English law can be said to have adopted an "objectivist" approach to defining the contours of this aspect of the law of attempt. An objectivist approach focuses on the *actions* of the defendant; these actions must "conform to objective criteria defined in advance. The act must evidence attributes subject to determination independently of the actor's intent" (Fletcher, 1978). In the law of attempt the defendant's actions must bring him "within striking distance" of committing the crime. Only at this point does the conduct generate apprehension; only then does it present a clear threat of harm justifying the imposition of criminal liability.

It is, however, no easy matter to determine whether a defendant has done acts which are "more than merely preparatory to the commission of the crime" and the courts have laid down a fairly open-textured test: they have held that the "Rubicon test" should be abandoned; a defendant need not have reached the point of no return. He must, however, have "embarked on the crime proper" (*Gullefer*, 1990). This means he must have actually started trying to commit the offence. This is, however, difficult to apply and, while the courts have paid regular lip-service to this test, judicial statements and the results of many cases are difficult to reconcile with it. For example, in *Campbell* (1991) it was suggested that the defendant could have been liable when he entered the building—although in terms of the crime charged, attempted robbery, this would hardly amount to starting to commit the offence. In *Attorney-General's Reference (No. 1 of 1992)* (1993) the defendant pulled a girl behind a hedge, lowered his trousers and lay on top of her but did not attempt penetration as his penis was flaccid. It was held that these actions were sufficient for the crime of attempted rape. However, given that rape requires penetration of the vagina or anus by the defendant's penis, it is difficult to see how a person who has not tried to penetrate a woman can be said to have "embarked on the crime proper".

Duff (1996) argues that the essence of an attempt is an attack on some legally protected interest. Reported cases since the 1981 Act do provide some support for such an approach in that courts seem more willing to hold that acts can be more than merely preparatory when there has been a confrontation with the victim or property. For instance, in *Jones* (1990) the defendant got into the victim's car and pointed a gun at him. It was held that his actions became more than merely preparatory when he entered the car (confronted or "attacked" his victim). Similarly, in attempted burglary cases (where the essence of the crime is entering a building as a trespasser), where there has been a "confrontation" with the building there can be sufficient conduct for an attempt (*Boyle and Boyle*, 1987: breaking a door; *Tosti*, 1997: examining a padlock; *Toothill*, 1998: knocking on proposed victim's door). In these cases "confrontation" tends to equate with physical proximity rather than Duff's notion of an "attack". It is difficult to see how examining a padlock could be regarded as an "attack" on the building. In cases where there has been no confrontation with the victim, it has been held that the conduct was merely preparatory (*Campbell*, 1991: had not entered the post office; *Rowley*, 1992 and *Geddes*, 1996: had not met with boys against whom the defendants were charged with attempting to commit offences; *Gullefer*, 1990: had not confronted the bookmakers from whom he was charged with attempted theft).

This prevailing theme of confrontation with the victim or property is no more than a general rule of thumb and clearly cannot be applied as a "test". Much depends on the type of offence allegedly being attempted. In *Rowley* (1992) it was indicated that an offence of attempted incitement of a child under the age of 14 to commit an act of gross indecency would be committed if a letter inciting such indecency was posted but not received. Clearly, there would be no confrontation in such a case. Further, this "confrontation" approach would probably only apply to crimes such as attempted murder, rape, wounding and burglary that are committed at a particular moment. With attempts to commit offences involving deception or evasion where there is more likely to be a "stratagem carried on over a period of time" (*Qadir and Khan*, 1997), it is unlikely that confrontation with the victim or property would be required.

A final, but crucial, point needs to be stressed. The above test is a legal test. Under section 4(3) of the Criminal Attempts Act 1981 it is for the judge to decide whether the defendant's actions *could* amount to an attempt. Thus if Campbell had entered the sub-post office the judge might have decided that this could be an attempt. In such circumstances it is then for the jury to decide as a matter of fact whether they *did* so amount to an attempt. With such a loose legal test and liability ultimately turning on the jury's interpretation of what amounts to "more than merely preparatory acts", there is maximum scope for policy considerations to prevail and for different juries to reach different verdicts and to be influenced, to different degrees, by inappropriate considerations.

(b) Conspiracy

While fairly substantial action is required for an attempt, all that is required for a conspiracy is an agreement between at least two persons to commit a crime (Criminal Law Act 1977, section 1(1); section 5 of this Act also preserves two species of common law conspiracy, namely, conspiracy to defraud [section 5(2)] and conspiracy to corrupt public morals or outrage public decency [section 5(3)]). The essence of the crime is the agreement itself; if this can be proved, no further conduct is required. So if two persons agree to rob a bank they are guilty of a criminal conspiracy as soon as they have reached an agreement. This is not punishing "evil thoughts" alone. Consistent with the general principle, there must be a physical manifestation of the evil intention—but here this requirement is satisfied merely by proof of an agreement (*Mulcahy*, 1868).

The real issue is whether such minimal conduct as a mere agreement to commit a crime ought to suffice for criminal liability. The rationale of "nipping crime in the bud" is insufficient here. Such arguments apply with equal force to attempts, yet to be liable for an attempt, we have seen that the post office robber in *Campbell* (1991) would need to have done more towards the actual commission of his crime. Why would he have been liable for conspiracy (and liable to the same punishment as for the attempt) if he and another had simply agreed to rob the post office and had done nothing in pursuance of that agreement?

Two main arguments are usually put forward to justify the law of conspiracy. First, it is asserted that collaborations between persons or groups increase the dangerousness of their actions. The shared commitment to perpetrating the crime makes it more likely that the crime will actually be committed by at least one of the parties. And it is more difficult for society to protect itself against collective criminal agreements, say, by organised crime, than against the antisocial designs of an individual. Greater apprehension is generated by criminal agreements; they pose more of a threat to society. Under the objectivist view of the criminal law, discussed above, an individual must come close to committing the crime before society is threatened, but the requisite threshold of threat and apprehension is crossed, both psychologically and practically, at a much earlier stage by a criminal agreement.

The second justification is that conspiracies may be regarded as more serious than attempts where there is an agreement to commit a series of offences. For instance, a crime network might be set up to organise the importation and distribution of prohibited drugs on a massive scale—and involving hundreds of persons. Such a collective criminal agreement is in itself far more serious and dangerous than any one isolated attempt to import drugs into the country. A conspiracy charge, revealing the larger criminal enterprise, will more accurately reflect the gravity of the conduct.

Whether such considerations are sufficient to justify punishing a mere agreement is an open question. In the USA many states insist upon an overt act in pursuance of the criminal agreement; one of the conspirators must actually do something towards committing the crime. While English law does not insist upon such a requirement, the fact remains that a mere agreement is almost impossible to prove unless some overt act has been performed from which the agreement can be inferred. But this point in fact exposes the law of conspiracy to yet another objection. We shall see later that the *mens rea* of most crimes can only be established by drawing inferences from acts; with conspiracy the *actus reus*, the agreement, can similarly be established by inference only in most cases. This means that in many cases conspiracy is completely a crime of inference—hardly a satisfactory state of affairs.

In many of the conspiracy cases, either the complete crime has actually been committed, or the overt acts relied upon as evidence of the agreement could well amount to an attempt. In *Knuller (Publishing, Printing and Promotions) Ltd* (1972) Lord Diplock stated that while a mere agreement did technically suffice for a conspiracy, in reality it was the overt acts done in concert that were truly dangerous and merited punishment. If this is so, one is left wondering whether a law of conspiracy is really necessary. The overt acts done in pursuance of a criminal agreement could well be dealt with by the law of attempt. If necessary, and particularly if the "dangerousness of collaboration" argument were accepted, the boundaries of the law of attempt could be pushed back to cover some preparatory actions when dealing with group criminality. Such a proposal would ensure that a significant physical manifestation of a criminal intention was a necessary prerequisite to the imposition of criminal liability.

(c) Incitement

The crime of incitement is a common law offence punishable on indictment with a fine and imprisonment at the discretion of the court. The essence of this offence is that the defendant must persuade, encourage or command another to commit a crime. The only "conduct" required is words or acts of persuasion. In *Fitzmaurice* (1983) it was held that the necessary "element of persuasion" was satisfied by a "suggestion, proposal or request [that] was accompanied by an implied promise of reward". If the person incited agrees to commit the offence, both are liable for conspiracy. If the incitee actually commits the crime, the inciter will be liable as an accessory to the complete offence—a point to be canvassed in the next section.

So, like conspiracy but unlike attempt, the actions of an inciter are far removed from the complete crime, making it questionable whether this offence has not pushed back the threshold of criminal liability too far. Why should mere words of persuasion involve criminal liability—particularly if nothing is done pursuant to those words? Are such words or actions manifestly dangerous? The incitee can, after all, resist such persuasion.

The justifications for the imposition of criminal liability upon such minimal conduct are similar to those already canvassed for the other inchoate offences, particularly conspiracy. The offence of incitement is necessary for timely police intervention to "nip the crime in the bud". An inciter has, by the fact of the incitement, indicated some degree of dangerousness; it is desirable to deter people from encouraging others to commit crime. Indeed, incitement can be seen as particularly dangerous because it may lead to more intelligent and careful planning and co-operation than if the hireling had simply acted on his own initiative. And finally, there is a view, not applicable to conspiracy, that the crime of incitement exists, in part at least, to protect the person incited from corruption (Gordon, 1978).

Whether these justifications are sufficiently convincing is a moot point. If the person incited agrees to commit the crime, there will be a criminal conspiracy; incitement thus amounts to no more than an attempted conspiracy—an offence expressly abolished by section 1(4) of the Criminal Attempts Act 1981. If the incitement is successful and the crime ultimately committed, the offence of incitement is redundant: the inciter would clearly be liable as a counsellor or procurer of the crime under the rules of accessorial liability. On the other hand, if the incitement fails and does not even mature into a conspiracy, the imposition of criminal liability for such minimal conduct does seem contrary to the general spirit of the law which normally requires fairly extensive action as a prerequisite for the imposition of criminal liability.

(d) Accessories
An accessory (or accomplice or secondary party) is a person who helps or encourages another (the principal offender) to commit a crime. Both can be liable for any offence committed. Section 8 of the Accessories and Abettors Act 1861 provides: "whosoever shall aid, abet, counsel or procure the commission of any indictable offence . . . shall be liable to be tried, indicted and punished as a principal offender." (A comparable provision exists for summary offences: Magistrates' Courts Act 1980, section 44.) Unlike incitement, the crime must actually have been committed. The accessory is liable for the same offence as the principal offender but the route to such liability is different. So if an accessory helps or encourages the principal offender to commit rape the accessory will also be convicted of rape despite the fact that he did not have sexual intercourse with the victim. This raises interesting fair labelling questions. Should a person who has not had sexual intercourse with the victim be termed a rapist? If an accessory encourages a principal offender to drive while drunk, the accessory is liable for the offence of driving with excess alcohol. Should a person who did not drive, and perhaps is unable to drive, be convicted of the offence of driving with excess alcohol? These matters will be revisited later. For the moment it is enough to note that the accessory's liability derives from that of the principal and so she is liable for the same offence: this is called "derivative liability".

It used to be thought that the terms "aid", "abet", "counsel" and "procure" bore distinct meanings (*Attorney-General's Reference (No. 1 of 1975)*, 1975) but it is now widely accepted that, with the possible exception of procuring, these terms are simply synonyms embracing all forms of helping or encouraging the principal offender of a crime. Indeed, the prosecution may charge an accessory in language which embraces all four terms without having to specify which precise category of accessory-ship is being alleged. While the House of Lords has stressed that it is desirable that the true nature of the case against the defendant should be made clear in the indictment (*Maxwell*, 1979), this recommendation appears to be "universally ignored" (*Taylor, Harrison and Taylor*, 1998). Given the advantage to the prosecution of not having to identify the precise role of the defendant, particularly in cases where there is uncertainty as to which of two persons actually was the principal offender, the present practice is not surprising. It does, however, raise the important issue whether defendants receive adequate notice of the precise case against them to enable them to prepare a proper defence.

As section 8 makes clear, an accessory, of whichever type, is liable to the same extent as the principal offender (and so can be punished to the same extent)—despite the fact that he has not himself directly committed the crime. For instance, in *Craig and Bentley* (1952) Bentley, who was in police custody, called out to Craig, "Let him have it". Craig shot and killed a policeman and was convicted of murder but escaped the death penalty because of his youth. Bentley, because of his encouragement, was also convicted of murder; he, however, was hanged. (His conviction was quashed 46 years later on the ground of deficiencies in the trial judge's direction: *Bentley*, 1999). The question for us to consider here is: how much conduct by an accessory is neces-sary to justify the imposition of criminal liability? How much help or encouragement must an accessory like Bentley give?

Consistent with the general principle, there must be some *conduct* by the accessory. The actions must amount to aiding, abetting, counselling or procuring the commission of the offence. The precise nature and extent of this conduct depends on the mode of participation in the crime. The approach of the English courts suggests that the type of conduct (and *mens rea*: see pp. 130–135) required varies according to the following modes of participation:

(i) Procuring
This refers to an accessory who instigates a crime: "To procure means to produce by endeavour. You procure a thing by setting out to see that it happens and taking the appropriate steps to produce that happening" (*Attorney-General's Reference (No.1 of*

1975)). So a defendant who surreptitiously laces her friend's drinks with double measures of spirits knowing her friend is about to drive home is liable for procuring the offence of driving with excess alcohol committed by the friend. With procuring causation must be established: there must be a causal link between the procuring and the commission of the offence (*Attorney-General's Reference (No. 1 of 1975)*, 1975). There need not necessarily be any consensus or meeting of minds with the principal offender. Indeed, as with the laced drink example, the principal may be completely unaware that she is committing a crime. As procuring involves "making the crime happen", it follows that the amount of conduct involved is whatever is necessary to ensure the commission of the offence.

(ii) Presence at crime without prior agreement
Where there is no prior agreement or consensus between the parties one is not dealing with "group criminality" (paradigmatically represented by criminal gangs or organised crime groups) and, accordingly, the law has been careful to circumscribe the criteria to be satisfied before there can be liability as an accessory. In *Allan* (1965) the defendant witnessed his friends committing a crime (an affray, which involves unlawful fighting). He had a secret intention to join in if his help was needed, but he outwardly did nothing and simply played the role of a passive spectator. It was held that he could not be liable as he had not actually encouraged the participants. Convicting him would have been getting uncomfortably close to convicting a person purely on the basis of his thoughts.

However, whilst some conduct is necessary, it is clear that the slightest act of assistance or encouragement can suffice. In *Clarkson* (1971) the defendants entered a room in an army barracks where a woman was being raped. They remained there watching the rape. It was held that their mere presence, even if that presence gave encouragement, was not in itself sufficient. There had to be "encouragement in fact". This could consist of "expressions, or gestures, or actions" signifying approval or encouragement. So if the defendants in *Allan* (1965) and *Clarkson* (1971) had cheered, clapped or shouted encouragement, this "conduct" could have been sufficient to render them criminally liable.

If one recalls the law of attempt where very substantial conduct is required, one is forced to ask: why is such minimal conduct as shouting encouragement sufficient for accessorial liability? One possible explanation is that even such minor assistance can "strengthen the resolve of the perpetrator" (Fletcher, 1978); it can give him the necessary fortitude to continue with the offence. We all know from our everyday experiences that we are sometimes prepared to take risks with the support of another that we are unprepared to take alone. Assistance or encouragement can thus increase the possibility of the offence occurring. While this can clearly be so in some cases, it hardly seems a plausible general explanation. The rapists in *Clarkson* (1971) appeared well committed to their rape and it is doubtful whether words or gestures of encouragement from Clarkson would have had any impact or effect at all. Further, this idea presupposes that the principal offender is aware of the encouragement or assistance he is receiving, and is thus capable of having his resolve strengthened. Yet in *Quick and Paddison* (1973) it was held that an accessory could assist a principal who was unaware of such assistance.

(iii) Consensual participation
In the above two modes of participation, the principal offender does not need to be aware of the accessory's assistance. More typical of true group criminality, however, is the situation where a crime is planned and executed by more than one person. Some may have provided assistance beforehand by ordering the crime to be committed or by providing the tools to commit the crime without being present at the scene of the crime. Others may be at the scene of the crime or nearby as a driver or lookout. The point about all these participants is that although the level of their contribution can vary greatly, they are all part of a consensual process that, with varying degrees of help, planning and assistance, has led to the commission of the offence. A criminal law prepared to punish mere agreements (conspiracies) must be prepared to punish any overt acts done in pursuance of that agreement when those acts lead to the ultimate harm. Accordingly, where there has been prior agreement, mere presence at the scene of the crime, pursuant to that agreement, is sufficient conduct. Similarly, mere advice, information, encouragement or the supply of tools prior to the commission of a crime will suffice. For instance, in *Bainbridge* (1960) the defendant was liable because he supplied oxygen cutting equipment to the principal offender who used it to break into premises. In *Calhaem* (1985) it was held that no causal connection was necessary for counselling as long as the offence

committed was "within the authority or advice" of the counsellor. In *Giannetto* (1997) it was stated that all a husband need say was "Oh, goody" in response to being told that another person intended to kill his wife in order to make him liable for the subsequent offence. In these cases the only rationale for punishing such minimal conduct is, again, that this advice or encouragement might have prompted the principal into action or strengthened his resolve. The supply of tools or advice might have had the same effect or made the commission of the crime easier or more certain. Further, with counselling there has been a meeting of minds. This can lead to momentum being gathered towards the commission of the crime and so the same justifications as those underlying the law of conspiracy are applicable here.

The requisite conduct can even be normal action in the course of a lawful business. For example, in *National Coal Board v. Gamble* (1959) a purchaser loaded his lorry with coal and had it weighed to ascertain the cost. On weighing the coal the weighbridge operator pointed out that the lorry was overloaded. The purchaser said he would risk it, whereupon the operator gave him the weight ticket enabling the purchaser to leave the colliery. This act was held to be a sufficient "positive act of assistance" to render the weighbridge operator (and thus the National Coal Board as his employer) liable as an accessory to the crime of driving an overweight lorry on the road. On this basis, if a shopkeeper sold an alarm clock knowing it was to be used for constructing a time-bomb, she would become an accessory to the offence committed by the bomber. Despite the fact that the principal offender could have obtained the alarm clock anywhere, the fact remains that the accessory has supplied an "essential article" to the commission of the crime (*National Coal Board v. Gamble*, 1959).

In all these cases there is a shared joint enterprise or meeting of minds; each member of the group, even though his or her particular actions are minimal, assumes responsibility for the actions of the other members of that group. However, one is only a "member of the group" when the group is acting in furtherance of a common or expected purpose. If one of the parties departs completely from the concerted action of the common design, the other parties are no longer responsible for that person's actions.

In *Powell; English* (1997) English and another man took part in a joint enterprise to attack and cause injury with wooden posts to a police officer. During the attack the other man unexpectedly produced a knife and stabbed the officer to death. It was held that, irrespective of his *mens rea*, English could not be liable for murder because the use of the knife was fundamentally different to the use of a wooden post. By using such a more dangerous weapon and so departing radically from the agreed joint enterprise, the other man was effectively acting on his own and English escaped liability. If, on the other hand, the principal offender had killed the officer with a blow from the wooden post, English (subject to having the requisite *mens rea*) would have been liable; this would have been an action within the joint enterprise and English, even though he struck no blow, would be responsible for such an "authorised act". In *Greatrex* (1998) it was held that whether the actions of one participant could be regarded as fundamentally different and thus outside the scope of the group activity was a matter of degree to be determined by the jury. In this case there was a concerted attack by six youths who were kicking the victim when the principal offender produced a bar and struck the victim on the head killing him. It was held that hitting someone with a bar was not necessarily qualitatively different from kicking someone with a shod foot, but it was a matter that should have been left to the jury.

Much group criminality, particularly where violence is inflicted, is not the product of careful planning but is the result of an instant fight where different modes of attack and/or weapons are spontaneously used. In *Uddin* (1998) there was a group attack on a victim using poles or bars when the principal offender produced a flick-knife and stabbed the victim to death. It was held that while the others might not have known of the knife, if, when it was produced, they continued to participate in the attack, the nature of their group action could be regarded as having changed and each would be liable for the resultant death.

This whole approach can be criticised for its emphasis on the detail and method of execution of the crime. If a group of youths agree to kick a victim to death and one of them produces a knife stabbing him to death, it seems absurd that the others should escape liability because the method of killing was different from that anticipated. While a knife is intrinsically more dangerous than a shoe, if an accessory has engaged in an attack on a victim (or supplied help or encouragement before the crime) intending death and death indeed ensues, it is difficult to see why the method of killing, or the instrument used, should make such a fundamental difference.

(iv) Failure to exercise control
Where the defendant has the right to control the actions of the principal offender, a failure to exercise this control may amount to the requisite encouragement or assistance. In *Harris* (1964) the supervisor of a learner-driver was convicted as accessory to the learner-driver's traffic offences when he failed to take steps to stop them. This principle has been importantly extended to employers who have a right to control the actions of their employees. In *J.F. Alford Transport Ltd* (1997) it was held that where a transport manager or managing director of a company who had a right to control the actions of employees deliberately refrained from exercising control, positive encouragement could be inferred. In such a case no positive conduct at all is necessary and, indeed, actual presence at the scene of the crime is not necessary. This approach is consistent with the views of Husak (1998) who rejects the act requirement in criminal law and would substitute a control requirement. In moral philosophy we are held responsible for all that is within our control; criminal responsibility should follow suit. Such an argument taken to its logical conclusion (which Husak indeed does) would permit criminal liability to be imposed for thought-crimes where there was evidence of a firm intention to commit a crime. As argued above, such an invasion of the privacy of a person's mind would be unthinkable. More realistically, Ashworth (1999) suggests that these "power of control" cases are in fact creating a new category of legal duty making liability for an omission to act permissible (see p. 49). Given the criminal law's general insistence on conduct and a consequent narrow circumscribing of the categories of legal duty permitting liability for omissions to be imposed (see pp. 50–51), one has to query the justifiability of imposing liability in these cases. Further, there is clearly uncertainty about the limits of this control principle. Am I in control of every person who enters my property (house or car) making me liable for whatever offence they commit, with my knowledge, therein? If so, the "law has, in effect, co-opted property owners as law-enforcement agents in respect of their property, and *in J.F. Alford Transport* employers were co-opted in respect of their employees' conduct at work" (Ashworth, 1999).

From the above analysis it can be seen that the amount of conduct required for accessorial liability varies considerably depending on the mode of participation. At one extreme one can be liable for an offence by doing nothing if one has a power to control the principal offender or be convicted of murder for saying "Oh, goody". At the other extreme one can escape liability for murder because the victim is killed by a knife instead of being hit to death as expected.

Such an approach is inevitable with the present commitment of English law to the principle of derivative liability. The crime has been committed. The policeman in *Craig and Bentley* (1952) was dead; the woman in *Clarkson* (1971) was raped. The question is one of deciding who should bear the responsibility for such a harm. Clearly many accessories ought to be held accountable because their actions may have contributed to the result. Craig might have fired his gun only because of the shouted encouragement from Bentley. In other cases the actions of the accessory may have enabled the principal to commit the offence more easily or safely. Even though they are minimal actions, if they contribute to, or facilitate, the ultimate commission of the crime, the accessory (assuming, of course, he has *mens rea*) ought to be held responsible.

However, even if one accepts this argument, one must still ask whether an accessory, who has done so little, ought to be held responsible *for the same offence* as the principal. Is such derivative liability justifiable? Assuming the contribution is not so great as to amount to a legal cause of the ultimate harm, should an accessory not be punished for the harm he or she has actually caused, namely, the harm of assisting or encouraging the principal offender? Bentley did not himself kill anyone. Even if he had encouraged Craig, did he deserve to be found guilty of murder? We clearly would blame a person for encouraging another to kill. Should that person not be punished for what he or she did, namely, that encouragement? According to such reasoning the accessory's true fault and danger to society reside in those actions of encouragement or assistance themselves. Following this reasoning, the Law Commission has proposed abandoning the present law of complicity where the accessory's liability is derivative upon the principal offence and replacing it with new inchoate offences of *"encouraging"* and *"assisting"* crime. This offence would carry the same maximum penalty as the offence being assisted (Law Commission, 1993a). If this proposal were implemented Bentley would have been liable for encouraging murder rather than murder itself. While any such new offence would need to be defined relative to the principal offence as, for example, encouraging murder is clearly worse than encouraging theft, this approach does have the attraction of emphasising the actual wrongdoing of the defendant. Punishment should be (but would not be, according to the Law Commission) geared to that conduct (assuming, of course, he possessed *mens rea*)—rather than the present position where shouting words of encouragement can be deemed to be equal to pulling the trigger and killing a person.

(iii) Meaning of conduct

(a) Voluntary acts
The conduct or actions of the defendant must be "voluntary". For example, if a defendant is roughly pushed into the victim, knocking her over, the defendant's "actions" are clearly involuntary—indeed, they are hardly *his* "acts" at all. Similarly, if a sleeping mother, sharing a bed with her child, rolls over and smothers the child, her actions will be held to be involuntary. A person can be held responsible only for his voluntary actions. If his physical movements are involuntary, there will generally be no criminal liability. Not only would punishment be undeserved in such cases, but also it could serve no deterrent function: involuntary action clearly cannot be deterred.

The real problem, however, has been to define the term "voluntary". The traditional definition of a voluntary act is that it is "a willed muscular contraction" (Holmes, 1881): it is a physical movement that results from an operation of the will. The mind is in control of bodily movements; it sends instructions to the muscles; the result is voluntary acts. Occasionally, however, the mind may not be in control of the body, and bodily movements may take place independently; such movements are involuntary acts: "The mind is . . . [the controlling] agent, whereas the body alone is only a dumb brute—and, as everyone knows, it makes no sense at all to hold dumb brutes responsible" (Gross, 1979).

This orthodox definition is not particularly helpful. If we decide to do something, say, hit someone or open a door, our movements become coordinated to our goal. Of course, there are muscular movements but we are not aware of them at a conscious level; we do not have to "instruct" our muscles to operate; such movements simply flow from our decision to act. And there is little point in arguing that the will must be controlling the muscles, albeit at a subconscious level—because this must also be true of many of the classical instances of involuntary conduct; the mother who rolled over in her sleep killing her child did not roll over because of the forces of gravity.

Hart (1968) suggested that the criterion of voluntariness should be whether the movements were "subordinated to the agent's conscious plans of action"; the issue would be whether they occurred "as part of anything the agent takes himself to be doing". Fletcher (1998) expresses it thus: "we do not perceive someone as acting unless we also perceive that the person is after something". If one means to open a door, then even though one is concentrating on something else, all physical movements geared towards opening the door are voluntary. But if, on the way to the door, one trips and, in falling, sticks out an arm to protect oneself, this movement of sticking out the arm would not be part of one's plan of action and would therefore be involuntary. Similarly, the mother rolling over in her sleep is clearly moving involuntarily; her movements are not any part of any action she means to take; she is not "after something"; she is unconscious and therefore does not take herself to be doing any action at all.

The criminal law, perhaps not surprisingly, has not truly attempted to face these complex problems. It has tended to adopt the approach that there is a continuum of "involuntariness" ranging from complete absence of consciousness, through persons acting in a confused or semi-conscious manner, to those who actually know what they are doing but claim their actions were "morally involuntary" because their will was overborne and they were forced to act as they did. The courts, in determining where to draw the line on this continuum, have been strongly influenced by the context, nature and dangerousness of the behaviour. Where the defendant has appeared overtly to be in control of his or her physical actions in cases where conduct has been claimed to be morally involuntary (for example, in situations of duress), the conduct has been deemed "voluntary", but the defendant might be allowed an "excuse" (see p. 96) exempting or reducing liability.

In other situations, however, the courts have refrained from developing clear principles thereby retaining maximum flexibility to judge the defendant's blameworthiness and dangerousness on an individual basis. In some cases where the defendant is engaged in a particularly dangerous activity, such as driving a car, the law has adopted the strict stance that only a complete

absence of consciousness will exempt from liability. For example, in *Attorney-General's Reference (No. 2 of 1992)* (1993) a lorry
driver, who crashed into another vehicle killing two people,
claimed that as a result of "repetitive visual stimuli experienced
on long journeys" he was in "a trance-like state" and "driving
without awareness". In the Court of Appeal it was held that
such a person should not be entitled to escape liability on the
basis of automatism because he was still able to exercise some
control in being able to steer the vehicle. Conduct would only be
involuntary where "there was a total destruction of voluntary
control".

More commonly, however, the law has not insisted on a
complete absence of consciousness or control but has deemed
conduct that is only "semi-conscious" or "semi-uncontrolled" to
be involuntary. This occurs particularly where the defendant's
conduct appears overtly abnormal and where a label or explanation for the behaviour can be attached, for example, sleepwalking or epileptic fit. This approach, however, has been extended
to less "obvious" cases. In *T* (1990) the defendant, to a charge of
robbery and causing actual bodily harm, claimed that she had
been raped three days previously and consequently was suffering from post-traumatic stress disorder; the offences had been
committed while she was in a dissociative state, namely, a
psychogenic fugue; she was not acting with a conscious mind or
will. At her trial it was held that, if accepted by the jury, this
would render her conduct "involuntary" and exempt her from
liability on grounds of automatism.

What is the outcome if conduct is adjudged to be "involuntary"? In the classic case of involuntary conduct, such as the
mother rolling over and smothering her child in her sleep, such
automatism exempts the defendant completely from all criminal
liability; she will walk out of court a free person. Being aware of
this, the courts have done two things to prevent too many
people escaping liability on the basis of automatism. First, they
have been careful to ensure that the defendant must have been
completely blameless. If the defendant were in any way at fault
in bringing about the involuntary behaviour (for example,
taking drink or drugs), she will be held liable (see pp. 43–44).
Secondly, the courts have realised that many people who act in
an "involuntary" manner might be dangerous; they could do it
again. Society might need protection from them. Accordingly,
the courts have tended to expand the definition of insanity so
that some cases of classic automatism might now be regarded as

cases of insanity. Where a defendant is found to be insane, she does not go free; she receives a special verdict—"not guilty by reason of insanity"—whereupon the courts have power to restrain her. Using this device, control, either for incapacitative or rehabilitative purposes, can be maintained over the defendant.

The issue is thus one of predicting dangerousness. How can we identify those who might behave in the same way again? In a line of cases culminating in *Sullivan* (1983) the courts developed the following test: if the involuntary conduct was caused by factors internal to the defendant then that conduct could recur; social protection demands that some control be exercised over the defendant; the insanity verdict needs to be invoked. On the other hand, if the conduct were caused by some purely external factor such as a blow on the head it is unlikely to recur and it is safe to release the defendant completely on the basis of automatism.

The following cases are traditionally thought to exclude voluntariness; whether the outcome is an acquittal on grounds of automatism or a court order on grounds of insanity depends on the cause of the involuntary behaviour:

Physical compulsion
For example, if a person is knocked off a bicycle and lands on a pedestrian, the cyclist's actions are clearly involuntary and she cannot be liable for any injuries sustained by the pedestrian.

Reflex movements of external origin
In *Hill v. Baxter* (1958) it was stated that purely reflexive movements of the arms and legs caused by being attacked by a swarm of bees would not be voluntary. Such a person, for instance, could not be said to be "driving" a car.

Concussion
A blow on the head or other physical trauma may sometimes produce a "black-out" or "confusional state", during which a person may engage in previously learned behaviour without being fully aware of what she is doing. While such a person is not completely unconscious, her ability to control her movements is sufficiently impaired to preclude criminal responsibility. Her actions are deemed to be involuntary. As seen earlier, the physical trauma of a rape which produced a dissociative state in *T* (1990) similarly counts as an "external

factor" giving rise to a defence of automatism. This can be contrasted with the Ontario decision of *Rabey* (1978) where the defendant received a "psychological blow" in the form of a rejection by a girl with whom he was infatuated. In a dissociative state he struck her with a geology rock causing injury. It was held that the "emotional stress suffered . . . as a result of his disappointment" was not an external factor. The dissociative state had its source in his psychological or emotional make-up and was therefore a disease of the mind which should lead to an insanity verdict.

Hypnosis
English law has not yet faced the problem of a defendant who commits a crime while under a hypnotic influence—although there are dicta indicating that such conduct would be involuntary (*Quick*, 1973). There is much scientific uncertainty as to the effect of hypnosis. There are claims, for instance, that one cannot hypnotise subjects to do acts they are unwilling to perform. Nevertheless, the view expressed in the Model Penal Code in the United States seems likely to prevail, namely, that "the dependency and helplessness of the hypnotised subject are too pronounced" to justify the imposition of criminal liability.

It could be claimed that "brainwashing" is analogous to hypnotism in that the subjects of both are in an altered state of consciousness. For example, in the United States, Patty Hearst, heiress to the Hearst fortune, was kidnapped and subjected to intensive brainwashing as a result of which she emerged as a revolutionary with a new name and robbed banks to finance the operations of the revolutionary group. However, the better view is that these were voluntary actions. Patty Hearst had an *altered* consciousness but there was still consciousness and control. There was not the "sharp break in consciousness that there is in cases of . . . hypnosis" (Moore, 1993). Of course, it might well be possible to afford Patty Hearst a separate defence on the ground that she was not to blame for her new altered character. However, acceptance of such an argument would open the door to claims that many persons should not be blamed because their characters were altered by an unfortunate or traumatic upbringing.

Unconsciousness
Where the unconsciousness is "normal", for example, our hypothetical case of the sleeping mother, or is externally caused,

as where a general anaesthetic is administered for therapeutic purposes, any physical movements are involuntary and will give rise to the complete defence of automatism. On the other hand, where the unconsciousness is the result of a neurophysiological disturbance such as a stroke or epilepsy, any resultant physical movements are now classed as the product of insanity.

Hypoglycaemia

Hypoglycaemia is a deficiency of blood-sugar which can be caused when diabetics take too much insulin. This can lead to impaired functioning of the central nervous system which can cause confusion, poor co-ordination and, sometimes, aggressive behaviour. In *Quick* (1973) and *Bailey* (1983) it was held that a defendant could not truly be said to be acting voluntarily during a hypoglycaemic episode. The condition is due to the injection of insulin which is an external factor and so there can be an acquittal on the basis of automatism. On the other hand, where the involuntary conduct is the product of *hyperglycaemia*—high blood sugar caused by an inherent defect and not corrected by insulin—an insanity verdict becomes appropriate (*Hennessy*, 1989).

Somnambulism

In one case a woman, dreaming her house was on fire, arose in a panic screaming "save my children" and threw her baby out of the window (Walker, 1968). In the Australian case of *Cogdon* (1951) Mrs Cogdon, in a somnambulistic state, dreaming that her daughter was being attacked by ghosts, spiders and North Korean soldiers, axed her to death. She was acquitted on the ground that her actions were not voluntary. Despite the fact that the acts of a sleepwalker are not entirely purposeless, the link between mind and bodily action is too distorted to justify the imposition of criminal liability. The sleepwalker is not acting with her normal conscious mind. However, as the cause of sleepwalking is "an abnormality of the brain function . . . or disorder, albeit transitory, due to an internal factor, whether functional or organic" (*Burgess*, 1991), an insanity verdict now becomes appropriate in such cases.

Epilepsy

The House of Lords has twice held that a person suffering spasms during an epileptic fit is, during that fit, insane (*Bratty*,

1963; *Sullivan*, 1983). In *Sullivan* (1983) the defendant, while recovering from an epileptic fit, attacked a friend and kicked him about the head and body. The House of Lords ruled that Sullivan's actions were caused by a disease of the mind; during his epileptic fit he was insane; it was irrelevant that the mental impairment was only temporary. Where the cause of the mental impairment was internal, as it clearly is with epilepsy, the insanity verdict was appropriate. This decision is most unfortunate. It seems absurd as well as highly insulting to epileptics to utilise the insanity verdict here. Nothing can be achieved by any of the orders that can be imposed pursuant to a finding of "not guilty by reason of insanity". The reality is that most such persons will simply plead guilty to the charge, as Sullivan himself did, and will often receive a non-custodial sentence.

Returning to the teleological (goal-directed) theory of action discussed above (p. 37), it has been suggested that a distinction could be drawn between "obviously non-purposive" conduct and actions that "look purposive" (Williams, 1983; Smith, 1983). A spasm or convulsion while in the throes of an epileptic fit would be "obviously non-purposive" and should result in an acquittal on grounds of automatism. On the other hand, Sullivan's conduct in kicking his friend "looked purposive"; these were not convulsions. In *Bratty* (1963), the other House of Lords epilepsy case, the defendant took off a girl's stocking and strangled her with it—again, conduct that "looked purposive". The problem with this distinction, however, is that the conduct of Mrs Cogdon as she axed her daughter to death similarly "looked purposive"—indeed, it was purposive within the context of her dreams.

The Law Commission (1989) has proposed a broader test exempting persons from liability if they act in a state of automatism which is defined as being in a condition whereby the person is deprived of effective control. It is difficult to see that such an open-textured test would represent any improvement on the current law and certainly provides no clear mechanism for distinguishing automatism from insanity.

A more radical solution to these problems could be to regard all the above cases as automatism (and not insanity) and to give the courts power to make appropriate orders, including the power to detain in hospital. For instance, in the old Scottish case of *H.M. Advocate v. Fraser* (1878) a sleepwalker was discharged on condition that he slept alone in future. Under section 37(3) of the Mental Health Act 1983 a magistrates' court has power to make a hospital order without recording a conviction providing the person is suffering from a major form of mental disorder and the court is satisfied that he did the act charged. While introducing a power of disposal where there has not been a conviction could contravene Article 5 of the European Convention on Human Rights (Baker, 1994), a provision such as section 37(3), with suitable amendment, could enable the courts to give effect to the present proposal. In most cases of automatism (concussion, etc.) there would be no need to make any kind of order. But giving the courts such power, which could be utilised in cases such as *Bratty* (1963) and *Sullivan* (1983), would make it unnecessary for them to have to expand the concept of insanity to such an unacceptable extent in order to maintain some control over the defendant.

(b) Deemed Acts

Despite the basic rule that voluntary conduct is a necessary prerequisite to the imposition of criminal liability, in certain circumstances this requirement is waived or, at least, "stretched" to a point where the law is simply "deeming" a person to have acted voluntarily. This occurs in the following situations:

(i) Involuntary conduct preceded by fault

The criminal law is concerned with the punishment of the blameworthy. In most of the cases of involuntary conduct discussed above no blame can be laid at the defendant's door. It is generally not a person's fault that a blow to her head causes concussion or that she lashes out her arms during a nightmare. The requirement of voluntary conduct relieves such persons of responsibility. But if it were the defendant's own fault that brought on the involuntary conduct or the resultant harm, the law will not allow her to escape liability by sheltering behind the facade of automatism. Thus, even though a person's conduct might actually be involuntary at the time she caused the harm, she will nevertheless be held liable if it were her fault that she got herself into that situation. One can view this in one of two ways. Either the defendant is being punished for her voluntary conduct prior to the crime, or, because of the preceding fault, the requirement of voluntariness is dispensed with and she is simply deemed to have acted.

This principle is illustrated by the case of *Quick* (1973). The defendant, a diabetic, took his insulin but thereafter ate hardly any food and consumed a quantity of alcohol. During the resultant hypoglycaemic episode he assaulted a victim. It was held that while hypoglycaemia could give rise to a defence of automatism, if the defendant were to blame for bringing about his condition he would be liable. It was stated that such a defendant is "at fault" in bringing about his state of automatism when he does something (such as take a drug) or fails to do something (such as fail to eat after taking insulin) and he knows, or ought to know, that there is a risk of resultant involuntary conduct. In *Bailey* (1983) a diabetic ate insufficient food after a dose of insulin to combat its effect. It was held, rather surprisingly, that the risk of this leading to aggressive or unpredictable behaviour was not "common knowledge, even among diabetics". Accordingly, if the defendant could not be expected to know of these risks, he could not be blamed for any resultant involuntary conduct. Similarly, in *Hardie* (1984) it was held that a defendant who took Valium could escape liability for his subsequent involuntary conduct because it was not known to the defendant, nor generally known, that Valium could, in some cases, cause "unpredictability or aggressiveness". On the other hand, the risks involved in excessive consumption of other drugs (such as heroin or LSD) or alcohol are well known: accordingly, any defence of automatism would fail in such cases.

This approach inevitably leaves many questions unanswered. For instance, Mrs Cogdon had been sleepwalking in her daughter's room the very night previous to killing her and had awoken to find herself violently brushing dream-spiders off her daughter's face. She therefore knew of the risk that she could walk in her sleep—and could walk into her daughter's room; she even knew she could violently brush her daughter's face. Can we therefore blame her for axing her daughter to death the next night? What would be the true basis for such blame—that she knew she was a somnambulist, that she did not lock herself or her daughter up that night, or that she had not hidden her axe away (presumably there were knives or other instruments in the house capable of being used against dream-North Koreans)? Arguably, it was the difficulty in coming to terms with these issues that persuaded the courts that the safest course (in terms of social protection) was to class such conduct as being the product of insanity (*Burgess*, 1991) thereby giving themselves the power to make such restraining orders as may be appropriate in the circumstances.

(ii) Status Offences

Some crimes are defined in such a manner that there is no express requirement of conduct; the crime is committed when a certain state of affairs exists, or when the defendant is in a particular situation or condition or is of a defined, prohibited status. For instance, it is an offence simply to belong to a proscribed organisation such as the IRA (Terrorism Act 2000, section 11(1)). As this section covers those who joined prior to the date of the commencement of the Act, it looks as though it is punishing the mere status of being a member of the IRA. However, consistent with the principle established in the preceding section, liability in such cases is justifiable (in terms of criminal law principles—whether such an offence ought to exist at all is another matter, discussed on pp. 244–256) if it is the defendant's fault that the prohibited status or state of affairs has come about. For example, closer inspection of the above statute reveals that this provision is aimed at punishing conduct. Section 11(2) provides a defence if one became a member before the organisation was proscribed and if one has not taken part in any of its activities while the organisation is proscribed. So what is being punished in reality is the act of joining the proscribed organisation or participating in its activities if one had joined at an earlier date.

But where there is no "conduct" and it was not the defendant's fault that the prohibited state of affairs has come about, liability is contrary to established principle. In the infamous case of *Larsonneur* (1933) the defendant was convicted of being a prohibited alien who was "found in the United Kingdom". The fact that she had been deported from the Irish Free State and brought to England in police custody was described as "circumstances which are perfectly immaterial". She was "found here"; the fact that she did not voluntarily come here was irrelevant. This notorious case has been defended on the ground that the defendant "was probably the author of her own misfortune" (Lanham, 1976), in that she attempted in England to contract an arranged "marriage of convenience" with the result that an order was made requiring her to depart from the United Kingdom. She then went to the Irish Free State where she persevered in her attempt to contract the marriage of convenience. It was therefore her fault that she was deported back to England. However, as it is not unlawful to enter into a marriage of convenience it is difficult to see how she was "blameworthy" other than in a rather generalised sense bearing little or no connection with her subsequent offence. Further, even if it was foreseeable that she would be deported from the Irish Free State, was it foreseeable that she would be deported back to the United Kingdom? Might she not reasonably have expected deportation back to her country of origin, France? Also, preceding fault is not mentioned in the judgment. All the circumstances leading up to her being found in the United Kingdom (on her enforced "return") were simply dismissed as "perfectly immaterial". (Interesting new research has revealed that there could have been another basis for rightly convicting Larsonneur: under the law as it then stood her going to the Irish Free State did not amount to a departure from the United Kingdom. She was therefore committing an offence under English law simply by being in the Irish Free State—Doegar, 1998).

In *Winzar v. Chief Constable of Kent* (1983) the defendant was brought into hospital on a stretcher. The doctor discovered that Winzar was merely drunk and asked him to leave. When he was later seen slumped in the corridor the police were called. They removed him to the roadway, "formed the opinion that he was drunk", and placed him in their car parked nearby. He was convicted of the offence of being found drunk on the highway, it being immaterial that he had been placed there involuntarily. It is possible to argue here that it must have been Winzar's fault that he was in that situation. The report of the case does not specify how he got to be taken to hospital, but the most likely explanation is that he had been found in some public place, or, perhaps, had summoned medical assistance when he was only drunk and not in need of such attention. However, it can also be argued (though perhaps with less conviction) that Winzar could have been found drunk in his own home by a neighbour or friend who summoned the medical assistance, in which case he would not have been at fault as we cannot blame someone for getting drunk in the privacy of their own home. Further, there is no hint at all in the judgment of the court that it was relevant how or why Winzar was brought to hospital; no mention was made of preceding fault.

In *Strowger v. John* (1974) the defendant was convicted of an offence, contrary to section 12 of the Vehicles (Excise) Act 1971, of failing to display a valid excise disc on his car windscreen. The disc had fallen from the windscreen while the defendant was at work. It has been suggested that there was prior fault here as "the accused could, by careful inspection, have guarded against such an occurrence" (Leigh, 1982). However, such a claim seems implausible as the court found that "the licence had become detached without any negligence or default of the defendant". The defendant was, in effect, held liable in the absence of any voluntary conduct.

From these cases it appears that English law is prepared, occasionally, to impose criminal liability in the absence of conduct or preceding fault. Husak (1998) has argued there is nothing objectionable in such an approach provided a person has control over the status or situation. Our sense of justice would be outraged by a law that made it a crime to have measles—a condition one is powerless to prevent. On the other hand, it would be perfectly acceptable (in terms of criminal law principles—as opposed to civil libertarian concerns) to make it a criminal offence to be a member of a prohibited organisation as such membership is within one's control. It can also be argued (Simester, 1998) that some of the central objections to the above cases are not in reality objections to imposition of liability without an act, but rather the fact that strict liability was imposed without the defendant being blameworthy. Whether offences of strict liability can be justified will be considered later (p. 135).

(iii) Vicarious Liability
In certain limited circumstances the law is prepared to hold a person criminally responsible even though he did nothing himself, but because he is vicariously responsible for the acts of another. This is not the same as accessorial liability where the defendant must act himself in the sense of, at least, helping or encouraging the principal offender. With vicarious liability the acts of one person are simply attributed to another even though that other might be completely unaware that a crime is being committed. In effect this is, like the cases in the preceding section, punishing people for their status or for being in a particular situation.

Traditionally, this concept has been broadly limited to certain situations in which an employer is held liable for the criminal acts of his employee committed within the scope of the latter's employment. This can occur in one of three ways. First, a statute might expressly provide for vicarious liability. For example, section 163(1) of the Licensing Act 1964 provides: "a person shall not . . . either himself *or by his servant or agent* . . ." do certain things. Secondly, in relation to licensee cases, the courts have developed the "doctrine of delegation". Under the Licensing Acts there are many offences which can only be committed by the holder of a licence (the licensee). If the licensee delegates general responsibility to her staff, their acts (and their *mens rea*) are imputed to the licensee. For example, in *Howker v. Robinson* (1973) a barman in the lounge-bar of licensed premises sold liquor to a boy aged fourteen. It was held that the licensee had delegated responsibility for running the lounge-bar to the barman and, accordingly, the licensee was liable. The acts of the barman were deemed to be the acts of the licensee. Finally, the courts can interpret words in a statute so that the act of an employee is deemed to be the act of his employer. Take for example the word "sell". Section 2 of the Food and Drugs Act 1955 makes it a criminal offence to "sell" improper food. "Sell" is a legal term referring to a legal contract of sale. Under such a contract, the sale is by the owner of the goods (owner of the shop, store, company or whatever) to the customer. So if a store assistant delivers improper food to a customer, the employer is deemed to have sold the goods (*Coppen v. Moore No. 2*, 1898). In a similar vein (but, perhaps, without the same legal logic) the courts impose criminal liability on companies for many strict liability offences committed by their employees. This is of particular importance in pollution offences where the only effective way of enforcing the law is by making the company itself liable. (*National Rivers Authority v. Alfred McAlpine Homes East Ltd*, 1994). Vicarious liability has also been applied to hybrid offences which are prima facie strict liability offences but allow the defendant a due diligence defence (see p. 143). However, it is clear that vicarious liability will not necessarily apply to all offences of strict liability. Whether it does apply or not is a matter of statutory interpretation bearing in mind the policy of the law and whether the imposition of vicarious liability will assist enforcement of the law (*Seaboard Offshore Ltd v. Secretary of State for Transport*, 1994). (Companies can also be directly liable for offences involving *mens rea*: see pp. 144–149)

Offences of vicarious liability have been criticised on the basis that the criminal law, being an institution of blame and censure, should target the individual wrongdoers and not employers. It could result in companies or employers being penalised for the wrongs of an employee when they might have done everything within their power to prevent the wrongdoing. In *Harrow LBC v. Shah* (1999) the owners of a shop took every possible precaution to ensure their employee did not sell lottery tickets to persons under the age of 16. When the employee did make such a sale the owners were criminally vicariously liable.

On the other hand, the rationale of vicarious liability is that it is the employer who is responsible for appointing the employee, who has control and authority over him or her and who is making the profits from the operation. As has been seen, it can be argued that a control principle is more important than an act principle in criminal law (Husak, 1998). On this basis it is the employer who must be responsible for ensuring that employees commit no criminal offences within the course of their employment. The threat of criminal liability will prompt the employer into maintaining careful authority over the employee. If the employer were not criminally liable responsibility could simply be delegated to others and immunity from prosecution acquired. Further, in many cases, particularly in the field of pollution, it is a failure in the company's system and operations that leads to the offence and not only would it be pointless, but also unfair, to punish the individual worker. (For further arguments in favour of punishing companies, see p. 148.) In short, it is not difficult to justify vicarious liability especially when applied to strict liability offences. For such crimes, no finding of fault on the part of the actor is required and so there would seem to be little point in requiring an establishment of fault on the part of the employer.

(c) Omissions

The conduct requirement of most offences is generally satisfied by proof of positive action. But, in certain circumstances, a passive failure to act may constitute the requisite conduct. Some crimes are specifically defined so as to involve criminal liability for failing to act: for example, failing to provide for a child in one's care or failing to file one's income tax return. But for other crimes a mere failure to act will not constitute the requisite "conduct" unless there is a legal duty to act. Thus a stranger can sit on a park bench and watch a small child drown in a shallow pool; she will incur no criminal liability even though she could have rescued the child with ease. In the Netherlands a few years ago a national furore broke out over a case where more than 100 sunbathers watched a nine-year-old girl struggling and drowning in a pond. Despite the girl's friends screaming for help, nobody made any effort to rescue her (*The Guardian*, 1993). However, the mother of that girl would not be able to refrain from action with the same impunity. She would be under a duty to rescue her child in such circumstances. Breaching such a duty would constitute the requisite "act" of the crime of homicide (either murder or manslaughter, depending on her *mens rea*).

English law, rooted in the tradition of individualism, has been loath to compel people to act. The fact that there is a clear moral obligation on the stranger to rescue the child is insufficient. One is only under a duty to act when one is under a legal obligation. Apart from cases where one is under a legal statutory obligation to act (as in the earlier examples), the law only imposes a legal duty to act where a defendant has assumed, or is in a position of, responsibility whereby others reasonably expect that she will act (or would do so if appraised of the facts). There are four main situations where such a common law duty to act has been held to exist.

First, where a *special relationship* exists between the parties, each becomes under a duty towards the other. For example, parents are under a duty to aid their children; husbands and wives are under a duty to aid each other. The basis of this duty might be that the blood or marriage relationship is so strong as to generate a legal duty to preserve life (*People v. Beardsley*, 1907), but the better rationale is that the interdependence that springs from shared family life or close communal living creates a reasonable expectation of assistance which generates the duty to act (Fletcher, 1978). Thus one would generally be under a duty to aid one's lover and probably even a flat-mate (depending on the relationship), but not one's separated spouse or emancipated son or daughter (*Shepherd*, 1862) (although, again, the situation or relationship might be such that there was still a duty to act).

Secondly, where one person *voluntarily assumes a responsibility* towards another whereby that other reasonably expects assistance if necessary, a legal duty to act will have been created. The cases here have mainly concerned defendants who have assumed responsibility for elderly or infirm persons by taking them into their homes (*Instan*, 1893; *Stone and Dobinson*, 1977), but the principle would apply in other cases as well. For example, if two persons engage in a dangerous joint enterprise such as mountaineering, their relationship of mutual reliance would generate a duty to act (*LaFave and Scott*, 1986). In *Sinclair* (1998) it was indicated that a duty might arise where a close friend of a drug addict paid for and supplied the addict with methadone and remained with him throughout a period of unconsciousness prior to his death.

Thirdly, a duty to assist others may arise out of *contract* (*Pittwood*, 1902). A lifeguard employed at a swimming pool is obliged to rescue swimmers in trouble. Because of his contract of employment, the swimmers reasonably expect assistance from him.

And, finally, where the defendant has *created a dangerous situation* he becomes under a duty to minimise the harmful consequences flowing from that dangerous situation. In *Miller* (1983) the defendant, while squatting in someone else's house, fell asleep on a mattress without having extinguished his cigarette. He awoke later to discover the mattress was smouldering. He did nothing about the fire, but simply moved to another room and went to sleep again. The house caught fire and the defendant was charged with arson, contrary to sections 1(1) and (3) of the Criminal Damage Act 1971. As he only had *mens rea* at the time he saw the fire and did nothing, the *actus reus* had to be established at that time. It was held that as the defendant had started the fire he was under a duty to take whatever steps were within his power to counteract the danger he had created—either putting the fire out himself or calling for the fire brigade. Such an approach is consistent with the general principle relating to the assumption of responsibility outlined earlier. Even when our actions are unintentional, they are nevertheless *our* actions and we bear a responsibility for them. Where others are placed in danger from these actions, they expect us to "do something". There is an expectation of reasonable assistance which can generate a duty to act. In *Khan and Khan* (1998) it was indicated that a drug dealer who supplies heroin to a person could possibly owe a duty to such person—but whether a duty arose in such circumstances was a matter for the jury to decide. This abdication of responsibility to the jury is unfortunate as whether there is a legal duty to act must logically be a matter of law for the judge to determine.

So in the above limited situations the law is prepared to hold people criminally responsible for their failures to act. How can this be reconciled with the fundamental principle that the law is only concerned with punishing conduct, voluntary human action?

Gross (1979), has argued that liability for omissions is not an exception to the general requirement that there must be conduct. Using the earlier example of the child drowning in a shallow pool, he would argue that the requisite conduct is the sitting on the park bench without rescuing the child. The sitting on the park bench is the conduct, but it is only criminal when done in circumstances where someone to whom one owes a duty is in need of rescue. Many legitimate activities (for example, driving) become criminal when performed in an unacceptable manner (for example, dangerously). While the stress in omissions "is on what must be done additionally if there is not to be liability" (in the main example, rescuing the child), "liability nevertheless is *for doing* certain things without doing certain other things" (sitting on the park bench without rescuing the child). Gross uses the example of failing to file an income tax return. The conduct that is being punished here is *residence in the state* without filing a return.

The more usual explanation, however, is that passivity is just as much "willed conduct" as is activity. "Conscious non-motion is a greater assertion of personality than casual acting" (Fletcher, 1978). The person on the park bench is "acting", albeit negatively. It is a significant act of will to remain motionless in such circumstances.

If it is thus possible to justify liability for omissions as not being inconsistent with the fundamental conduct requirement, why is such liability restricted to those areas where there is a legal duty to act? Why is there no general duty to act? The argument here is that morality surely condemns the stranger who watches the child drowning when he could easily rescue her; such a person has effectively killed that child. The law ought to reflect such a morality. Further, if one of the objects of the criminal law and punishment is to stimulate socially approved conduct then the imposition of criminal liability in such cases would encourage people to act.

If a general duty to act were introduced, it could operate in one of two ways. It could exist as a separate offence carrying a minor penalty as in many Continental Criminal Codes. Thus the sunbathers in the Netherlands would not be convicted of murder or manslaughter but of a special offence of failing to rescue carrying a maximum penalty of three months' imprisonment. Alternatively, a general duty to act could replace the existing categories of legal duty, and breach of this general duty would constitute the requisite "conduct" for more serious offences. The stranger's failure to act would thus, like the mother's failure, result in a conviction for murder or manslaughter, depending on her *mens rea*. This more radical approach is unlikely ever to be adopted because, in addition to the objections to creating a general duty to act, canvassed below, there would be special problems here in relation to causation and *mens rea*. It could be difficult to argue that the stranger causes (in law) the death of the child whereas the mother, by failing to exercise her special responsibility for her child, does substantially cause (in law) the death of the child. One of the tests of a cause is whether it is something "exceptional" that alters the status quo. The mother's relationship to the child is part of the status quo. Because she is the mother her failure to act is "exceptional"; it alters the status quo and can be a cause. On the other hand, because there is no special relationship, the stranger's failure to act does not alter the status quo and so is not a legal cause of the consequence. Similarly, it has been argued that the stranger cannot have the requisite *mens rea*. She might, at most, want the child to drown, but wanting something to happen is not the same thing as intending it to happen. However, such a view is not totally convincing. One can intend anything over which one has control. One cannot intend that it will be sunny tomorrow—but the stranger can intend the death of the child because it was within her power and control to prevent that death.

The arguments against the introduction of a general duty to act are regarded by English law as overwhelming. The central argument relates to individual liberty and the view that the law should not encroach upon people's privacy and liberty by forcing them to act. The picture painted is that of a person taking a quiet Sunday morning walk through the park and being called upon to rescue one hapless victim after another. Other objections are of a more pragmatic nature. If a hundred people stood on a beach watching someone drown, would all one hundred be liable and be prosecuted? How much help would need to be given? After dragging the drowning man from the sea, would one be under a duty to provide mouth-to-mouth resuscitation and then drive him to the nearest hospital if necessary? How much danger would the rescuer be expected to risk? What if the rescuer's efforts exacerbated the situation and worsened the plight of the imperilled person?

Many of these objections can be easily countered. If there were a general duty to act, it would be limited by a criterion of reasonableness: the rescuer would only be expected to do what was reasonable in the circumstances. And with regard to the individual liberty argument, it must be remembered that our interests in doing as we like are continually being countered by opposing, greater interests. And which is the greater interest: one's right to sit on a park bench minding one's own business, or the right of the child to life? Perhaps, individual liberty can be best fulfilled "in a community which accepts that human interdependence, mutual support, and the fulfilment of interpersonal obligations are necessary for the fullest development of individuals" (Ashworth, 1991).

Perhaps the law's reluctance to impose criminal liability for omissions is based upon an intuitive feeling that it is simply not as bad to "let die" as to "kill". It is morally wrong, but not *as* wrong, to watch the child drown as to hold her head under the water. On this basis it might be desirable for omissions to be punished to a *lesser extent* than positive "action". Acceptance of this view would pave the way to the introduction of a new special offence of "failing to rescue". This crime would not carry a severe penalty, but its very existence on the statute book would have the symbolic value of underwriting the importance that ought to be attached to the value of human life and bodily safety—even of strangers.

4. BLAMEWORTHINESS

(i) Rationale

We have already seen that paradigmatically criminal liability is only imposed upon a *blameworthy* or *culpable* actor whose conduct has caused a forbidden harm (see earlier, p. 17). It is not enough that a defendant has simply done the forbidden act or caused the prohibited harm. She must have done so in circumstances in which she can properly be blamed for her conduct. Without such blame or fault she is regarded as "innocent"—and a civilised society is offended at the notion of punishing the innocent. Further, punishment of the blameless would probably be an ineffective deterrent: the law cannot hope to deter innocent actions, and those who are blameless are in no need of help or rehabilitation; and their very "innocence" indicates that they present no threat to others and so society has no need to protect itself from such persons. In short, not only would it be unjust, but also there would be little purpose served in punishing the blameless.

(ii) Indicators of blame

We saw in Chapter 1 how people are viewed today as a moral agents and not simply as instruments of causing harm. They are regarded as *responsible* for their actions. Being a responsible agent means being capable of reason and capable of understanding the social and legal norms to which one is subject; it means possessing free will. Such persons can thus control their actions and can choose whether to comply with the law or not. (The law thus firmly rejects a school of thought advocating determinism. According to this view people are not free agents always in control of their actions and choosing how to act; instead, their actions are seen as "determined" by preceding events and conditions.)

It follows that because people are responsible agents exercising control and choice over their actions, we are able to judge these actions. We can evaluate and discriminate between different actions and attribute praise or blame to the actor—in a manner that would be quite inappropriate if dealing with a non-responsible agent. In an artificial sense one might praise or blame a baby for being good or not, or praise or blame a dog for being quiet or not—but we do not hold the baby or the dog *responsible* for their actions in any meaningful way because their actions are not the product of reason, control and choice. We can judge the *result* (and disapprove of the noise made by the baby or the dog), but not the *agent* because of its non-responsibility.

This notion of responsibility and view of people as moral agents led to wide acceptance of the notion that blame and punishment is only justified if a person has *chosen* to commit a crime. If I deliberately throw my glass on the floor breaking it, you can blame me for my actions because you can disapprove of my choice to act in that way. But if I, acting in a normal, careful manner, were to slip on a loose carpet and drop my glass and break it, blame would be inappropriate; I was not in complete control of my actions and did not choose to break the glass.

This process of choosing to break the law is, of course, a mental process. Such persons are said to have a morally blameworthy *state of mind*—or, in legal shorthand, *mens rea*. Where a person acts with *mens rea* he or she is a responsible agent who has chosen to break the rules; he or she is thus blameworthy and deserves punishment. Viewed this way, *mens rea* refers to a cognitive state of mind (which includes realising consequences could occur). However, as explored earlier (p. 19), there is a broader "normative theory of criminal culpability" under which an assessment of blameworthiness is not limited to states of mind. Rather, it involves an evaluation of the defendant's actions, taking into account all the circumstances including the defendant's state of mind. Culpability or blame is the opposite of "merit" or "praise" (Snyman, 1995). It is a disapproving value judgment. Viewed this way, the presence of *mens rea* indicates that the defendant is blameworthy, but there can be other indicators of blame. However, before exploring these others, we should examine this main indicator, *mens rea*, in more detail.

(a) *Mens rea*

Mens rea is the mental element required by the definition of a particular crime. It does not refer to any single state of mind. As seen in the preceding section, it clearly embraces those who have made a decision and chosen to break the law (intention). However, *mens rea* is not limited to such states of mind. It also covers those who act realising there is a chance (perhaps only a small chance) of their conduct causing the prohibited result ("subjective" recklessness). And in some cases it could even extend to persons who do not anticipate causing any harm, but who really ought to have realised the risks and whose actions indicate indifference to the result ("objective" recklessness).

Mens rea also covers other states of mind unrelated to intending or foreseeing consequences, for example, *knowing* or *believing* that goods are stolen (Theft Act 1968, section 22), *dishonesty* (Theft Act 1968, section 1), *fraudulent* trading (Companies Act 1985, section 458). However, with result crimes in particular, increasingly it is intention and recklessness that have come to be regarded as the core *mens rea* concepts. It is these concepts that are most often inserted in modern legislation and the courts, in interpreting older statutes, have tended to recast older *mens rea* terms in terms of intention or recklessness. For example, in *Sheppard* (1981) the word "wilfully" in section 1 of the Children and Young Persons Act 1933 was interpreted as meaning intentionally or recklessly (neglecting a child). In *Savage; Parmenter* (1992) the word "maliciously" in section 20 of the Offences against the Person Act 1861 was interpreted as meaning recklessly (foreseeing injury).

Many crimes may be committed if the defendant has either of these two main species of *mens rea*. For example, section 1(1) of the Criminal Damage Act 1971 provides that the offence of criminal damage may be committed either intentionally or recklessly. With such crimes it is, of course, unnecessary to distinguish intention from recklessness; either species of *mens rea* will suffice. But certain other crimes are more limited in their *mens rea* requirements. For example, section 18 of the Offences against the Person Act 1861 provides that for the offence of wounding or causing grievous bodily harm the defendant must act "with intent to cause grievous bodily harm". A similar provision is to be found in the Criminal Attempts Act 1981, section 1(1): one can only attempt to commit a crime if one intends to commit the offence (even if the actual offence itself can be committed recklessly). For these latter crimes it is essential to define intention with some precision in order to distinguish it from recklessness.

(i) Intention

A person clearly intends a result when he wants it to happen—when it is his aim or objective. This is so even if the chances of the result occurring are slim: if the defendant shoots at his victim half a mile away knowing he could easily miss, he still intends to kill his victim if that is what he is trying to do.

But what of a defendant who does not want or mean to cause a result but who realises it will almost certainly occur? The classic example here is the man who plants a bomb in an aircraft to explode in flight; his object is to obtain insurance money; he knows passengers are virtually certain to be killed but he hopes that through a miracle they will avoid death. Does he intend the death of the passengers? And what of a defendant who again does not mean to cause a result but who realises that it is a likely or highly probable result of his actions? For instance, he might be playing a variation of Russian roulette with four out of five chambers of his revolver loaded; he points the gun at his victim and pulls the trigger—knowing there is an 80 per cent chance of the victim being killed. Does he intend to kill?

For several decades intense controversy has raged through English law concerning the meaning of intention and whether it covers these two situations. In *Hyam* (1975) Mrs Hyam poured petrol through the letterbox of the house of her lover's new mistress in the hope of frightening her into leaving the neighbourhood; she ignited the petrol knowing people were asleep in the house. When two children died in the fire and Hyam was charged with murder the jury were directed that the necessary intention for murder was established if they were satisfied that Hyam foresaw death or grievous bodily harm as a highly probable result of her actions. It was not necessary to prove that she wanted that result or that she had aimed at that consequence. The House of Lords upheld this direction, arguably endorsing the view that the word "intention" did bear such a broad meaning throughout the criminal law.

Such an approach was plainly unacceptable. It involved attributing a highly artificial and unnatural meaning to an everyday concept—something best avoided, especially in the criminal law where most issues of guilt are ultimately decided by ordinary lay persons, namely, the jury or lay magistrates. Further, assigning such a broad meaning to the word "intention" made it impossible to distinguish intention from recklessness. If a consequence were foreseen as highly probable, this was intention; if it were foreseen as merely probable or possible, this was recklessness. The imposition of criminal liability clearly should not be dependent upon such fine and impracticable distinctions. And, finally, such a broad meaning of intention was morally confusing. Most commentators felt that there was a significant moral difference between wanting a result to occur and merely foreseeing its occurrence as highly probable (Williams, 1983). While the actor in both situations is in control and is willing to produce the particular evil consequence, the actions become more reprehensible if they are deliberate and purposeful. People's objectives or aims clearly influence our perceptions of their characters as a moral agents. It is the striving to cause harm to another that marks the actions as distinctive. Further, harm is more likely to occur when the actor is trying to produce it and purposeful action involves a deliberate flouting of the legal order. More blame is appropriate than in cases where the actor does not mean to achieve the consequence but foresees it as a likely by-product of the actions. Accordingly, many commentators felt that the word and concept "intention" should be reserved for those actors who actually tried to produce the forbidden consequence. Such cases could then be marked out as more serious offences where the defendant would deserve greater punishment.

Responding to these criticisms the House of Lords was forced to retreat from the position adopted in *Hyam* (1975). In *Moloney (1985)*, where defendant shot his stepfather while engaged in a challenge to see who was quicker on the draw with shotguns, the House of Lords held that in most cases judges should refrain from elaborating or paraphrasing the meaning of intention; it should simply be left to the jury's good sense to determine whether the defendant acted with the necessary intent. This approach was endorsed by the House of Lords in *Hancock* (1986), a case which involved striking miners pushing a large lump of concrete from a bridge on to a convoy of cars below causing the death of a driver. Whether a defendant intended a result was a question of *fact* that only the jury, by concentrating on the particular facts before it, could resolve. While it is thus impossible to know what intention means in the criminal law, we can guess that many juries will opt for the common-sense definition, namely, "as 'a decision to bring about a certain consequence' or as the 'aim'" (*Mohan*, 1976). To underline this view, Lord Bridge, delivering the leading judgment in *Moloney* (1985), held that foresight of a consequence as probable, highly probable or likely was *not* the equivalent of, or an alternative to, intention. Juries might *infer* from such foresight that the defendant possessed the necessary intention but they would not be bound to draw such an inference; ultimately, the meaning of intention was completely a matter for them.

In *Moloney* (1985) Lord Bridge added an important qualification. In "rare" and "exceptional" cases it might be necessary to give guidance to the jury as to how, and in what manner, they could draw inferences from the facts to determine whether the defendant had the necessary intention. This would occur in those cases where the defendant had a purpose other than causing the prohibited harm—but where that result was an inevitable or likely consequence. For instance, Hyam's purpose was to terrorise her lover's mistress into leaving town; death or serious injury was a very likely by-product of her actions; guidance or elaboration to the jury would be necessary. The same would be true of both *Moloney* (1985) and *Hancock* (1986). In *Hancock* (1986) Lord Scarman recognised that such cases are not at all "rare" and "exceptional", and accordingly guidance to the jury will be necessary in most cases where the defendant has a primary aim in acting other than causing the prohibited harm.

Lord Bridge in *Moloney* (1985) stated that, in such cases, if a result were foreseen as "little short of overwhelming" or a "moral certainty" this would "establish" intention. In other words, intention was *defined* as including these states of mind. For all other cases (where a direction was necessary) he laid down guidelines to be employed: the jury should consider whether the relevant forbidden result was a "natural consequence" of the defendant's actions, and whether the defendant foresaw it as being a natural consequence of his actions. If so, then it would be proper for the jury to draw an inference from this that the defendant intended the forbidden consequence.

These guidelines were disapproved by the House of Lords in *Hancock* (1986) because they failed to refer to the *probability* of the consequence occurring which "may be vitally important". The greater the probability of a consequence occurring, the more likely that it was so foreseen and, if so, the more likely that it was intended. But, even in such cases, it must be emphasized that this degree of probability of the result occurring was only one factor to be considered by the jury with all the other evidence in determining whether the defendant intended a result. In *Hancock* (1986) the idea that foresight of a "moral certainty" *was* intention was ignored. In all cases foresight of whatever degree of probability was only *evidence* from which intention *could* be inferred.

In *Nedrick* (1986), where the facts were similar to those in *Hyam* (1975), the Court of Appeal attempted a "crystallisation" of these decisions by holding that the jury were "not entitled to infer" intention unless they were sure that death or serious bodily harm as a "virtual certainty (barring some unforeseen intervention)". Where a defendant realises that the consequence is "for all practical purposes inevitable", the inference that he intends that result "might be irresistible".

In *Woollin* (1998) the House of Lords attempted to tighten and clarify the *Nedrick* (1986) direction but, unfortunately, ambiguities in the leading judgment by Lord Steyn have only served to obscure the law even further. In this case a father lost his temper with his baby son and threw him across a room. The child hit his head on something hard and died. Referring to the *Nedrick* (1986) direction, Lord Steyn, at one point in his judgment, stated that "a result foreseen as virtually certain is an intended result". This is laying down a legal definition of intention. Foresight of a virtual certainty is not simply *evidence* from which intention *may* be inferred. It is a test of what intention *is*. However, at the conclusion of his judgment he approved the *Nedrick* (1986) direction but replaced the word "infer" with a new word: "find". Under this amendment the *Nedrick* (1986) direction now reads that "the jury are not entitled to find the necessary intention unless they feel sure that death or serious bodily harm was a virtual certainty (barring some unforeseen intervention) as a result of the defendant's actions and that the defendant appreciated that such was the case". This is *not* a definition of intention. It is simply a confirmation of the pre-existing law that there must be foresight of a virtual certainty before the jury is permitted to find intention. Such foresight is an evidential "precondition" (Wilson, 1999) to a finding of intention but the fact that there is such foresight does not mean the jury *have* to find intention. In appropriate cases they can still conclude that, despite the defendant foreseeing the consequence as virtually certain, there was nevertheless no intention. That there is such a "get-out clause" (Wilson, 1999) is confirmed by Lord Steyn's conclusion that "the decision is for the jury upon a considera- tion of all the evidence in the case".

These cases reveal two things. First, the judges have been keen to withdraw from the broad definition of intention laid down in *Hyam* (1975). Normally (for example, in cases of a direct attack upon the victim), no direction need be given to the jury. In the cases where a direction is necessary, nothing less than foresight of a virtual certainty will suffice before intention can be found.

But, secondly, there has been an unwillingness to deny the jury some moral elbow-room. In some cases there is a "moral threshold" (Norrie, 1999) between what the defendant foresaw as virtually certain (a legalistic notion) and what she "really" intended (a moral judgment). When deciding whether a person intended a consequence, we are, to an extent, judging their behaviour in context. We are looking at their role in the sequence of events and deciding whether to attribute moral responsibility (for the crime charged) to them. These cases, by leaving intention undefined, are trying to retain maximum flexibility so that juries do not have to resort to perverse verdicts to convict those felt deserving of conviction. Many violent protesters or terrorist bombers who do not necessarily *mean* to kill, for example, could escape liability for murder if a clear and narrow definition of intention were laid down. But now, juries have a free hand to convict where they feel it to be appropriate.

Equally, this lack of definition enables juries, not only to expand, but also to contract their definition of intention to meet the justice of the particular case. For example, the context in which Moloney killed his stepfather, bearing in mind that they had a close loving relationship, could be relevant in persuading a jury not to find intention. Similarly, in *Steane* (1947) the defendant, in order to save his family from a concentration camp during the war, made pro-German radio broadcasts. He was charged with the offence of doing acts likely to assist the enemy with intent to assist the enemy and escaped liability on the ground that he had not made the broadcasts with the requisite intention, but, rather, had acted with intent to save his family. If decided today, the context, surrounding circumstances and understandable motive of the defendant could permit a jury not to find intention despite the fact that Steane must have foreseen as a virtual certainty that his acts would assist the enemy. In *Chandler* (1964) the defendants, opponents of nuclear weapons, planned a non-violent demonstration to immobilise an aircraft at a RAF station. They were convicted of an offence under the Official Secrets Act 1911 which required proof of "a purpose prejudicial to the safety or interests of the state". Their claim that their intention had been to benefit the country was rejected. As in *Steane* (1947) it was the context, political setting and motive of the defendant that was allowed to determine what the intention was.

This approach of allowing the jury scope to take account of the context of the acts, the motives of the defendant, and the pre-existing relationship between the parties has been described as "legal argument [which] is a kind of moral shadow-boxing or ventriloquism which deals with moral issues, but at one remove" (Norrie, 1999). Such an approach of leaving critical moral issues to the jury is in fact not uncommon in the criminal law. In theft, for instance, the issue of "dishonesty" involves value judgments; ethical stances have to be taken—and the jury, as the mouthpiece of community values, is probably the most appropriate body to express such judgments. There is no reason in principle why such an approach should not be appropriate to the ascertainment of the meaning of intention.

These decisions on the establishment of intention, however, leave the law in a state of confusion and uncertainty and open the door to inconsistency in jury verdicts. Possessed with identical facts, one jury might conclude that Hyam intended death or grievous bodily harm while another jury could reach the opposite conclusion. This lack of definition and certainty is highly undesirable and simply invites prejudice, discrimination and abuse. It involves the abandoning of all standards in an area of law where it is crucial that standards be clearly laid down. The principle of legality insists that people be clearly informed in advance about what is acceptable or unacceptable conduct. While the interpretation of intention is always going to be flavoured by the context in which the actions are committed, the concept of intention does involve a consideration of less far-ranging factors than those involved in the determination of dishonesty, mentioned earlier. In the interests of certainty and predictability it is surely for *the law* to determine what intention means—and in laying down that definition community values should be reflected. To the extent that the attribution of intention and the assignment of moral responsibility do not coincide—which would be the case if Steane were held to have intended to assist the enemy—the defendant should be afforded an excuse. Thus the better approach in *Steane* (1947) would have been to have held that Steane did intend to assist the enemy but that he should escape liability on grounds of duress. This was the approach adopted by the majority in *Re A (Conjoined Twins)* (2000) where an order was made authorising doctors to separate conjoined twins even though this would certainly result in the death of the weaker twin. It was held that the doctors would have an intention to kill but would be afforded a defence of necessity. However, the third member of the Court, Robert Walker L.J., allowed himself the "moral elbow-room", discussed above, and stated that, despite the consequence being inevitable, the doctors would lack the necessary intention because the death of the weaker twin "would not be the purpose or the intention of the surgery".

One final problem must be mentioned. Most of the above cases were cases involving murder. Until *Woollin* (1998) it had been broadly accepted that "intention" bore a constant meaning throughout the criminal law. However, Lord Steyn in *Woollin* (1998) was careful to limit his judgment to the meaning of intention in the crime of murder, adding that intention need not necessarily have "precisely the same meaning in every context in the criminal law". Of course, if *Woollin* (1998) is interpreted as merely introducing a semantic change ("find" in place of "infer") that has not altered the substance of the law, this limitation to the crime of murder is unimportant. However, if a change in the law has been effected (a definition of intention introduced), this would mean that "intention" has a chameleon-like quality with its meaning varying between different crimes: it is defined for purposes of the law of murder, but for all other crimes *Nedrick* (1986) continues to apply with juries having latitude whether to find intention when a consequence is foreseen as virtually certain. (Indeed, this is an argument that Lord Steyn did mean to change the law. Why else would he have imposed this limitation?) Such an approach would be unacceptable and only increase uncertainty throughout the criminal law. It is difficult to see that there is any sound policy reason why intention should not have a fixed meaning for all crimes employing the concept.

Given the present uncertainties, there is a strong case for a legislative definition of intention. However, it will be difficult to produce a test of intention acceptable to all. One approach would be to accept Lord Steyn's dictum that foresight of a virtual certainty is the *test* of intention. A similar test, favoured by many commentators, is the Law Commission's proposal that a person acts "intentionally" with respect to a result when it is his purpose to cause it or "he knows that it would occur in the ordinary course of events if he were to succeed in his purpose of causing some other result". (Law Commission, 1993b). Such a test does at least lay down a standard. A diligent jury will know what it is working towards. Inferences, based on probabilities and so on, will still need to be drawn. But they will be inferences towards a clearly specified goal, rather than the present position where, applying the *Moloney* (1985)/*Hancock* (1986)/*Woollin* (1998) guidelines, the jury is forced to draw inferences from all the evidence to try to establish something that is totally undefined.

On the other hand, if the earlier arguments concerning the moral significance of striving to achieve a result are accepted, it could be more appropriate to limit intention to situations where the actor aimed at, or tried to achieve, the result. This would have the advantage of achieving a correlation between the legal and the ordinary meaning of intention and would ensure that some of the most serious crimes which require proof of intention (such as murder and causing grievous bodily harm with intent) were more narrowly limited to their paradigms that involve persons who mean to cause the prohibited harm. Those who fall outside the paradigm and merely foresee the harm (however high the degree of foresight) could instead be liable for lesser offences (such as manslaughter and inflicting grievous bodily harm).

One final point needs mention here. Intention must be subjectively ascertained. It is not a matter of what the defendant ought to have intended. The jury must somehow get into the mind of the defendant and find out what he actually did intend (Criminal Justice Act 1967, section 8). Such a task is, of course, impossible; we do not have "intention-meters" to plug into a person's brain. So what the jury has to do is draw inferences from the facts; they must consider all the circumstantial evidence—the conduct of the defendant before, during and after the crime, his motives, etc.—and from all this infer what he must have intended. The result is that unless the defendant is markedly different from an ordinary person (say, because he is suffering from schizophrenia), the jury will tend to conclude that if an ordinary person would have intended a certain result from his actions, then the defendant must also have had a similar intention. This is, in effect, an "objective test" of intention: the defendant is deemed to have intended that which a reasonable person would have intended in the circumstances. Nevertheless, while this might be so in practice, it is important that section 8 of the Criminal Justice Act 1967 endorses a subjective test of intention. It ensures that the exceptional defendant (say, one suffering from some abnormality) will be treated on an individualized basis. The question will be: what did *he* intend? It will not be: what would some hypothetical, normal defendant have intended?

(ii) Recklessness

The law has long regarded the reckless wrong-doer as blameworthy and deserving of punishment—but the law has not always been (and still is not) consistent as to the meaning of recklessness.

After a somewhat uncertain and vacillating history, the law appeared to have settled down by the late 1970s to approve a subjective meaning of the concept of recklessness. Under such a test recklessness involved the conscious running of an unjustifiable risk (*Cunningham*, 1957). The defendant must himself have foreseen the possibility or chance of the consequence occurring, and the risk taken must have been one that was unjustifiable or unreasonable to take in the circumstances.

For instance, in *Stephenson* (1979) the defendant crept into a hollow in the side of a large straw stack to sleep. Feeling cold, he lit a fire of twigs and straw inside the hollow. Not surprisingly, the stack caught fire and was damaged. Now, while most people would clearly recognise the risks involved in such an activity, Stephenson was able to establish that he suffered from schizophrenia which could have prevented him from foreseeing or appreciating the risk of damage from his act of lighting the fire. Accordingly, he had not been reckless.

Such a subjective test of recklessness is clearly reconcilable with the theory of responsibility outlined earlier (p. 55), explaining why we blame people for their actions. A subjectively reckless actor is responsible for his actions. He is in control of his actions and, knowing the possible consequences, has chosen to take unjustifiable risks. We can plainly disapprove of such a choice and blame him for his conduct. We can also hope that punishment will deter him and others from taking similar risks on subsequent occasions. Following this reasoning, we do not blame Stephenson for his actions. Because he was unable to realise what the possible consequences of his actions would be, he did not choose to risk causing harm; to him there was no risk. Accordingly, he was not fully responsible for the consequences of his actions.

But what if Stephenson had not suffered from schizophrenia but had simply not bothered to think about the risks involved in his activities? He might simply have been extremely tired, depressed, drunk or just foolish. Must we still respond: he was not aware of the risks; he did not choose to risk causing harm; he is blameless? Consider, for instance, the defendant in *Spratt* (1991). From the window of his flat in a housing estate he fired pellets from an airgun towards the forecourt of the estate. He claimed he was firing to see how far the pellets would go and was aiming at a sign on the rubbish chute. He claimed he failed to think about the possibility of anyone being on the forecourt. In fact, children were playing there and one of them was struck on the leg and arm by pellets, sustaining injury. Must we simply respond: Spratt did not recognise the risks; he never thought about injuring anybody; he thus made no choice to risk causing harm and is blameless?

These questions were emphatically answered in the negative by the House of Lords in *Caldwell* (1982) and in *Lawrence* (1982) when Lord Diplock, delivering the leading judgment in both cases, ruled that a defendant was reckless if he: (1) did an act which created an obvious risk of the consequence occurring—an obvious and serious risk according to *Lawrence* (1982), and (2) when he did the act he either gave no thought to the possibility of there being any risk, or recognised that there was some risk involved but nonetheless went on to do the act.

This test of recklessness (referred to hereafter as "*Caldwell* recklessness") constituted an important extension to the law of recklessness. No longer was liability dependent upon a defendant subjectively recognising the risks involved in his actions; a defendant who has completely failed to consider risks, such as the defendants in *Stephenson* (1979) and *Spratt* (1991), could now be adjudged reckless. For instance, in *Elliott v. C* (1983) a 14 year-old girl who was in a remedial class at school and who had not slept for an entire night poured white spirit on the floor of a garden shed and then threw two lighted matches on the spirit; the shed was destroyed by fire. It was established that because of her age, lack of understanding and experience, and exhaustion, she did not recognise the risk of destroying the shed; even if she had thought about the matter, she would not have realised the risks. However, it was held that the risk was an "obvious" one—obvious to a "reasonably prudent person". Accordingly, she was reckless in not giving any thought to such an obvious risk.

At first, the House of Lords held that this new test of recklessness was applicable throughout the criminal law (*Seymour*, 1983). Since then, however, there has been something of a retreat from *Caldwell* recklessness with the House of Lords in *Reid* (1992) emphasising that recklessness can bear different meanings in different contexts in the criminal law. For example, while *Caldwell* recklessness applies to criminal damage, the more "subjective" *Cunningham* (1957) recklessness applies to non-fatal offences against the person and accessorial liability. Unless there are sound reasons of principle for this approach (which there are not), it hardly seems satisfactory that recklessness should have a variable meaning especially when that meaning cannot often be predicted in advance.

At first, especially after cases such as *Elliot v. C* (1983), it was thought that this *Caldwell* recklessness test was laying down a completely objective standard making it largely indistinguishable from negligence (pp. 71–73). However, it is now clear that while it represents a major swing towards objectivity, *Caldwell* recklessness can still be described as being, in some senses at least, "subjective" and as a "state of mind". There are two reasons for saying this. First, if a defendant does consider the risk, but then rules it out as not possible, he will not come within the new test because he is not someone who has "given no thought to the possibility of there being any risk" (he has considered the possibility) nor has he acted "recognising that there was some risk involved" (he has dismissed the risk). For example, in *Chief Constable of Avon and Somerset v. Shimmen* (1987) the defendant, a Martial Arts expert, was showing off his skills to some friends. He aimed a kick at a plate-glass window contending that he had the necessary muscular control and skill to avoid breaking the window. His skill failed him and the window was broken. While it was held that Shimmen was liable for causing criminal damage, this was because he did in fact recognise that there was a risk even though he was taking precautions to try to eliminate it. However, it was conceded that a defendant who makes a genuine mistake and thinks that there is no risk will not be reckless. This approach was confirmed in *Reid* (1992) with Lord Ackner giving the example of a driver of a left-hand drive car, who, in reliance on his passenger's (mistaken) assurance that the road ahead is clear, pulls out to pass when a car is in fact approaching. Such a driver who genuinely believes there is no risk, because his passenger has assured him of this fact, is not reckless.

The second reason for asserting that *Caldwell* recklessness is still, in some respects, a state of mind and not synonymous with negligence is somewhat more elusive, but nonetheless important. In *Lawrence* (1982) it was stated that recklessness necessitated a finding of "moral turpitude" which was not necessary for negligence. While this clearly does not refer to cognition or advertence to consequences (which is the usual territory of the terminology "objective" and "subjective"), it seems to refer to a mental state or attitude of indifference or not caring. A defendant who, through momentary forgetfulness, fails to consider a risk might be negligent but will not be reckless if, for example, he throws open his car door in a residential street without first checking that the road is clear. On the other hand, a defendant on scaffolding who tosses bricks to the street below demonstrates an attitude of reckless indifference to the safety of those below. Thus whether someone is reckless under the *Caldwell* test depends on the context, setting, circumstances and degree of danger involved and whether from those actions in that context etc. one can infer an attitude of indifference. Such inferences will not always be easy to draw but, arguably, are no more difficult than trying to infer whether someone actually foresaw a risk.

Nevertheless, despite these qualifications, the fact remains that the *Caldwell* recklessness test, by moving away from cognition (advertence to consequences), does represent to some a major swing towards "objectivity" in the criminal law and has been ferociously attacked by some commentators (Williams, 1981; Smith, 1981) and rejected by the Law Commission who would re-introduce a cognition-recklessness test throughout most of the criminal law (Law Commission, 1989; Law Commission, 1993c).

The case against objective liability in the criminal law as exemplified by the *Caldwell* (1982) test of recklessness is simple. Responsibility is based upon choice; the defendant must choose to do harm (which includes *consciously* running the risk of causing harm); the defendant who simply fails to think or consider possibilities has not exercised such a choice; he is thus not blameworthy and does not deserve punishment. It is also argued that punishment is pointless under a deterrent theory of criminal law because the notion of deterrence presupposes that defendants have thought about the consequences of their actions; one who is unaware of the risks involved in his actions will hardly be deterred from so acting.

On the other hand, it is possible to support this shift towards objectivity in the criminal law. The fundamental question is whether we blame persons who fail to consider obvious risks and simply go ahead and act. Lord Diplock compared such a state of mind with that of a man who has foreseen the risks of his actions and concluded: "Neither state of mind seems to me to be less blameworthy than the other" (*Caldwell*, 1982). We do surely blame persons who fail to consider the consequences of their actions. It is this failure to bring to bear one's faculties to perceive risks that is blameworthy. We all have a responsibility to avoid creating obvious and unjustified risks to the safety of others; it is the failure to exercise this responsibility that is blameworthy. If a worker on a high building simply threw bricks down to a crowded street below, injuring pedestrians, we would surely not be impressed by his plea: "I just didn't think; my mind was elsewhere". Our response would be: "You ought to have thought; we blame you for not thinking". A failure to consider the possible consequences of one's actions expresses a certain attitude towards those consequences: it demonstrates a lack of concern about them. Duff (1980) gives the example of the bridegroom who forgets his wedding. This could only be because he regarded the whole event as quite unimportant. We are surely entitled to blame people when their lack of concern and their indifference poses risks to the safety of others.

However, such an argument is only plausible if the actor had *the capacity to do otherwise*. We can blame Spratt because he was capable of recognising the risks involved in his actions and ought therefore not to have fired his airgun. But we surely cannot hold responsible and blame the schizophrenic in *Stephenson* (1979) or the young backward girl in *Elliott v. C* (1983). They were not capable of foreseeing the consequences of their actions and therefore could not have assumed the responsibility we expect most people to shoulder; their actions did not demonstrate indifference and lack of concern; they were simply the inevitable product of their inadequacy. We can sometimes blame people for their inadequacies if it were their fault they were in such an inadequate condition (for example, if they had voluntarily consumed drugs or too much alcohol), but no civilised society should blame people for inadequacies over which they have no control. It follows that such persons ought not to be blamed for the consequences of actions that are purely the result of such an inadequate condition. There are hopeful dicta supporting this approach to be found in *Reid* (1992) where Lord Keith of Kinkel, for example, stated that a person would not be reckless "where his capacity to appreciate risks was adversely affected by some condition not involving fault on his part".

So, provided the defendant was capable of appreciating the risks involved in his actions, it follows that there ought to be little objection to blaming and punishing those who fail to think and whose actions manifest indifference to the interests of others. Indeed, there are further considerations supporting punishment in such cases. The "subjective" (cognitive) theory of criminal liability (which endorses the notion of "subjective" recklessness) assumes that the state of a person's mind is ascertainable: that somehow it is possible to establish what was in his mind when he committed the crime, possibly months or even years previously. While this same problem exists with regard to proof of intention, it is even more acute here. Lord Diplock described the distinction between consciously running a risk and failing to appreciate a risk as an impracticable distinction when the only person who knows what was in the defendant's mind is the defendant himself—and even he probably cannot recall accurately. He stated that he was simply not prepared to perpetuate such "fine and impracticable distinctions" (*Caldwell*, 1982).

And, finally, it is possible to support punishment in such cases on utilitarian grounds. The punishment of a defendant who fails to consider obvious risks might encourage him or others in the future to be more careful. It can prompt persons to take care before acting, to use their mental faculties and to draw upon their experiences so as to anticipate the consequences of those actions. We shall delay exploring the validity of such claims until later when the whole deterrent basis of the criminal law will be subjected to closer scrutiny.

(b) Negligence

A person is negligent if his conduct fails to conform to the standard expected of an ordinary reasonable man in his situation, *i.e.* if on a purely objective basis he fails to exercise the degree of care, skill or foresight that such a reasonable man would exercise.

Negligence is often classed as a species of *mens rea* on the basis that it is a state of mind: it is the failure to think about the consequences of one's actions. Not thinking refers to a state of mind, albeit a blank state of mind. However, such a view cannot be accepted for two reasons. First, it is semantic nonsense to describe a blank state of mind as a state of mind unless it could be counted as an attitude of indifference, in which case it would be *Caldwell* recklessness. According to this view, unconsciousness would need to be described as a state of mind. Second, English law has long recognised two degrees of negligence. There is simple negligence which involves the same standard as that employed by the civil law, and there is gross negligence which involves a major departure from the standards of the reasonable person. If negligence were an empty mind, how could there be degrees of emptiness and negligence? Accordingly, it is better to regard negligence not as part of *mens rea* but as a separate factor indicating blameworthiness.

As seen in the preceding section, the prevailing view until recently was that criminal liability ought generally to be based upon subjective *mens rea*. It was widely felt that punishment for negligence was generally inappropriate. Accordingly, negligence has not traditionally been regarded as an appropriate basis for the imposition of criminal liability in English law. At common law the only exceptions were careless driving (now driving without due care and attention or without reasonable consideration for other persons contrary to section 3 of the Road Traffic Act 1988) and manslaughter which requires gross negligence. However, with the proliferation of statutory offences regulating commercial and other aspects of modern daily life, there has been an increasing trend towards the creation of offences based on negligence: for example, insider trading (Criminal Justice Act 1993, section 52(2)(a)); supplying intoxicating substances to under-age persons (Intoxicating Substance (Supply) Act 1985, section 1(1)) and harassment (Protection from Harassment Act 1997, sections 1(1) and 2(1)).

However, while the formal position that crimes of negligence are few and far between still remains, the reality is more complex. Over recent years the number of crimes that are in effect crimes of negligence has grown as a result of an increasing trend to convert crimes of strict liability (crimes where no blame need be established—see pp. 135–143) into crimes of negligence by providing a "due diligence" defence. For example, with the offence of possessing prohibited drugs contrary to section 28 of the Misuse of Drugs Act 1971 the prosecution only has to prove that the defendant was in possession of the substance. It does not have to prove that the defendant knew that the substance was a prohibited drug. The defendant, however, will escape liability if he can prove (and the onus is on him) that he did not know nor suspect *nor have reason to suspect* that the substance was a controlled drug. Although the prosecution does not have to prove the necessary culpability, in effect this has become a crime of negligence in that the defendant will escape liability if he can prove that he was not negligent.

As should be clear from the preceding section, the "lurch towards objectivity" in *Caldwell* (1982) has brought that species of recklessness closer to negligence. However, it is important to reiterate the distinction between the two tests. First, a defendant who rules out a risk is not reckless but can be negligent. For example, in *Lamb* (1967) the defendant had a revolver with a five-chambered cylinder that rotated clockwise each time the trigger was pulled. The revolver had two bullets in the chambers but neither bullet was in the chamber opposite the barrel. Lamb pointed the revolver at his best friend in jest and pulled the trigger without meaning to do any harm. Unfortunately for all concerned, but most particularly for the friend, the pulling of the trigger rotated the cylinder and so placed a bullet opposite the barrel so that it was struck by the firing pin. The bullet was discharged, killing Lamb's friend. Because Lamb had checked that no bullet was opposite the barrel, he could be regarded as having made a mistake and ruled out the risk and so would not be reckless. There is no doubt, however, that he would be negligent. The reasonable person would simply not take such unjustifiable risks. The second feature distinguishing the two concepts is that while negligence simply involves failing to conform to the standards of the reasonable person, recklessness, as we saw, involves something more: it involves "moral turpitude" (*Lawrence*, 1982) and the running of an obvious *and serious* risk (*Lawrence*, 1982) manifesting an "attitude of indifference" (Duff, 1990).

So, while recklessness involves a blameworthy state of mind, negligence involves a "purely objective" failure to act according to a set standard. As blame is generally regarded as a prerequisite to the imposition of criminal liability and punishment, negligence is *generally* not regarded as an appropriate basis for the imposition of criminal liability. However, there is a strong view that more use could be made of negligence as an indicator of blame in the criminal law. Where the harm is great and the risk is obvious then, provided the defendant had the capacity to take precautions, criminal liability could be appropriate (Ashworth, 1999). Indeed, even the Law Commission (1996), who has long been committed to a subjectivist view of the criminal law, now concedes that when the harm risked is as serious as death, gross negligence liability can be justified. For example, pointing loaded guns at people and pulling the trigger is such a dangerous activity that we are surely justified in blaming and wanting to punish Lamb. This is particularly true with respect to those activities where the risks of serious harm are well-known, as is the case with dangerous weapons and with certain environmental and driving offences. It is incumbent on those engaging in activities widely recognised as dangerous to take care. Punishment for negligence could operate as an effective deterrent here.

This same debate has for the last century, and particularly over the last three decades, been conducted in a slightly different setting, namely, in relation to the law of mistake.

(c) Lack of mistake

If a defendant makes a mistake and does not think he is doing things that cause or constitute the prohibited harm, we might wish to exempt him from blame. Whether this is so depends on the type of mistake that has been made.

For most crimes the defendant must have *mens rea* in relation to the *actus reus*. This means he must have *mens rea* in relation to each of the elements of the *actus reus* (the so-called definitional elements). For instance, the *actus reus* of rape is committed when a man has sexual intercourse (*i.e.* vaginal or anal penetration) with a woman or a man without consent. To be convicted of rape a defendant must have *mens rea* (either intention or recklessness) in relation to both these definitional elements. But problems occur if he makes a genuine mistake and thinks the person is consenting when they are not.

If responsibility and criminal liability were based purely upon "subjective" *mens rea*, such a defendant ought to be acquitted— no matter how unreasonable his mistake. However, until recently the law was not prepared to adopt such a stance. Ever since *Tolson* (1889) the law insisted that a mistake had to be reasonable if the defendant was to escape liability. If the mistake was not based on reasonable grounds the defendant would be held liable. This was in fact making negligence the basis of criminal liability. A defendant who made such an unreasonable mistake lacked subjective *mens rea*, but was negligent and was being punished for that negligence.

However, in the last three decades there has been a sharp swing away from such an approach and, instead, there has been an insistence on "subjective" *mens rea*. This movement was heralded by the famous House of Lords decision in *Morgan* (1976). In this case a husband invited a number of companions home to have sexual intercourse with his wife. He suggested to them that if she struggled they were not to take it seriously as that was her way of increasing her sexual satisfaction. The men all had intercourse without the wife's consent. At their trial for rape they claimed that because of the husband's story they had honestly believed she was consenting. The trial judge directed the jury in accordance with the then established law that the men would only escape liability if their belief that the woman was consenting was based on reasonable grounds. The House of Lords held that this direction was wrong. If the men honestly believed that the woman was consenting they lacked *mens rea*. The reasonableness or otherwise of their belief was irrelevant— thus, in effect, ousting negligence as a basis for the construction of criminal liability. (It ought perhaps to be pointed out that while the House of Lords held that the trial judge's direction in law was incorrect, it nevertheless dismissed the appeal holding that a properly directed jury would have dismissed the defendants' story as a "pack of lies" and would clearly have convicted.)

Another famous illustration of this shift away from basing liability on negligence is to be found in the Court of Appeal decision of *Williams (Gladstone)* (1984). The defendant saw a man dragging a youth along a street and striking him. Leaping to the rescue of the youth, he punched the man who sustained injuries to his face. Had the facts been as he believed them to be, he would have escaped liability on the basis that he was acting in "self-defence" of the youth (see later pp. 86–95). However, he had made a mistake. The man, who had seen the youth seize a woman's handbag, was in the process of lawfully restraining him with a view to taking him to a police station. Under the old law the defendant would have escaped liability only if his mistake had been a reasonable one (*Albert v. Lavin*, 1982). However, following the approach endorsed in *Morgan* (1976), it was held that the unreasonableness of the belief was irrelevant because that would involve convicting the defendant on the basis of his negligence. The crime with which the defendant had been charged (Offences against the Person Act 1861, section 47—see later, pp. 178–179) required proof of the following definitional elements: (i) that the defendant committed an act; (ii) which was unlawful, and (iii) resulted in the application of force to the victim. For criminal liability, *mens rea* had to exist in relation to all three elements. Because of his mistake the defendant thought he was acting *lawfully*. He thus lacked *mens rea* and so escaped criminal liability.

This line of reasoning has now received clear endorsement by the House of Lords in *B v. DPP* (2000). In this case the defendant, a 15 year-old boy, invited a 13 year-old girl to perform oral sex with him. He was charged with the offence of inciting a child under 14 to commit an act of gross indecency, contrary to section 1(1) of the Indecency with Children Act 1960. The boy honestly believed the girl was over 14 years of age. Their Lordships held that such a belief meant that the defendant had no *mens rea* with regard to an *actus reus* element (the child being under 14). The reasonableness of his belief was irrelevant. To insist on reasonableness would be effectively to convert the crime into one of negligence which would be unacceptable given the "general shift from objectivism to subjectivism in this branch of the law".

All the above cases concerned mistakes as to clear *actus reus* definitional elements (whether the victim was consenting or was over 14 years of age) or mistakes as to an element of a justificatory defence. In the next section we shall see that defences are traditionally classified as being either justifications or excuses. Conduct is justified when it is, in effect, approved of or, at least, not wrongful. A person acting in self-defence is not committing a wrong; in restricting unprovoked aggression he is doing what we expect him to do and so is acting lawfully. The above cases have declared that one of the *actus reus* elements is the need for *unlawful* action. The defendant who makes a mistake and thinks he is acting lawfully lacks *mens rea* in respect of this *actus reus* element.

The House of Lords in *B v. DPP* (2000) did not, however, cite or discuss another line of cases concerning defendants who make mistakes as to whether they have an *excuse* for acting as they do. When conduct is excused, the actions of the defendant remain wrong and unacceptable (*i.e.* unlawful) but because she has an excuse, we blame her less or not at all. For example, in *Graham* (1982) it was held that the defence of duress (regarded as a classic example of an excuse) would only be available to one who *reasonably* believed that she was being subjected to severe threats. It is possible to support this divergence of approach. A person who makes a mistake as to a justificatory defence element mistakenly believes she is doing a good or, at least, lawful thing: blame and censure is inappropriate. But, when a person, because of a mistake, does what they know to be a wrong, unlawful act (stealing because of perceived duress), the law is right to insist on a higher standard that only a plausible (reasonable) mistake will exempt the defendant from blame. Extra care is needed from people who know they are doing wrong. The problem with this approach, however, is that the distinction between justifications and excuses is not always that clear-cut and classifying lack of justificatory defences (but not excusatory ones) as part of the *actus reus* requirement is little more than trickery by sleight of hand.

This rather dry doctrinal analysis with insistence on subjective *mens rea* in relation to each *actus reus* element sidesteps the central issue whether we are only justified in blaming those who actually realise they are causing a harm or doing a wrong. Perhaps the law on mistake should be more "context-sensitive" making "reference to the circumstances of the act, to D's responsibilities, or to social expectations of conduct in that situation" (Ashworth, 1999). For example, persons such as police officers or members of the armed forces who inflict force on others believing they are acting in self-defence perhaps have an extra responsibility, because of their training, to reflect on their reasons for acting—and so the law should insist on a reasonable mistake requirement. Similarly, the context in which the crime of rape takes place—the close proximity between the parties necessarily providing an opportunity for the man to ask whether the other is consenting in cases of any doubt—again suggests that only reasonable mistakes should exculpate.

Of course, it is possible to go further than the limited argument that in some contexts and some circumstances only reasonable mistakes should exempt defendants from liability. There is the deeper argument that in all cases we are entitled to expect a certain level of conduct from people and we are justified in condemning failures to achieve that standard. These are the arguments considered earlier (pp. 66–68) when discussing the cases of *Caldwell* (1982) and *Lawrence* (1982) and whether criminal liability is appropriate in situations where a defendant might not be aware of the consequences of his actions but ought to have been. The two lines of authority are technically reconcilable: the defendants in *Morgan* (1982) and *Williams (Gladstone)* (1984) could well be said to have considered the risks involved in their actions but to have ruled them out, thus not coming within the net of *Caldwell* (1982) recklessness. However, in spirit, the two sets of cases are diametrically opposed, with *Caldwell* (1982) and *Lawrence* (1982) holding responsible and blameworthy those who *ought* to have considered risks—and *Morgan* (1976) and *B v. DPP* (2000) exempting from responsibility and blame all who did not subjectively realise they were doing wrong. It is unlikely that such tensions within the law will be easily settled—and certainly cannot be regarded as concluded by dogmatic statements about "a general shift from objectivism to subjectivism" (*B v. DPP*, 2000)—but if the criminal law is ever to develop in a coherent manner, central conflicts such as these will need resolution.

(d) Lack of defence

(i) Introduction

We have seen in the preceding sections that the law blames persons with *mens rea*. But even this is not an invariable rule. A person might have intended to cause a harm but we would not blame her if she, say, punched another in the face to save her own life. In other words, viewing the matter negatively: we do not blame a defendant if she is (through no fault of her own) incapable of complying with the law or has a valid excuse or justification for her actions (or, perhaps in certain situations, we might blame her less). These exemptions from liability are, in Anglo-American law, termed "defences".

Most defences in English law are "general defences": they are complete defences to any criminal charge. Others, however, are partial and particularised defences: for example, provocation is a defence only to the crime of murder but does not result in a complete exemption from liability; the defendant is instead convicted of manslaughter.

English law has long adopted the view that all defences are either excusatory or justificatory. However, some other legal systems (such as South Africa) and some recent English commentators (Gardner, 1998) suggest that there are three types of defence: preconditions of responsibility; justifications; and excuses. The reason for separating off the first of these is that before there can be any moral evaluation of the defendant's actions and culpability, there is a "fundamental precondition of responsibility" to be satisfied: the defendant must be responsible for his actions as a moral agent. One must be sure that they are *his* actions in the sense he bears a *basic* responsibility for them. For example, if a defendant, through no fault of her own, acts in a completely involuntary manner with no awareness of what she is doing, she is not a responsible moral agent and is simply not amenable to the criminal law's evaluative judgments as to culpability. Again, we would exempt from any consideration of liability the conduct of an insane person who lacked capacity to comply with the law's commands. While these defences have traditionally been regarded by English law as excuses, it is argued that if authorship of the actions is denied, the defendant has done (in the sense of being responsible for) no wrong; there is nothing to excuse. Responsibility, in this basic sense, for one's actions is necessary in order for those actions to be amenable to justification or excuse.

Such an analysis, however, is problematic. The cases where the precondition of responsibility is not satisfied are those involving automatism, insanity, lack of age and involuntary intoxication. While some actors in these categories can properly be described as lacking basic responsibility for their actions, the fact remains, as already seen in relation to automatism (p. 37), that the law tends to the view that there is a continuum of involuntariness—with the context, nature and dangerousness of the behaviour influencing where the line is to be drawn. In some cases semi-conscious behaviour has been held to be capable of being involuntary (*T*, 1990); the actor does bear *some* responsibility for the actions. Similarly, with lack of age, it simply makes no sense to say that the average nine-year old child bears no basic responsibility for his actions in the sense that they are not *his* actions. In these cases there is some responsibility for the actions but because the behaviour was only semi-conscious or because of the youth of the actor, we are prepared to excuse the behaviour and exempt the actor from blame. The argument that the preconditions of responsibility should be treated separately from excuses faces further obstacles. Lacey (2000) adds diminished responsibility to this list of persons who are "beyond the purview of criminal law's proscriptions and other communications". But, again, as the very label "diminished" (as opposed to a complete lack of) responsibility suggests, there is some residual actor-responsibility. The reality, again, is that such persons do bear basic responsibility for the actions, but to the extent their responsibility is diminished, they are afforded an excuse. Further, if one is to take this precondition approach seriously, extreme cases of voluntary intoxication should result in a complete defence on the basis that the actor bears no basic responsibility for the acts. South African law adopts this approach where it was stated in the leading case in relation to a "dead drunk" person that there was "no question of an act . . . there is no trace of control and it is therefore unnecessary to philosophise about fault; there is simply no room for fault. There is similarly no question of criminal capacity." (*Chretien*, 1981). Such an approach is (and should not be) accepted by English law. As we shall see, English law adopts the view that a person who voluntarily consumes drink or drugs does bear a basic responsibility for any actions committed even while "dead drunk". It is the blameworthy act of getting drunk that informs the construction of the later acts. Finally, if the precondition approach is taken to its logical conclusion many other categories of person should be exempted from liability as not being the author of their actions. Thus, South African law allows provocation and emotional stress to exclude the voluntariness of conduct (*Arnold*, 1985) when the better approach is that the actor has "acted" (*i.e.* bears a basic responsibility for the actions) but, because of the provocation, is excused (or partially excused).

It must be stressed that it is important whether these cases are classified as preconditions of responsibility or as excuses. If the former approach is accepted, the test becomes a purely subjective one: is there basic actor-responsibility? The causes of non-responsibility, whether insanity, age, drunkenness or provocation, etc., and whether the actor is to be blamed for such non-responsibility, are irrelevant. If, however, these cases are regarded as excuses, policy considerations relating to blame can be let in and, subject to an exploration of the rationale of excuses (below, p. 96), there can be an insistence on the defendant being free from blame before being entitled to an excuse. There can be a moral evaluation of the actions with perhaps a requirement that an excuse will only be available if a reasonable person would have acted in the same way in the circumstances. Because of the importance of allowing policy to dictate the contours of blame (which is, after all, the pivot around which criminal liability does and should revolve in most cases), and because of the above problems associated with the precondition approach, this book will continue to adopt the more orthodox Anglo-American stance, which also better reflects the present English law, and regard these cases as ones raising excuses. However, as will be explored shortly, there might be a case for recognising two different categories of excuse: one relating to the clearer preconditions of responsibility, which could be termed *status excuses*, and the other covering *non-status excuses*. Such a sub-division of excuses could permit a more fine-tuned approach to be adopted. With status excuses there could be an insistence on the defendant being free from blame (a prerequisite of all excuses) but, recognising the different aetiology of the defences, one could dispense with any objective requirement that a reasonable person would have reacted in the same way.

What is the difference between a justificatory and an excusatory defence? When conduct is justified it is, in effect, "approved" of or, at least, tolerated as acceptable conduct. Any harm caused by the defendant is outweighed by the fact that he has thereby avoided an even greater harm or has furthered some greater societal interest (Robinson, 1982). For instance, a defendant acting reasonably in self-defence or a police officer using reasonable force to effect an arrest will have a justificatory defence for his conduct. He has done no wrong. Each is promoting a greater interest, namely, restricting unprovoked aggression, and ensuring the law is enforced, respectively.

Because justified conduct is acceptable conduct, it follows that there is no need to try to prevent such conduct recurring. Not only is the defendant blameless, but also a deterrent or incapacitative sentence would be quite inappropriate. Further, one is entitled to assist a defendant in his justified conduct. He is "behaving correctly"; one is always permitted to assist others in such behaviour and, for the same reason, one is not entitled to use force to resist such justified conduct (subject to what has been said above concerning unreasonable mistakes—see earlier, pp. 74–76). So, for example, one cannot use force to resist a lawful arrest as this would involve an undermining of the greater interest being protected, namely, the enforcement of the law.

With excuses the focus is on the actor rather than the conduct. With an excusatory defence, the conduct of the defendant remains unacceptable or wrong but, because of some precipitating event or excusing condition or characteristic of the defendant, we hold her not responsible (or not fully responsible) for the wrong act. Her excuse renders her blameless (or less blameworthy) and therefore it would be unjust to punish her at all (or to the full extent for the crime committed). So, for example with non-status excuses, we do not blame someone for giving in to the sort of threats that all reasonable people would have given in to. Such a person has an excuse for her actions. Similarly, with status excuses we do not blame someone for being insane or for being only eight years old; such a person has an excuse for her actions. But, the fact nevertheless remains that a wrong has been done to the victim and so society might feel it necessary to protect itself from repetition of such conduct. So, despite the insane person being "blameless", society might wish to commit her to a secure mental hospital, and although the eight-year-old is not "blamed" for the harm he causes, society may choose to retain some control over him by the institution of civil care proceedings. And, finally, because a "wrong" has been done to the victim, it follows that one may not assist such an excused defendant as this would be helping to perpetrate an evil and, similarly, one can use force to resist an excused attack. If an insane defendant attacks one, reasonable force is permitted to resist such aggression. The insane defendant is committing a "wrong" to the victim and one is always permitted to counter such unacceptable conduct.

We are now in a position to examine these justificatory and excusatory defences in more detail.

(ii) Justification
In what circumstances is conduct justified on the basis that it avoids a greater harm or promotes a greater societal interest? Two examples of a justificatory defence were given above, namely, self-defence and public authority (for example, the use of reasonable force by the police in effecting a lawful arrest). In order to obtain some insight into the workings of justificatory defences, two defences, consent and self-defence, will be examined in more detail.

(i) Consent In certain circumstances the victim's consent is a defence to a criminal charge. If you consent to my cutting open the skin on your toe in order to remove a thorn, my conduct becomes justified, acceptable conduct. The greater interest here is the value of human autonomy. Individuals are free and responsible agents and respect must be given to their right to consent to physical injury, etc., being committed against them. However, in certain circumstances the interests of society are deemed to prevail over any value attached to human autonomy and consequently consent may not be given to certain types of harm.

This was the reasoning adopted by the House of Lords in *Brown* (1993) when it held that consent was a defence to common assault (which involves only a minimal degree, or threat, of injury). Where the level of injury caused is so minor the law can afford to protect interests in autonomy. However, where more than trivial injury results and actual or grievous bodily harm results, consent is only a defence if there is social value attached to the activity. Where the activity is regarded as socially desirable or acceptable, the law permits one to consent to serious injuries. Thus we regard a medical operation as a socially valuable activity and so one can consent to serious injury in the course of proper medical treatment. Whether there are any limits to the sorts of medical treatment that can be consented to is uncertain. For example, some people suffer from a rare disorder (apotemnophilia) and want to have their limbs amputated. Some of these persons find the whole concept sexually arousing. Others want the operation because they regard themselves as incomplete with four limbs and will only feel normal when one limb is amputated. It was recently discovered that a surgeon in Scotland had performed two amputation operations on persons in the latter category (British Medical Journal, 2000). No criminal prosecution was brought. While the issue has never been tested, it is unlikely that the mere fact of being a registered medical practitioner will necessarily provide immunity from criminal liability in all such cases. Further, it is clear that one cannot consent to one's own death even at the hands of a qualified medical practitioner; euthanasia has not been accepted by our society.

Another socially acceptable activity is sport and so injuries sustained in rugby, football, boxing and other sports are deemed to have been consented to, provided the injuries are sustained "in the course of play" (*Billinghurst*, 1978). Indeed, while one cannot directly consent to one's own death, if death results from, say, boxing (as it has), the deceased will be deemed to have consented to the injury that led to the death. The rationale for allowing consent here is that lawful sport is a socially desirable and beneficial activity to be encouraged. Such sports are "manly diversions, they tend to give strength, skill and activity, and may fit people for defence, public as well as personal, in time of need" (Forster, 1762). Many would today strongly disagree that boxing provides sufficient social benefit as to justify its continued legalisation. However, the practical problems of criminalising such a widely condoned activity clearly outweigh any arguments of principle.

Another category of injuries that may be consented to is those inflicted in the course of body alteration: cosmetic surgery, male circumcision, tattooing and piercings of the body for purposes of personal adornment, for example the piercing of ears and tongues to insert decorative jewellery. The social utility in such activities is less obvious although presumably personal "beau-tification" is the prevailing interest being protected in some of these cases. In *Wilson* (1996) the defendant, at his wife's instiga-tion, used a hot knife to brand his initials on her buttocks. It was held that, as the wife regarded this as "the acquisition of a desirable piece of personal adornment" and as it was similar to tattooing, the wife's consent should be respected; it was not in the public interest to criminalise the defendant's conduct.

Finally, it has been held that the public interest demands that in appropriate situations such as the school playground, barrack room or factory floor, people must be deemed to have consented to "rough horseplay". For example, in *Jones* (1986) some school-boys escaped criminal liability after they threw the victim some ten feet into the air causing serious injuries, including a rup-tured spleen which had to be surgically removed. Had the victim asked to be thrown in the air, one could accept that there is no public interest in denying the right to consent. But, in this case the law deemed a boy, who was trying to run away, to have consented. It is difficult to understand what public interest could justify this. Boys might be boys but bullying, which is what this amounts to, is something the criminal law should not tolerate when serious injury results.

On the other hand, where the conduct in question is not approved of and is deemed not to be in the public interest, no consent may validly be given to the causing of anything less than trivial injuries. Occasionally, legislation criminalizes con-duct irrespective of consent being given. For example, the Prohibition of Female Circumcision Act 1985 makes female circumcision an offence and the consent of the female is no defence. More usually, however, it has been for the common law to determine whether the public interest should prevail over individual autonomy. Thus one cannot consent to injuries inflicted in the course of fighting (other than lawfully organised boxing or wrestling) (*Attorney-General's Reference (No. 6 of 1980)*, 1981). Such fighting, whether in the street, a pub or on private property is unlawful and each party may be liable for any injuries inflicted on the other. There is a strong public interest in the maintenance of order. There can only be the weakest autonomy interest in expressing oneself through violence (macho pride, showing off, fear of being branded a coward, etc.) The public interest accordingly "trumps" the personal interest. A similar approach has been adopted to more unconventional forms of body piercing. While the piercing of ears, nose and tongue has become acceptable and therefore can be legally consented to, the extent to which one can consent to all such injuries is severely limited by cultural, historical and moral factors. In *Adesanya* (1974) a mother was convicted of aggravated assault offences when she cut the cheeks of her sons in accordance with her tribal custom. In *Oversby* (1991) it was held that while body piercing for decoration was not an offence, piercings for obscene purposes or piercing one's lover's penis for sexual pleasure was a criminal offence, irrespective of consent (Bibbings and Alldridge, 1993).

In a similar vein the House of Lords in *Brown* (1993) held that one could not consent in law to injuries (amounting to more than a battery) inflicted in the course of consensual sadomasochistic activities. In this case the appellants, a group of sado-masochistic homosexuals, regularly met to participate in inflicting pain on each other. Many of their activities involved genital torture such as inserting fish hooks through another's penis or dripping hot wax into the urethra of the other's penis. These activities were all engaged in for sexual pleasure. They had all been consented to and, indeed, requested. They were "controlled" in that code words could be used to terminate the activity; instruments were sterilised to reduce the risk of infection; none of the injuries necessitated medical treatment. In *Emmett* (1999) a similar approach was adopted in a case involving heterosexual sado-masochism between a couple who were living together. While this case suggests that one might be able to consent to some forms of actual bodily harm, it was nevertheless made clear that one could not lawfully consent to sadomasochistic injuries which are more than transient or trivial.

Does the European Convention on Human Rights have a role to play here? Article 8 enshrines a right to respect for private life which ought surely to encompass the private sexual activities in these cases. Indeed, *Brown* (1993) was challenged on this basis in the European Court of Human Rights in *Laskey, Jaggard and Brown v. U.K.* (1997). The European Court conceded that there was a violation of the right to respect for private life in Article 8(1) but ruled that criminalisation in cases involving "violence" was justifiable under Article 8(2) which permits invasions of privacy if it is "necessary in a democratic society . . . for the protection of health or morals".

In so ruling, the European Court effectively endorsed the highly moralistic stance of the House of Lords in *Brown* (1993) that "pleasure derived from the infliction of pain is an evil thing" (per Lord Templeman). If someone inserts a pin through your ear, that is legal. As a society we have accepted the culture of ear-piercing. The purpose is making oneself more attractive and we appear to value (indeed, encourage through advertising) adornments to increase "attractiveness". However, if someone sticks a pin through your penis because you gained sexual excitement thereby, that person commits a crime.

We shall see later (pp. 248–252) that, generally speaking, legal moralism has gone out of fashion. We usually need a better reason to criminalise conduct than that we find it disgusting. For instance, we need to establish that the conduct "harms" another and it is difficult to say that a person is "harmed" by an injury that was requested. However, *Brown* (1993) demonstrates that when judges find an activity sufficiently "disgusting" public interest in the maintenance of "standards" soon predominates over individual autonomy interests in expressing one's sexuality in the manner one finds most appropriate. The effect of this decision is to condemn all sado-masochists, who wish to be involved in the causing of more than minimal harm, to a life of celibacy. It seems hard to believe that a person's interest in sexual self-expression is so much less important than an interest in looking beautiful or engaging in other, approved-of "manly diversions". Responding to such criticisms, the Law Commission (1995) has proposed that (with exceptions) consent should be a valid defence in all cases where injury is caused unless there has been an intentional or reckless causing of "seriously disabling injury". If implemented, this would meet many of the above objections but still does not resolve the deeper issue of whether the law is justified in overriding the autonomy interests of a person who freely chooses to consent to such a very serious injury. Whether such a paternalistic attitude is justified is a matter considered later in this book (pp. 249–250).

(ii) Self-defence The phrase "self-defence" is misleading as the defence covers not only protection of oneself, but also acts done in defence of one's property and in defence of others. We all have a right to resist threats to ourselves or any interests with which we are closely identified, including proprietary interests which can be regarded as "interests of personality" (Kadish, 1976). However, the title "self-defence" is retained here—because of its wide acceptance in common parlance.

Analysis of the scope of the present English law on self-defence is rendered problematic because this is one area of substantive criminal law that will certainly be affected by the European Convention on Human Rights which has been incorporated into English law by the Human Rights Act 1998. Article 2(1) declares that "everyone's right to life shall be protected by law" but that deprivation of life will not contravene the Convention "when it results from the use of force which is no more than absolutely necessary . . . in defence of any person from unlawful violence".

There is controversy over the extent to which this provision will affect the law. First, Article 2 only applies when the force used in defence results in the death of the aggressor. It does not cover the use of force that results in injuries short of death or in damage to property. Secondly, the present English law on self-defence applies not only to threats of violence but also to attacks on property. For example, one can use reasonable force against a burglar. Under Article 2, however, one is only allowed to kill to protect oneself against "unlawful violence". As a result of these differences two approaches are possible. The whole law of self-defence could be interpreted in a manner consistent with the Convention jurisprudence meaning that there would be one set of rules applying in all situations involving self-defence. (Emmerson and Ashworth, 1999). The alternative view is that English law could end up with two sets of rules: one where the defensive force does not lead to the death of the aggressor or where there is an attack not amounting to "unlawful violence" (where the current English law would apply) and another where the aggressor is killed in response to unlawful violence (where the jurisprudence on Article 2 would apply).

There is one final controversy surrounding the potential scope of the Convention. There is agreement that under Article 2 the citizen has a right to have his life protected by the state and so the provision clearly applies to killings by the agents of the state, most notably the police and the army. This is important as many of the cases have involved policemen or soldiers killings suspected criminals or terrorists. But does Article 2 apply where one citizen kills another? Buxton (2000) argues that it does not because the Convention only requires a state to have in place a system of law that gives "adequate protection against the prospect of being killed by other Englishmen". Ashworth (2000b), however, argues that Article 2 will be interpreted to apply in such cases as it would be contrary to the Convention to accord less protection to people from attack by other citizens than from attack by officials. It should be pointed out, however, that it would not necessarily be irrational to have different standards here. As we shall see, Article 2 lays down a much stricter test of when it is permissible to kill another in self-defence. Because of their training and experience it could well be proper to expect soldiers and policemen to conform to a higher standard than ordinary citizens.

Given these uncertainties, the focus in the following section will be on the present English law but reference will be made throughout to any potential impact of the European Convention on Human Rights on these rules.

The law and the policy underlying that law is best revealed by examining a famous American case (*Goetz*, 1986) and exploring how English law would respond to such a factual scenario. In December 1984 Bernhard Goetz was riding on the New York subway when he was suddenly surrounded by four black youths. One of them demanded five dollars. Goetz, who had been mugged some three years previously and had become somewhat obsessed with that incident, drew a .38 pistol and shot the four men he thought were about to rob him. Two of the youths were shot in the back. One of the youths was shot a second time as he lay slumped in a seat. Three of the youths were carrying screwdrivers, but this fact was unknown to Goetz. After the shooting Goetz fled. All four youths were seriously injured; one was paralysed from the waist down. Despite being initially hailed as a hero, the "subway vigilante" Goetz was eventually charged with attempted murder, assault, reckless endangerment of other passengers in the subway and with unlawful possession of a firearm. If this case were heard in the English courts, would Goetz be able to plead successfully that his actions were justified on grounds of self-defence?

"Vigilantism is private enterprise in the justice business" (Will, 1985). It is clearly the function of the law to preserve law and order and protect the innocent. While people might have reservoirs of rage waiting to burst out and might fantasize about killing and humiliating those who threaten or offend them, the reality is that we do not live in the Wild West or in a Clint Eastwood movie—but in a so-called civilised society. And in such a society it is imperative that the right of the individual to self-help be restricted. Being allowed to use force in self-defence is an exception to the basic tenet that we all owe a duty to others not to injure or kill them. However, this obligation only lasts as long as the government is able to protect its citizens (Hobbes, 1651). When the government is no longer able to afford protection a citizen is entitled to resort to self-help. Accordingly, in many situations self-help is necessary because it would be impracticable or unrealistic to rely upon the arrival of official help. It follows that for this self-help to be justified, it must be *necessary*. If it were necessary for Bernhard Goetz to do all he did in order to protect himself, then his actions were justified and he is free from blame. But if the force used were not necessary to repel the attack—if he was a vigilante taking the law into his own hands or a disturbed individual striking back in hatred or vengeance—then his actions cease to be justifiable and we can blame him for his excessive response.

The paradigmatic situation involving self-defence is where, as in *Goetz* (1986), the defendant is being attacked by an aggressor. There are, however, exceptional cases where the rules of self-defence can be stretched to allow defensive action against a non-culpable person. For example, if one is attacked by someone who is insane or in a state of automatism, one may use defensive force to protect oneself. In *Re A* (*Conjoined Twins*) (2000) twins were conjoined (Siamese twins). If they were separated the weaker twin (Mary) would be killed but the stronger one (Jodie) would have good prospects of survival. Without a severance both would die. The Court of Appeal ruled (against the wishes of the parents) that doctors could decide to perform the operation even though this would necessarily involve the death of Mary. Part of Ward L.J.'s analysis was in terms of self-defence. Jodie was entitled to have her life defended by an operation causing the death of her sister whose existence was threatening Jodie's life: "The reality here . . . is that Mary is killing Jodie." Doctors were entitled to remove "the threat of fatal harm to her presented by Mary's draining her lifeblood". Accordingly, it might be better for the rules on self-defence to concentrate on the defendant's normative position rather than on the culpability of the other person (Horder, 1998). Nevertheless, most of the present law has been structured as a response to the paradigmatic self-defence situation. In determining whether defensive force was necessary, the law has been primarily concerned with balancing the competing interests of the initial aggressor and the defender—but as the aggressor was the culpable one responsible for starting the violence, the law has (mostly) tended to tip the scales in favour of the defender. This is tacit acceptance of a moral theory of forfeiture: the aggressor by his wrongful attack has to some extent forfeited his right to bodily integrity and even life. Four issues call for determination. The bias in favour of the defender goes a long way towards explaining how these issues have been resolved in English law.

First, was *any* defensive action necessary? The four youths in *Goetz* (1986) might never have posed any physical threat to Goetz at all. Had he declined their request for five dollars they might have done nothing. On the other hand, irrespective of what might actually have occurred, Goetz was scared; to him the threat was real and he believed he was about to be mugged. English law used to insist that the defender's belief that defensive action was necessary had to be reasonable. Only if a reasonable person in Goetz's situation would also have believed he was about to be physically attacked would defensive action be permitted. Such an approach is surely correct. If the reasonable person would have made the same mistake there can be no question of our blaming Goetz (in relation to this first issue). The law ought to recognise, and indeed praise, those who act in a reasonable manner.

However, as we saw earlier in relation to the law of mistake (pp. 73–77), the law has now moved away from this objective standard of reasonableness. The idea is that if the defendant genuinely believes that defensive action is necessary then he or she is not blameworthy and must be judged according to that belief (*Williams (Gladstone)*, 1984) This means that if Goetz were paranoid or neurotic and believed he was about to be attacked when, say, a youth on the subway had merely asked him the time, we would have to judge his conduct as though he were actually about to be attacked. In balancing the interests of aggressor and defender this seems to be excessively biased in favour of the defender—especially as there is no actual aggressor in the example. As was argued earlier, the objective requirement of reasonableness is there to isolate the blameless from the blameworthy. The fact that someone has acted unreasonably, or has made an unreasonable mistake, is one of the indicators of blame and ought not to be swept aside in such a manner. In those cases affected by the European Convention on Human Rights it is likely that English law will be forced to change direction. The jurisprudence from the European Court of Human Rights on Article 2 has insisted that there be a reasonable belief in the need for force (*McCann*, 1996). The approach adopted in *Williams (Gladstone)* (1984) would be clearly contrary to this stricter standard.

The second important issue is whether one is under a duty to retreat, if possible, when faced with aggressive force. Goetz, for instance, did not try to escape although he could probably have retreated to the other end of the subway car, where some twenty other passengers were gathered. Would this failure to retreat mean that defensive force was unnecessary? There is a conflict here between two opposing views. The first view insists that one should be allowed to hold one's ground and not be forced by an aggressor to the "ignominy, dishonour, and disgrace of a cowardly retreat" (Beale, 1903). The defendant's right to autonomy—the right to be where he or she chooses to be provided he or she is acting lawfully—must be respected. The opposing view is that in a civilised society, while cowardice might be regrettable, it is infinitely worse to resort to violence that could possibly be averted. The defendant's right to autonomy must be balanced against the victim's right to life and bodily integrity; the law should encourage people to retreat from situations that could end in violence. Following the Hobbesian view (above p. 88) self-help is only justified when the government is no longer able to protect the citizen and, accordingly, people should retreat and seek official help whenever possible.

The English courts have, perhaps understandably, tried to steer a middle path between these two extremes and have held that while a person is not under a positive duty always to retreat, the defender ought to demonstrate that he or she does not wish to fight. A failure to retreat will be one of the factors to be taken into account in determining whether the defensive action was reasonable and necessary (*Julien*, 1969; *McInnes*, 1971). On this basis, if the Goetz case were being heard in an English court, the failure to retreat would certainly indicate that defensive force was unnecessary, but it would by no means be conclusive of that fact.

The third issue concerns the immediacy of the threatened violence. It is often stated that the anticipated attack must be imminent and that one is not justified in using force to repel violence that will only occur in the future. But the courts, again desirous of providing extra consideration to the defender as opposed to the aggressor, have held that anticipatory self-defence can be justifiable in certain circumstances. In *Attorney-General's Reference (No. 2 of 1983)* the defendant's shop had been damaged and looted during the 1981 rioting in Toxteth. Fearing further attacks, he manufactured ten petrol bombs to protect himself and his shop. These expected attacks never materialised. The defendant was charged with possessing an explosive substance contrary to section 4 of the Explosive Substances Act 1883. However, the Court of Appeal ruled that his actions were justified on the grounds of self-defence. He was possessing the bombs for a "lawful object" (self-defence) and therefore could not be liable as section 4 exempts those who act with a "lawful object" from liability. If one is allowed to defend oneself in the face of an attack, one must be allowed to prepare oneself for such defensive force. The defendant is not confined for his remedy to calling the police or boarding up his premises.

The implications of this decision are potentially alarming. One of the charges brought against Bernhard Goetz was unlawful possession of a firearm. Presumably, following the reasoning in *Attorney-General's Reference (No. 2 of 1983)*, arming oneself for one's own protection against a genuinely anticipated attack is a justifiable act. Goetz, because of his previous mugging and because of widely held views as to the dangerousness of New York subways, would probably be able to establish such a genuine fear and could therefore escape liability on this count. Clearly, some anticipatory defensive action must be permitted but not as much as the *Attorney-General's Reference (No. 2 of 1983)* could allow. Perhaps the better approach would simply be to insist that the threatened force must be reasonably imminent. Possibly, an exception could permit the carrying of an offensive weapon in public for self-defence if there was "an imminent *particular* threat affecting the particular circumstances in which the weapon was carried" (*Evans v. Hughes*, 1972). At the time of taking his gun into the subway Goetz was not fearing a reasonably imminent attack; there had been no particular threat to him. Accordingly, his plea of self-defence on this count ought to fail.

The final issue relating to self-defence concerns the proportionality of the defensive response. The general rule is that the response must be proportionate to the attack; the defender may only use such force as is reasonable in the circumstances to repel the attack. Assuming some defensive force from Goetz was necessary, the issue becomes whether he could have averted the danger with lesser force—say, with a push or a punch or even by threatening the youths with his gun without firing it. Was it reasonably necessary for him actually to fire the gun?

Again, however, in balancing the interests of defender and aggressor the scales have become weighted in favour of the defender. In *Shannon* (1980) the Court of Appeal ruled that if the defendant thought that what he was doing was necessary, that was "most potent evidence" that only reasonable defensive action had been taken. In a crisis a defendant could not be expected to weigh up precisely the measure of his necessary defensive action. This seems to suggest that as long as the defender is truly acting in self-defence (as opposed to responding in angry retaliation or pure aggression), the degree of force used is immaterial (*Palmer*, 1971). For a period English law took this to its logical conclusion holding that as long as the defendant thought he was using only a reasonable amount of force, there could be no liability (*Scarlett*, 1994). More recent cases (*Owino*, 1996), however, have rightly emphasized that the defendant's views are not decisive. The issue is whether, in the circumstances as the defendant believed them to be, the level of force used was in fact reasonable. But, of course, in assessing what is objectively reasonable the jury must still take account of the fact that in situations of crisis the person attacked cannot be expected calmly to "weigh to a nicety the exact measure of necessary defensive action" (*Palmer*, 1971). Accordingly, the question in the hypothetical English Bernhard Goetz case is whether, in the circumstances that he believed himself to be, Goetz's response was reasonable and proportionate. His belief that his response satisfied this standard is not determinative but the jury would have to take into account the fact that, in the crisis situation he believed himself to be in, a calm, carefully measured response cannot be expected.

It might be thought that the insistence of Article 2 of the European Convention on Human Rights that defensive force be "absolutely necessary" might result in a stricter test. Indeed, in *Andronicou v. Cyprus* (1998) it was stated that the response must be strictly proportionate on the facts that were reasonably believed by the defendant. In this case police officers stormed a flat in which a girl was being held hostage and opened fire with machine guns. While this seems a somewhat excessive response, it was nevertheless concluded that some indulgence must be allowed in crisis situations and so there was no violation of Article 2.

This whole approach, especially by the English courts, is controversial. One view is that the traditional rules on self-defence reflected a male view of the world such as two gunfighters facing each other on a dusty street in a Western movie. The recent relaxations in the law of self-defence could be welcomed as opening up the defence to a wider range of persons. In particular, a possible beneficial by-product is that there is now a chance that some battered women who kill or injure their abusers could successfully plead self-defence. Research has suggested that many battered women who kill do so to avoid threats of death or serious injury to themselves or their children (McColgan, 1993). Some courts in the United States and Canada have started affording a defence in such circumstances. For example, in *Diaz* (1983) a woman succeeded in a plea of self-defence after she shot her sleeping husband who had raped and beaten her and then threatened to kill her. Such a person could possibly come within the above self-defence rules on the grounds that she believed defensive action was necessary and was allowed to "strike first" and, given the greater physical strength of many men and the levels of violence to which she had been exposed, the degree of force used could (just possibly) be construed as reasonable. However, such battered women would still have to overcome the problem that they did not retreat. For example, in *Alhuwalia* (1992) the defendant, after ten years of excessive abuse and facing threats of further violence the next morning, poured petrol over her sleeping husband and set him alight, killing him. If she had attempted to escape liability on grounds of self-defence (which she did not) she would have had to counter the objection that she could have sought official protection or left the home. She would, of course, have argued that she had already obtained two court orders restraining her husband; these had in no way stopped him from inflicting violence on her. Further, she would have contended that "retreating" was not a feasible option for her. For cultural (and, perhaps, religious reasons) she was committed to holding her marriage together and why should she be forced to leave her own home? It is easy to say that a woman must retreat, but to where? What of the children? (O'Donovan, 1991). Nevertheless, despite the strength of these claims it seems unlikely that self-defence will be extended to women other than those under fairly immediate threat of serious violence.

The opposing view is that these developments in the English law of self defence should be regarded with deep suspicion in that they appear to give carte blanche to anyone to use force, whenever they like, purely on the basis that they *believe* it is necessary. For example, in *Finch and Jardine* (1982) two police officers wrongly thought they had seen a dangerous escaped criminal. Believing anticipatory force to be necessary they nearly beat to death that person, who was in fact a totally innocent man. They escaped all liability on grounds of self-defence because: (i) they thought defensive force was necessary; (ii) clearly the police cannot be expected to retreat in such cases; (iii) anticipatory action was justified as the only way of incapacitating such a dangerous criminal (if he had been), and (iv) they thought it was necessary to use as much force as they did to ensure that he was really incapacitated. Since *Owino* (1996) this case might be differently decided if it was felt that the force used was disproportionate to the danger. However, this question has to be assessed on the basis of the situation the police officers believed themselves to be in. As they believed they were apprehending a highly dangerous and armed criminal, it is possible that a jury could still find their response to be reasonable and proportionate in those circumstances.

If the police had made a *reasonable* mistake (that is, the sort of mistake all reasonable people would have made in the circumstances) we would not blame them; they would have been acting perfectly properly. However, dispensing entirely with the concept of reasonableness is perhaps opening the door to the "trigger-happy" to shoot first and then afterwards claim that it was all a terrible mistake. It is, quite simply, taking the theory of forfeiture too far. Justifying such killings is asserting that no wrong has been done. The initial aggressor was culpable and so "persons can swat the wrongdoer like a fly and toss his remains in the garbage" (Dressler, 1999). However, the value which ought to be placed on human life and the right to life enshrined in the European Convention on Human Rights dictate that any theory of forfeiture should be narrowly circumscribed by a tighter test of when self-defensive force is necessary. Section 3 of the Criminal Law Act 1967 specifies that only reasonable force may be used in the prevention of crime. In most cases of self-defence the aggressor will be committing a crime (although this will not be true in some cases of anticipatory self-defence) and therefore the defender will, in acting defensively, also be acting to prevent a crime. Similarly, section 117 of the Police and Criminal Evidence Act 1984 provides that a police constable may only use reasonable force in exercising conferred powers. It is unfortunate that the courts have tended to ignore these provisions and have not insisted on the contours of the four issues discussed above being limited by the concept of reasonableness.

A final point deserves mention. If a plea of self-defence succeeds, the defendant's actions are justified and he escapes liability. If the plea fails, he is fully liable for the crime charged. One possibility, which has not yet been adopted by English law, is that where the defendant was acting to defend himself or his property but the defence fails—say, because he used too much defensive force—then, although his actions are not justified, he should have an excuse or a partial excuse. Particularly in the context of homicide, the doctrine of partial excuse could be most useful here: the defendant's liability could be reduced from murder to manslaughter. The Australian courts used to adopt such an approach to excessive self-defence (*McKay*, 1957; *Howe*, 1958) until they started to follow a line similar to English law (*Zecevic*, 1987). This solution would be particularly useful in cases where burglars are killed or seriously injured as happened in a recent highly publicised case where a Norfolk farmer, Tony Martin, shot and killed a burglar. He fired a shotgun at close range and without any warning. Given the excessive nature of his response it is hardly surprising that the jury rejected his plea of self-defence and convicted him of murder. Under the present English law this must be right. Human life must be valued ahead of property interests. It is difficult to see how killing someone (or injuring them seriously) can be a reasonably proportionate response to an attack on property interests. A defendant whose defence fails (because, say, the response was excessive) is blameworthy—otherwise his defence would have succeeded. But, because Martin was acting to protect himself or his property, he is less blameworthy than another who acted coldly and deliberately (assuming he was acting defensively and not as an "executioner": Yeo, 2000). A lesser level of criminal liability (manslaughter) and less punishment is therefore appropriate.

(iii) Excuses

Many "excuses" are simply not recognised by English law as a matter of substantive law. For example, there is no defence of entrapment, killing under duress or provocation in cases other than murder but, of course, these "excuses" may be used as mitigating factors when sentencing an offender or may be recognised by prosecutorial discretion (level of charge or whether to charge at all) (Ashworth, 1999). In what circumstances does the substantive law excuse conduct on the basis that because of some precipitating event or excusing condition or characteristic of the defendant we exempt him from full responsibility and blame for the wrongful act? We have already seen in introducing the concept of excuses that there are two types of excuse: status excuses and non-status excuses.

(i) Status Excuses. The status excuses currently recognised by English law are automatism, insanity, diminished responsibility, lack of age and intoxication. With all these defences it is the abnormal or different condition of the defendant that is the basis for excusing his conduct. Because of this condition, these actors cannot conform to the law's commands or cannot understand the wrongfulness of their actions. Their capacity is deeply affected and to that extent they are relieved from blame or full blame. However, in order to secure this relief from blame, it is necessary that the defendant not be at fault in bringing about this condition. Thus we saw earlier (p. 43) that if a defendant was at fault in bringing about a state of automatism, no defence is available. Similarly, intoxication can only be a full defence if it is involuntary, for example, if the defendant's drink is laced. If the defendant voluntarily consumed drink or drugs, he is, at most, entitled to a reduction in liability. Because the gist of status excuses is that the defendant lacked full capacity through no fault of her own, the focus of the enquiry is a subjective one concentrating of the defendant herself. References to how a reasonable person would have reacted are inappropriate.

Because of its close relationship to the requirement of voluntary action, automatism has already been discussed (pp. 38–42). Some of the remaining status excuses provide a complete defence (insanity, lack of age and involuntary intoxication) while others (diminished responsibility and voluntary intoxication) are only partial excuses. Insanity, diminished responsibility and intoxication will now be explored.

(a) Insanity. Responsibility connotes full control over one's actions, an understanding of the implications of those actions and a power to choose whether or not to abide by the law. An insane defendant lacks such full control, understanding and power of choice. Accordingly, he is not responsible for his conduct and is excused from criminal liability.

Lack of control or understanding and the ability to make effective choices can be caused by external factors, internal factors or a combination of the two. Where the cause is external, such as a blow to the head causing concussion, the law is content to exempt the defendant fully from responsibility and allow his acquittal on grounds of automatism (see earlier, pp. 38–42). If the cause is external but is the defendant's fault, such as consuming hallucinogenic drugs, the law will hold the defendant responsible and blame him for consuming the drugs. On the other hand, where the lack of control or understanding or ability to choose has an internal, or partly internal, pathological cause, the law is torn in two directions: on the one hand, it recognises that it would be unjust to punish such a person who is sick rather than wicked but, on the other hand, this very illness could cause him to act in the same way again; he is thus regarded as potentially dangerous and perhaps in need of restraint. Accordingly, where a person is found to be insane the result is the "special verdict" of not guilty by reason of insanity. In murder cases the judge must then order the defendant to be admitted to a "special" secure hospital specified by the Home Secretary. The defendant will be detained there for as long as the Home Secretary directs—possibly for the remainder of his life. The position used to be the same in non-murder cases but now the judge has a discretion to make a hospital order, a guardianship order, a supervision and treatment order, or an order for the absolute discharge of the defendant (Criminal Procedure (Insanity and Unfitness to Plead) Act 1991).

Of course, some defendants are so severely mentally ill as to be unable to stand trial. Where a person is too mentally ill to be able to participate meaningfully in his trial, he can be found unfit to plead and dealt with in the same way as if the special verdict had been returned. Before such an order can be imposed there must be a "trial of the facts" to ensure the jury is satisfied the defendant did the acts constituting the *actus reus* of the offences in question. (It is likely that this "trial of the facts" breaches Article 6 of the European Convention on Human rights which guarantees the right to a fair trial and has been interpreted to mean that the defendant must be able to participate effectively in criminal proceedings against him: *T v. United Kingdom*, 2000.) The result is that the insanity defence is only employed by those who were insane at the time of the commission of the crime but who at the time of the trial are no longer manifestly insane.

The legal test for establishing insanity as a defence was laid down in 1843 by the McNaghten Rules which require that the defendant, at the time of committing the act, must have been "labouring under such defect of reason, from disease of the mind, as not to know the nature and quality of the act he was doing; or if he did know it, that he did not know what he was doing was wrong".

This involves a three-fold test. First, the defendant must be suffering from a *disease of the mind*. While one might have thought this was a matter for psychiatric determination, the judiciary, fearful that too many dangerous defendants might escape completely the clutches of the criminal justice system through the defence of automatism, have been careful to emphasise that "disease of the mind" is a legal concept and its interpretation has been strongly influenced by policy considerations. Accordingly, it has been construed to mean that there was something internal to the defendant that caused the conduct. With internal causes, for example, schizophrenia, there is a danger of repetition. The defendant is potentially dangerous and it is important that the courts retain the power to exercise control (for example, hospitalisation) over him. The insanity verdict triggers this power of control. This requirement that "disease of the mind" involves an internal cause of action has led to the unfortunate result that many persons, such as sleepwalkers, epileptics and some diabetics, have been inappropriately held to have been suffering from a disease of the mind and swept within the ambit of the insanity defence. (For a fuller discussion, see pp. 38–42 above.) Classifying such persons as insane can only be regarded as false labelling.

The second requirement under the McNaghten Rules is that the disease of the mind must cause a *defect of reason*. The ability to reason must be affected; it is not enough that the defendant simply failed to use her reasoning powers because of absent-mindedness or confusion (*Clarke*, 1972).

Finally, it must be established that as a result of the disease of the mind and defect of reason the defendant either *did not know the nature and quality of his acts* or did not know the acts were *wrong*. This final requirement makes the test extremely narrow.

In effect, it only covers those defendants who, in extreme states of mental illness, are unaware of what they are doing or of the significance of their actions. Classic examples of not knowing the nature and quality of one's actions are: throwing a baby on a fire thinking it is a log of wood; cutting off someone's head thinking it will be great fun to see him searching for it when he wakes up—and so on. The "wrongness" limb of the McNaghten Rules has been interpreted to mean that the defendant must not know that the action is legally wrong. For example, she must be so mentally ill as not to understand that murder or burglary are criminal offences. Strictly applied, a defendant who was so severely mentally ill as to come within either of these limbs would generally be unfit to stand trial. Research has concluded, however, that psychiatrists tend to interpret the "wrongness" limb broadly to include cases where the defendant thought her actions were morally justified. As the wrongness limb is the most commonly utilised branch of the test, this expansion to include typical situations of religious delusions (for example, believing the victim is possessed by the devil) has been an important mechanism in preventing the insanity defence from being virtually useless (Mackay and Kearns, 1999).

This psychiatric broadening of the concept of wrongness raises a central dilemma. The courts have been clear that all the issues presented by the McNaghten Rules are legal matters and so legal definitions of "disease of the mind" and "wrongness" have been developed. However, section 1 of the Criminal Procedure (Insanity and Unfitness to Plead) Act 1991 makes it clear that no verdict of not guilty by reason of insanity can be returned except on the written or oral evidence of two or more registered medical practitioners (at least one of whom has to be approved under section 12 of the Mental Health Act 1983). Research has concluded that in the vast majority of cases (about 86 per cent) the jury had no role. Based on the agreed expert evidence they were simply directed (with both prosecution and defence agreement) to return a verdict of not guilty by reason of insanity. This same research found that a significant number of psychiatric reports concluded that the defendant was insane but either did not mention, or did not explain the defendant's mental condition in relation to, the McNaghten Rules (Mackay and Kearns, 1999). Such an approach is in fact consistent with the interpretation of Article 5(1)(e) of the European Convention on Human Rights that persons of unsound mind may only be deprived of their liberty if there is "objective medical expertise" and a clear correlation between the medical and legal definitions of mental illness (*Winterwerp v. The Netherlands*, 1979). However, while in practice medical evidence has become determinative of the issue in most cases, the fact remains that the test of insanity is still formally a legal one with the legal status of the medical evidence not made explicit. With the judiciary interpreting the McNaghten Rules "with all the clinical detachment of a tax statute" (Sutherland and Gearty, 1992) and still having the ultimate power whether to direct the jury to follow the medical evidence, it is not surprising that the McNaghten Rules have recently been held by a court in Jersey to breach the Human Rights Act (*The Times*, February 14, 2001). Indeed, in those cases where the psychiatric and legal tests of insanity differ radically (for example, in relation to sleepwalkers, diabetics and epileptics) further challenges can be anticipated.

In the past, most defendants who stood trial were unwilling to plead insanity. In the years preceding the 1991 Act there were only about four findings of insanity per year (Mackay and Kearns, 1999). Imprisonment was regarded as preferable to indefinite detention in a "special" hospital. If the charge were murder, the defendant might well be convicted of manslaughter on the basis of diminished responsibility. In such an event, and for all other charges, the defendant might even escape prison by receiving a hospital order under the court's powers contained in the Mental Health Act 1983. Since the 1991 Act there has been some increase in the use of the insanity defence with an average of nearly nine findings of insanity per year. In 52 per cent of these cases the defendant received a community disposal, particularly supervision and treatment orders (Mackay and Kearns, 1999). Once it is realised that the courts are prepared to make use of their increased powers it can be anticipated that more defendants will attempt to plead insanity as a defence.

Should the insanity verdict be retained? To some commentators it has become nothing more than "an ornate rarity, a tribute to our capacity to pretend to a moral position while pursuing profoundly different practices" (Morris, 1982) and, accordingly, should be abolished. The gist of the argument is as follows: about one-third of all prisoners suffer from some form of mental disorder (Ashworth, 1991); for. these persons the insanity defence is not available; if mental illness is an excusing condition, the law is being applied in a grossly uneven manner. But, more fundamentally, ought mental illness to be an excusing condition at all? Many people might be mentally ill and commit a crime but there is little evidence to suggest that the one causes the other. The classic position is that the insane are mad and not bad. But why cannot the same person be both mad and bad? At a different level, Morris (1982) argues that while there might be a relationship between mental illness and crime, a stronger relationship exists between adverse social circumstances and criminal behaviour. Being born to a one-parent family living on welfare in an inner-city area is a stronger pressure towards committing crime than any mental illness. Why is there an insanity defence but no defence of "social adversity"?

It must be noted that under the civil law insane persons can be committed to hospital against their will. The fact that such a person has committed a crime is irrelevant to such civil commitments. Under these abolitionist proposals, where a person has committed a crime he would be criminally prosecuted in the normal way. If he had *mens rea* he would be convicted, and then any mental illness would be taken into account at the sentencing stage. His sentence, of course, could not then exceed that available to a sane defendant convicted of the same offence. If, on the other hand, *mens rea* could not be proved—because of mental illness or for whatever other reason—the defendant would have to be acquitted, but, of course, if he were perceived to be dangerous, civil commitment proceedings under the Mental Health legislation could be instituted.

Adopting such a solution, it is argued, would avoid the present confusion of roles and conflict between the disciplines of law and psychiatry. At present psychiatrists have to appear as witnesses in criminal courts and answer legal questions such as: did he know the nature and quality of his act? This is an unanswerable question unless the psychiatrist is prepared to distort his testimony to fit the "manifest absurdity of the McNaghten test" (Royal Commission on Capital Punishment, 1953). Under the proposed solution lawyers could argue in court about matters they understand: moral choice, guilt and innocence. And at the sentencing stage or in the civil commitment proceedings the psychiatrist could give meaningful testimony in terms of appropriate treatments and so on.

In 1982 Idaho became the first state in the United States to abolish the insanity defence (Idaho Code, section 18–207, Supp. 1983). All issues of insanity were eliminated from the criminal trial; the defendant is either found guilty or not guilty depending on proof of *mens rea* or other matters affecting the elements of the offence charged. Mental illness only becomes relevant at the sentencing stage. It ought perhaps to be mentioned that Idaho's abolition of the insanity defence was not so much in response to the arguments suggested above, but was a result of the mood of anger and public outrage in the United States following the acquittal of John W. Hinckley on the ground of insanity, following his attempt to assassinate President Reagan. Idaho is a very conservative and isolated state; there was a strong belief that the insanity defence was never more than an attempt to "hoodwink" the jury; it was open to fraud and misrepresentation and usually employed only as a last resort by guilty defendants; it resulted in dangerous defendants being released as "cured" far sooner than they would have been had they been sentenced on the basis of guilt.

It is to be hoped that English law never chooses to go down this route. Judge Bazelon stated in one of the most famous United States insanity cases that "our collective conscience does not allow punishment where it cannot impose blame" (*Durham v. United States*, 1954). And this surely is the central and proper function of the insanity defence as an excuse. We excuse the weak and hold them blameless (or less blameworthy). We excuse a defendant subjected to duress; we recognise the plight of the helpless; it is a concession to human infirmity. So too with insanity. The mentally ill are clearly "weak". Our whole culture endorses the view that respect ought to be paid to human autonomy and dignity and compassion should be shown for the weak. The insane offender is so "obviously different" from most people that we are prepared to excuse him. Also, the insane offender is immune to the deterrent messages of the law and so punishment for individual deterrence is pointless. And even in terms of general deterrence, the main function of conviction and punishment is to stigmatise the wicked in order to affirm minimum standards of conduct. The general public is unlikely to identify with an insane offender; he is too different and no lessons can be learnt from his experience.

Accordingly, it is submitted that the insanity defence ought to be retained as an excuse in the law. Of course, the McNaghten Rules are far too narrow and need to cover many more defendants suffering from mental illness. The Rules have been largely abandoned in the United States and serious reforms proposed in this country (Butler Committee, 1975). Discussion of such proposals is beyond the reach of a book of this nature but, in assessing any reform proposals, one final issue, alluded to earlier, must be addressed. Should insanity operate as an excuse for the defendant's crime that involves proving that her mental illness *caused* the commission of the offence? Or should insanity be regarded as a status (rather like the status of infancy) that exempts the insane person from prosecution and punishment under the criminal justice system: "human beings who are insane are no more the proper subjects of moral evaluation than are young infants, animals or even stones" (Moore, 1985)? This latter view, which is similar to the "precondition of responsibility" approach rejected above (p. 78), however, presents major problems. In dispensing with the causation requirement, it involves exempting from criminal liability a person who rationally committed a crime merely because she happened, coincidentally, to be mentally ill. Such an approach would distort the function of the criminal law which is an institution of blame (involving the assignment of responsibility *for acts committed*) and punishment. The criminal law is not there to make sweeping and stigmatising judgments about the condition and status of people if that was not connected to the commission of the crime. (That is the role of the Health Authorities under the civil law.) Insanity as a criminal defence must operate as an excuse where responsibility for conduct is lessened. Accordingly, a substantially reformed insanity defence as an excuse for conduct is a necessary part of the construction of the criminal law.

(b) Diminished responsibility. Diminished responsibility is a partial excuse to murder only, reducing liability to manslaughter. The excusing characteristic of the defendant is that he must have suffered from "such abnormality of mind (whether arising from a condition of arrested or retarded development of mind or any inherent causes or induced by disease or injury) as substantially impaired his mental responsibility for his acts" (Homicide Act 1957, section 2). Such a defendant is still partially responsible for his actions but, to the extent that he is partially irresponsible, he is afforded a partial excuse which, if successful, enables the judge to avoid the mandatory sentence of life imprisonment for murder and impose a lesser sentence instead.

The test of diminished responsibility laid down in section 2 is highly problematic and raises fundamental questions as to the role of mental disorder in assessing criminal responsibility and whether such mental impairment should be determined medically by psychiatrists or legally and morally by judges and juries. In theory, the section involves a three-fold process. First, the abnormality of mind must arise from one of the bracketed causes (arrested or retarded development, etc.) and in *Byrne* (1960) it was stated that this was a matter to be determined by expert medical evidence. This is particularly problematic because none of the bracketed causes have established psychiatric meanings. Indeed, research suggests that psychiatric reports often fail to indicate which of the bracketed causes has led to the abnormality of mind (Dell, 1984). Accordingly, more recent Court of Appeal decisions have started to provide legal definitions of the bracketed causes (*Sanderson*, 1994) which has led to the conclusion that "the words in parenthesis are legal rather than psychiatric concepts" (Mackay, 1999). The result is that it is for psychiatrists to testify whether the defendant was suffering from arrested or retarded development, etc., even though these are legal concepts. It is interesting to note that these judicial attempts to define the aetiology of abnormality of mind have coincided with a fall in the number of successful diminished responsibility pleas and an increase in the number of murder convictions possibly indicating increased scepticism by psychiatrists at their role in such cases. Secondly, it has to be established that the specified bracketed cause has resulted in an "abnormality of mind". In *Byrne* (1960) it was stated that this is "a state of mind so different from that of ordinary human beings that a reasonable man . . . would term it abnormal" and that it is "wide enough to cover the mind's activities in all its aspects" including "the ability to exercise will-power to control physical acts". This suggests an approach based on morality rather than psychiatry. Whether the reasonable man would regard a state of mind as being "so different" that it can be termed abnormal is clearly a matter for the jury as the mouthpiece of ordinary people. Further, the inclusion of those lacking ability to control their actions has allowed the defence to be opened up to a wide array of different types of person who kill: those acting under an "irresistible impulse", mercy killers, women suffering from pre-menstrual syndrome and battered women—despite the fact that in these cases there is often virtually no medical evidence of mental abnormality. Thirdly, it must be established that this abnormality of mind caused a substantial impairment of mental responsibility. The notion of "mental responsibility" is "either a concept of law or a concept of morality; it is not a clinical fact relating to the defendant" (Butler Committee, 1975). Similarly, whether there has been a "substantial impairment" of such responsibility is not a medical issue. Both these questions can only possibly be answered by the jury.

However, in practice, medical experts go beyond testimony as to the bracketed causes and offer evidence on all three of the above matters. Indeed, psychiatric evidence can be conclusive: in cases where all the medical evidence supports diminished responsibility the prosecution can accept a plea of guilty to manslaughter by diminished responsibility (*Cox*, 1968) with the result that there is now a contested trial with jury involvement in only 15 per cent of all diminished responsibility cases (Mackay, 2000). In short, while section 2 is laying down a largely legal test, it is psychiatrists who are mainly making the determination whether the test is satisfied.

Two further points relating to the operation of section 2 deserve mention. First, for policy reasons (below, p. 107) the courts have been careful to insist that an "abnormality of mind" cannot be caused by drink or drugs. This policy was extended in *O'Connell* (1997) to cover a defendant who had been taking sleeping drugs on prescription. While the policy of not permitting the voluntary consumption of alcohol or illegal drugs to afford any excuse is understandable, it is generally thought that this exclusion should not extend to an unexpected reaction after taking prescribed drugs (above, p. 44). Secondly, it is becoming increasingly common for defendants to plead both diminished responsibility and provocation as alternative partial defences. For example, as we shall see, in *Ahluwalia* (1992), one of the leading cases on battered women pleading provocation, the defendant having failed in her provocation plea, finally had her conviction for murder reduced to manslaughter on grounds of diminished responsibility. At first sight these two pleas seem far removed from each other: the focus in diminished responsibility is on the defendant's mental abnormality; in provocation the loss of self-control must be compared with how a reasonable person would have responded in the same situation. However, the increasing tendency of the courts in provocation cases to permit mental abnormality to be regarded as relevant in assessing whether it was reasonable for such a person to have responded in that way has gone a long way to collapse the distinction between the two defences. Indeed, the majority in the leading House of Lords decision of *Smith* (2000) openly admitted that there was a significant overlap between the two defences.

Diminished responsibility "operates in a largely pragmatic manner but is riddled with discrepancies and conceptual confusion" (Mackay, 2000). Nevertheless, especially as long as the mandatory sentence for murder is retained, there is clearly a role for such a partial defence. Although it is not necessary to establish a causal link between the mental abnormality and the killing (arguably such a requirement should be essential: see p. 103), there are some defendants who are manifestly so mentally disturbed and different from the rest of us that some recognition of their impaired responsibility seems appropriate. The argument runs that if it takes collusion between psychiatrists, prosecutors, judges and juries to achieve this result, then so be it. However, apart from the fact that it is impossible to defend a law that has to operate through collusion, there are many mentally disturbed killers who are exempted from the conspiracy and found guilty of murder. Incoherent law opens the door to unequal treatment. In *Sutcliffe* (1981) both the prosecution and defence were content that the "Yorkshire Ripper" plead guilty to manslaughter on grounds of diminished responsibility. Such an outcome would have been uncontroversial in less high-profile cases. However, the judge declined to accept the plea insisting on a full trial which resulted in a murder conviction. Such discrepancies in practice are hard to defend.

A further problem with the present diminished responsibility defence is that it has been used as a "left-over" category enabling the law to avoid confronting central issues such as whether there should be a defence of mercy-killing and whether battered women should be allowed to plead self-defence or provocation. Between 1982 and 1991 there were 22 homicide cases involving mercy-killing with a murder verdict being returned in only one case (Ashworth, 1999). This practice and the existence of diminished responsibility as an escape-route simply takes pressure off law reformers having to confront the central issue whether there should be some form of defence available for mercy killers.

The time has come for a radical rethink of the role and content of the diminished responsibility defence. Any reformulation needs to address the central issue whether it is a medical or a legal test and the respective roles of psychiatrists and juries. A further important consideration is whether the defence exists merely to avoid the mandatory sentence for murder. The Select Committee of the House of Lords on Murder and Life Imprisonment (1988–89) recommended abolition of the mandatory sentence for murder but retention of diminished responsibility for fair labelling reasons. Following this, consideration should be given to extending diminished responsibility as a partial defence to other crimes. If those who lack full responsibility for their actions deserve excusing to a degree this should plainly apply to other serious offences such as attempted murder and causing grievous bodily harm with intent. However, embarking on this route would be such a slippery slope (should diminished responsibility be a partial excuse to rape?) that for the foreseeable future attempt at law reform seems unlikely.

(c) Intoxication. Intoxication can be caused by the consumption of either alcohol or other drugs (or a combination of the two). While the precise effect of each drug on the human central nervous system is different, alcohol and many other drugs have the initial common effect of releasing inhibitions causing some persons to do things they would not normally do. In such cases the actor is still fully aware of what he is doing and, accordingly, the law generally refuses to recognise such partial intoxication as any form of excuse. The law simply adopts the view that a "drunken intent is nevertheless an intent" (*Sheehan and Moore*, 1975). Where drink has been voluntarily consumed such an approach is inevitable. The actor has not lost all control and the ability to reason; he has chosen to drink and can still be adjudged responsible for his actions and, to the extent that his abilities are impaired, he can be blamed for such impairment and not excused. The vast majority of crimes of violence are committed by persons who have been drinking (Cretney and Davis, 1995). On purely practical grounds it would be impossible to allow the consumption of, say, three or four pints of beer to operate as an excuse. The evidential problems posed by such an approach would be insuperable—and, of course, it could actually encourage drug consumption followed by crime.

What is the position, however, when it is not the defendant's fault that he is drunk? In *Kingston* (1994) the defendant's drink was laced with drugs. In a state of intoxication he indecently assaulted a fifteen-year-old boy. He did know what he was doing (*i.e.* he did have *mens rea*) but claimed the only reason he did it was because of the drugs. As seen earlier (p. 18), the House of Lords held that because Kingston committed the *actus reus* with the necessary *mens rea* he should be liable irrespective of the fact that he bore no "moral fault" for his actions. Clearly swayed by policy and practical considerations (too many people would claim the defence which would be difficult to disprove), the House declared that it would be difficult to justify an excuse here. Such a defence would effectively be one of irresistible impulse derived from a combination of innate drives (Kingston had paedophilic tendencies) and external disinhibition (caused by the drugs). Allowing such a defence would conflict with the clear rule of English law that it is no excuse that one acted from an irresistible impulse of purely internal origin. This argument, however, misses the central point. As canvassed above, many people might have anti-social and criminal tendencies. If the paedophile gives way to his tendencies and sexually abuses children he deserves blame and punishment. A defence of irresistible impulse is totally inappropriate. But if the only reason he commits the crime is because a third party removes his control mechanisms, his actions become, in effect, involuntary and blame and punishment become inappropriate. We allow a defence of duress to those who commit crimes because of the threats of others; we should similarly allow a defence to those who only commit crimes because of the actions of others. Sullivan (1996) has argued that such destabilisation should afford an excuse—but only where it results in a lapse on the part of a person of otherwise good character. His argument is that Kingston should only be allowed an excuse if he had no previous convictions (or character-based acquittals) for similar offences. This, again, misses the crucial point: he might have had earlier convictions but have managed restraint for years. On this occasion Kingston was blameless.

The position is somewhat different where the involuntary intoxication causes the actor to commit a crime in such a state of intoxication that he lacks *mens rea*. Here the law adopts the view that as there is no *mens rea* and the defendant cannot be blamed for his intoxication, a complete defence is justified. This reasoning has been extended to persons who voluntarily take a drug which is not generally known to cause extreme intoxication. Thus in *Hardie* (1984) it was held that Valium and other sedative or soporific drugs must be treated differently from alcohol and other drugs that cause "unpredictability or aggressiveness" because the effects of Valium and such drugs were not generally known.

The real problem faced by the law, however, is not such cases where drink or drugs causes imprudence or has been secretly administered, but rather the rarer cases where there has been a voluntary excessive consumption of alcohol or drugs or where a more powerful hallucinogenic drug such as LSD has been taken. In such cases the drugs can have the effect of impairing ability to foresee consequences. One can become so intoxicated that one loses awareness of what one is doing. For instance, in *Brennan v. HM Advocate* (1977) the defendant consumed between 20 and 25 pints of beer, a glass of sherry and a quantity of the drug LSD. He then stabbed his father to death with a knife. In such a state of extreme intoxication, his claim that he was unaware of his actions becomes plausible. And clearly, at the time of stabbing his father, Brennan was not responsible for his actions; he lacked control over them; he possessed no ability to reason and make choices. Indeed, all the hallmarks of responsibility were missing.

Some Commonwealth courts have indeed taken this view to its logical conclusion and held that if a defendant is so drunk as to lack *mens rea* there must be a complete acquittal (*Chretien*, 1981 [South Africa]; *O'Connor*, 1980 [Australia]). Such a purist, doctrinal approach ignores, however, important policy considerations that, given the strong association between violence and drink, there are public protection arguments against affording a complete acquittal in such cases. Indeed, one can argue that these "dead drunk" defendants, such as Brennan, are, in a sense, responsible for the deaths or injuries that they cause. Where a person chooses voluntarily to consume drink or drugs he can be held responsible for anything that happens while in such a state of voluntary intoxication. In our culture everyone knows the potential consequences of excessive drinking or drug-taking. Everyone can therefore be deemed to know the risks involved and can be blamed for such risk-taking.

Accepting this view that blame is appropriate, the next question becomes: how much blame? Should drunken offenders be blamed to the same, a lesser or even a greater extent than their sober counterparts? It is instructive in this respect to consider the legislative response in South Africa to the *Chretien* (1981) decision that drunken defendants who lacked *mens rea* should be exempted from all liability. The Criminal Law Amendment Act 1 of 1988 creates a new special offence covering those who commit prohibited acts but lack *mens rea* because of intoxication. Such persons are liable to the *same* penalty which may be imposed for the crime for which they have been acquitted and case law has established that the intoxication cannot be a mitigating factor for this offence (*Maki*, 1994). Indeed, section 1(2) of this Act provides that intoxication may be regarded as an aggravating factor. Given the close association between drink and crime, especially crimes of violence, such a public protectionist stance, with its deterrent underpinnings, is understandable. However, from a desert perspective the emphasis is on the degree of responsibility and blame to be attached to the defendant and English law has adopted the view that, while it is appropriate to blame the defendant for becoming so intoxicated, in many cases his responsibility is reduced. He is less in control of his actions than his sober counterpart. He is also probably less dangerous as his drunkenness will deprive him of any steadfast resolve to commit the crime. In a sense, the position of a drunken defendant who is unaware of his actions at the time of the crime is analogous to that of a reckless wrongdoer—who deserves punishment but not to the same extent as the intentional wrongdoer. Thus, while Brennan was clearly to be blamed for becoming so intoxicated and then killing his father, he was not as blameworthy as a sober person who deliberately kills another.

In most cases the law has deemed it to be unnecessary (and, in fact, not possible) to allow intoxication to operate as a partial excuse at the substantive level. This is particularly true in relation to drunken mistakes (*O'Grady*, 1987: mystifying comments to the contrary in *Richardson and Irwin*, 1999 cannot be regarded as consistent with the bulk of authority). The reduced level of blameworthiness can be reflected at the sentencing level. Such an approach has the added advantage of allowing fine-tuning in the sentencing to reflect the actual extent of the drunkenness. But this approach could not be adopted in relation to the crime of murder which carries a fixed penalty (formerly the death penalty and now life imprisonment). Accordingly, the law developed a rule that intoxication could be a defence to crimes of "specific intent". These are crimes that can only be committed intentionally, of which murder is a prime example. Other such offences include causing grievous bodily harm with intent, theft and burglary. Where, however, the crime can be committed recklessly, for example, manslaughter, malicious wounding or inflicting grievous bodily harm, and assault, the crime is classed as one of "basic intent" and intoxication is no defence. Getting drunk and casting off the "restraints of reason and conscience" (*Majewski*, 1977) is a reckless thing to do. The requisite *mens rea* of the crime, recklessness, is established by proof that the defendant voluntarily got himself intoxicated (*Majewski*, 1977).

This whole approach is, of course, policy-driven by a desire not to "let drunks get away with it". While in a lay sense of the word one can agree that "getting drunk is a reckless thing to do", it hardly constitutes "recklessness" in the *Cunningham*

(1957) sense of the word. *Cunningham* recklessness involves foreseeing the possibility of the harm occurring. Most defendants who drink themselves into oblivion do not possess such foresight. Indeed, it was largely to overcome this problem that recklessness was redefined in *Caldwell* (1982). Applying his new objective test of recklessness, Lord Diplock in this case was able to conclude that the act of setting fire to the hotel created an obvious risk of endangering life and therefore the defendant was reckless; his lack of subjective foresight was irrelevant. However, with the *Caldwell* (1982) test of recklessness largely jettisoned in the field of offences of violence, we are left with the situation that the law wants to, and does, blame and punish drunken defendants but its artificial construct, *mens rea*, comprising intention and recklessness, is simply not up to the job. Despite adverse comments by the House of Lords in *Kingston* (1994), the true basis of liability here is blame or moral fault and not *mens rea*.

The practical effect of this rule is that for crimes of specific intent intoxication generally operates as a partial excuse. A drunken defendant can be excused liability for murder (a crime of specific intent) but convicted of the lesser offence of manslaughter (a crime of basic intent). (When a defendant is charged with a greater offence, for example, murder, a jury can acquit of that offence if not satisfied that the greater offence elements have been proved—the *mens rea* of murder—but convict of a lesser included offence—manslaughter—if satisfied that the lesser offence elements have been established.)

The illogicality of such an approach is manifest. The whole concept of "specific intent" was devised to enable drunkenness to operate as a substantive mitigating factor to certain crimes, particularly murder. But, as a result of the above definition, drunkenness is sometimes a partial excuse (where there is a lesser included offence of basic intent) but sometimes a complete defence—as with theft where no lesser included offence that can be committed recklessly exists. There is no rationale underlying such a distinction; the result is sheer chance.

The law is thus in a state of incoherence—largely because of a judicial reluctance to articulate openly the aims of the law in this respect. It is submitted that the true policy of the law here is (and should be) that we blame the drunken defendant for causing a harm, but we blame him less than his sober counterpart. Drunkenness is thus truly a partial excuse. The defendant is less responsible and deserves less punishment—for all offences. The law should accordingly adopt one of two approaches. The first possibility is to recognise that what the defendant is really being punished for is getting so drunk as to cause a prohibited harm. Accordingly, a special offence of "criminal intoxication" could be created. If a defendant in a state of voluntary intoxication commits a listed offence (for example, physical harm to another) he would be liable for this special offence, the punishment for which would be, say, two-thirds of that for the underlying listed offence (Law Commission, 1993c. The Law Commission [1995] finally rejected this proposal). Alternatively, if drunkenness were not to be used as a *substantive* mitigating factor (either because it were felt that this new offence would not convey sufficiently the seriousness of the defendant's actions or because, under the present law, not all crimes have a lesser included counterpart that can be committed recklessly), then it could be relegated to being a mitigating factor in sentencing. If this latter course were adopted, special provision would need to be made for murder to ensure that drunken defendants escape the mandatory sentence.

(ii) Non-Status Excuses. The main non-status excuses recognised by English law are duress, provocation and superior orders. It is important to understand the rationale of excuses because that will help shape the contours of some of the specific rules governing the defences. One view is that an excuse is a "concession to human frailty" (*Howe*, 1987). The problem with this view is that it endorses the "human frailty" of the defendant suggesting that while some mitigation at the sentencing stage might be appropriate, the defendant is not free from all blame and so should not actually be fully excused. An alternative view is that as responsibility involves offering defendants an effective opportunity to make a choice whether to commit a crime, persons who have no fair opportunity to make such choices are entitled to an excuse (Hart, 1968). So, for example, if a person is threatened with extreme violence unless he commits a crime, the pressure of this threat is so great that he is effectively denied the capacity to make a rational choice. The problem with this rationale is that it would make the assessment of excuses totally subjective. Pursuing the duress example, anyone who was scared (no matter how irrationally and unreasonably) would have to be afforded a defence because their capacity for practical reasoning was affected. A more modern way of explaining the gist of excuses is that the defendant has acted for reasons that are entirely socially understandable in the sense that we can empathise with their reasons for acting and accept that socially responsible persons could act in that way. Gardner (1998) puts the point even more strongly: "The gist of an excuse . . . is precisely that the person with the excuse lived up to our expectations". The advantage of this approach is that it allows the law to insist on certain basic levels of fortitude or restraint; these can be measured against the standards of the normal or reasonable person. The problem with this (and the other rationales) is that excuses then boil down to an evaluation of the reasons explaining why a defendant acted in a particular way which includes an evaluation of the emotions motivating the conduct (Lacey, 2000)—a can of worms perhaps best left unopened. It is far from easy to determine which reasons (or emotions motivating conduct) are such as to be empathised with or expected. For instance, fear and despair are reasons that are clearly socially understandable. Equally, jealousy and greed are unacceptable reasons for acting and so should not, and do not, provide any defence. Much more problematic is whether anger (lying at the heart of the provocation defence) is an emotion/reason that should excuse. Most people get angry sometimes; that is entirely understandable and to be expected. But is it understandable/to be expected that one would get so angry as to kill? It is this equivocality about the acceptability of anger as the reason for acting that has led to provocation only being a partial defence to murder.

These issues will be explored further as we turn to an examination of the two most important non-status excuses: duress and duress of circumstances (a complete defence) and provocation (a partial defence).

(a) Duress and duress of circumstances (necessity). The defence of duress by threats has long been recognized by English law. This is where the defendant has been threatened with death or extreme violence if he does not commit a crime. For example, in *A v. DPP* (2000) the defendant claimed that two youths had threatened to kill him unless he stole a woman's handbag. He snatched her handbag after a struggle. It was held that duress could be a defence to a charge of robbery.

However, until recently English law refused to admit a general defence of necessity. This would cover situations where the defendant commits a crime to prevent a greater evil. For example, in *O'Toole* (1971) an ambulance driver committed a traffic offence while rushing to answer an emergency call. It was held that no defence of necessity was available to him. However, while maintaining this overt stance the law did in fact, permit a necessity-like defence in the back door in certain limited circumstances. In cases involving medical treatment doctors were allowed in certain cases to commit what would otherwise have been a crime (for example, operating on a patient without their consent) in order to prevent a graver harm to their patients (*F v. Berkshire Health Authority*, 1990). Further, many statutes, either specifically or by the use of phrases such as "without lawful excuse", effectively permitted a defence of necessity. In the mid-1980s, however, the courts started expanding the boundaries of duress by threats to cover situations of necessity, terming the new defence "duress of circumstances". Within a decade this had become a well-established defence being governed largely by the same rules and parameters as the defence of duress by threats.

Accordingly, there are now two parallel defences in English law. *Duress by threats* (commonly termed simply "duress") covers, as seen above, cases where a person threatens the defendant with death or serious injury unless he or she commits a crime. *Duress of circumstances* (often called "necessity") covers cases where the defendant commits a crime to avoid "other objective dangers" (*Howe*, 1987) threatening himself or others. For example, in *Martin* (1989) the defendant, who was disqualified from driving, drove his son to work because his distraught wife was threatening to commit suicide if he did not do so. So, duress of circumstances is concerned, not with direct threats made by people, but with cases where the defendant is faced with a crisis or emergency whereby he or another will suffer serious injury or death unless an offence is committed. The threat or emergency must be extraneous to the offender. In *Rodger and Rose* (1998) it was held that a defence of duress of circumstances was not available to a charge of breaking prison where the defendants claimed that if they had not escaped from prison, they would have committed suicide.

While the term "duress of circumstances" has long been thought to be no more than a synonym for "necessity", there are indications from a recent, important Court of Appeal decision (*Re A (Conjoined Twins)*, 2000) that these might, in some respects, be separate defences. Duress and duress of circumstances are traditionally regarded as a concession to human frailty and are accordingly viewed as being excusatory in nature. It operates when a defendant is faced with serious violence if he does not commit a crime. He thus commits the crime to avoid the evil to himself or others. Such conduct is generally not justified: it is not "right" or acceptable conduct. The defendant ought not to have the power to choose to harm an innocent person rather than be harmed himself. Nevertheless, such a person is not fully responsible for his actions. We saw earlier (p. 112) that the notion of responsibility involves being able to choose to commit a crime or not. A person who has been subjected to overwhelming threats is unable to make such a free choice. He has been deprived of a "fair opportunity" (Hart, 1968) to choose to obey the law. He has been forced to make a "coerced choice from morally unacceptable options" (Horder, 1994a). His actions are "morally involuntary" (Fletcher, 1978) and he is excused from blame. Another way of putting this is that the defendant has acted for reasons that we can understand; we can accept that reasonable people could have acted in that way.

However, because the actions of the defendant remain "wrong", the law subjects them to intense "moral scrutiny" (Horder, 1994a) and has placed strict limits upon the circumstances in which such a person can be excused. In common with the other non-status excuses this has been achieved by invoking a standard of reasonableness in respect of most aspects of the defence.

On the other hand, it was indicated in *Re A (Conjoined Twins)* (2000) that necessity does not cover the same ground and may have a justificatory basis. With necessity the actor's mind is not so overborne as to make his choice morally involuntary. Rather, the defence is allowed where a rational choice has been made to avoid the greater of two evils. In this case it was held that where doctors owed conflicting duties to conjoined twins they were justified in choosing the lesser of two evils: the death of one rather than the death of both. Whether this thinking will be extended beyond cases of medical necessity where the conflict between a doctor's duties has to be resolved is unclear. Indeed, many of the classic situations of duress of circumstances can be seen in a justificatory light. This is where the harm caused is less than the harm threatened, for example, if property belonging to another were thrown into the sea to save the lives of those on a lifeboat. Further, many of the examples of necessity cited in *Re A (Conjoined Twins)* (2000) extend beyond medical necessity. However, for the moment, it would appear that whatever the defence is termed, the law on duress, duress of circumstances and necessity is, with one important exception, largely the same and can be summarized as follows:

First, the defence is only available when there is a threat of death or really serious injury. Thus while avowedly eschewing the balancing of evils approach, this strict triggering condition (and the fact that, as we shall see, duress is not a defence to murder) in fact ensures that the harm caused is always less than the evil threatened (except, perhaps, in cases where grievous bodily harm is caused as a result of a threat of grievous bodily harm). It would be premature to regard the *dicta* in *Re A (Conjoined Twins)* (2000), concerning the balancing of evils, as triggering a change of direction. In this case the greater evil was the death of both twins.

Secondly, English law has long been committed to the rule that the defence is available even if the threat is not actually real as long as the defendant reasonably believes it to be real (*Graham*, 1982). However, the recent case of *Martin (D.P.)* (2000) drew an analogy between duress and self-defence and held, as *Williams (Gladstone)* (1984) has held on self-defence, that the defence of duress will be available if the defendant honestly believes it is necessary, irrespective of the reasonableness of that belief. It is to be hoped that *Martin (D.P.)* (2000), which goes against a long line of authority, will not be followed. With excuses, we can only accept the person's reasons for acting when they have lived up to our expectations which can be measured against the standard of normal, reasonable people. With the excuse of duress the defendant is committing a wrong and should only be excused if he or she has a plausible—a reasonable—explanation for such wrongdoing.

Thirdly, the person subjected to the threat is expected to show reasonable steadfastness and not give in to the threat too readily. The classic formulation here is: would a sober person of reasonable firmness, sharing the characteristics of the defendant, have given in to the threats (*Graham*, 1982)? In *Bowen* (1996) it was stated that the test is whether there is a clear characteristic making the defendant less courageous. It is not sufficient that he or she is generally timid, pliable or vulnerable. But, if he or she belongs to a category of persons who are generally all more vulnerable, the jury can take this into account. Examples given in this case are young people, who may be more timid than adults, and pregnant women who, out of fear for their unborn children, might give in to threats more readily. A further relevant characteristic is that the defendant is suffering from a recognized psychiatric condition. However, while it is true that many psychiatric conditions can make people more susceptible to threats, the requirement that the defendant must suffer from a "recognised psychiatric condition" is unhelpful. Modern psychiatry has abandoned a cause-based system of classification and now adopts an approach of grouping symptoms and signs. Classifying someone as having a "recognised psychiatric condition" according to these criteria tells us little about that group of persons' ability to withstand threats (Buchanan and Virgo, 1999). In principle, a requirement of reasonable steadfastness seems sensible and would certainly be necessary if any type of threat sufficed. But, given that only a threat of death or serious bodily harm can trigger the defence (and bearing in mind that duress is not a defence to murder), this requirement seems far-fetched, if not superfluous. It envisages that some defendants must not choose self-preservation (Smith, KJM, 1999). If faced with a threat of death or grievous bodily harm unless, say, robbery is committed, it would require more than reasonable steadfastness to resist the threat (assuming all the other rigorous requirements of the defence are met). When would one ever classify as "timid, pliable or vulnerable" a person who commits a crime (other than murder) when faced with such a serious threat? It would require heroism to the point of foolishness for a defendant to choose to die or suffer serious injuries rather than give in and commit the lesser offence.

Fourthly, the threat must be imminent and the defendant must take reasonable steps to neutralize the threat by escaping or seeking protection from, say, the police (*DPP v. Lynch*, 1975). In *Abdul-Hussain* (1999) it was stated that the peril or threat must be "imminent" even if not immediate. This is meant to convey that the threat must be operating on the defendant's mind so as to "overbear his will" even if the execution of the threat is not immediately in prospect. The period of time between the inception of the peril and the defendant's act is a "relevant but not determinative factor". A vivid example was given in this case: if Anne Frank had stolen a car to flee from Amsterdam and then been charged with theft, she would not have been denied a defence of duress of circumstances "on the ground that she should have waited for the Gestapo's knock on the door". Whether the defendant has taken reasonable steps to neutralize the threats depends on the circumstances. For example, there might be grave risks involved in going to the police and police protection might be ineffective (*Hudson and Taylor*, 1971). The test is a flexible one to be answered by the jury: would a reasonable person in the defendant's situation have gone to the police? The interpretation of this imminence requirement is, of course, entirely dependent on the context in which decisions have to be made. In cases involving medical necessity it has been stressed that the principle is "one of necessity, not emergency" (*Re A (Conjoined Twins)*, 2000). In this case the death of both twins was not an immediate, or even imminent, prospect; they could well have lived for many more months. However, as their deaths within that period was a certainty, a severance operation that would kill the weaker twin was a necessity.

Fifthly, the defence is only available to those who are "truly blameless" in the sense that it was not their fault they were forced to choose between the two evils. Accordingly, duress (in either of its forms) is not available to those who have voluntarily joined a terrorist or violent organization as such persons "must be taken to anticipate what may happen to them if their nerve fails" (*Shepherd*, 1988). Even where the defendant gets involved in non-violent criminal activities, such as drug-dealing, the defence is not available if he is aware that he could be threatened with violence unless he commits a crime to raise money to pay drug debts (*Baker and Ward*, 1999).

Finally, and most controversially, duress and duress of circumstances are not defences to the crime of murder (*Howe*, 1987) or attempted murder (*Gotts*, 1992). A person subjected to duress "ought rather to die himself, than kill an innocent" (*DPP v. Lynch*, 1975, citing *Hale's Pleas of the Crown*). In the famous case of *Dudley and Stevens* (1884) three men and a boy had been drifting on a lifeboat on the open seas for 20 days. Eventually, after six days with no food and water the two defendants killed the boy who was in a weak condition and ate his flesh and drank his blood. Four days later they were rescued and subsequently convicted of murder (a sentence later commuted to six months' imprisonment). This denial of the defence raises questions of deep moral significance. Should all four have died rather than sacrifice the life of one of them? The problem with cases such as this (and moral quandaries based on such scenarios) is that they tend to lose sight of the fact that one is dealing here with an excusatory defence and not a justificatory one. There can never be a justification for killing an innocent person in such circumstances. Arguments about whose life should be sacrificed become irrelevant. Dudley and Stevens had no "right" to kill the boy or anyone else. Had he been strong enough, he would have been entitled to defend himself. The essence of an excuse, however, is that it is a "concession to human frailty" (*Howe*, 1987). If a person has a plausible excuse (hence all the rigorous requirements), we can understand his predicament and reasons for acting. If a person of reasonable firmness would have responded in the same way—which will only be the case in the most exceptional situations—surely we ought, while recognising that a "wrong" has been done, to exempt the defendant from blame and punishment.

With regard to the defence of necessity (to the extent that it differs from duress of circumstances), one, possibly narrow, exception has recently been allowed whereby a person may kill to save the life of another. In *Re A (Conjoined Twins)* (2000) it was held that doctors could perform an operation to separate conjoined twins even though this would necessarily mean the death of the weaker twin. Without the operation both would have died within three to six months. In such circumstances, it was held that doctors were allowed to choose the lesser of two evils (the death of the weaker twin rather than the death of both). However, it should be stressed that this ruling has not opened the door to allowing duress of circumstances as a defence to murder (which the Court of Appeal would not have had the authority to do). While Lord Brooke allowed such a defence where the person killed was already "designated for death", Lord Robert Walker used other bases for his decision and Lord Ward was careful to limit his judgment to cases where there was a conflict between a doctor's duties. A doctor is under a legal duty to do what is best for the patient. Here there were conflicting duties owed to the twins and, in exercising their duty, the doctors had to make a choice of the lesser of two evils. In such circumstances the operation would be "justified". It thus appears that while duress and duress of circumstances are no excuse to murder, in the extreme and exceptional circumstances of this case where the death of both persons is a certainty and it is clear which one could survive and which has to die, a defence of necessity as a justification to murder has been introduced into English law.

(b) *Provocation*. The essence of an excusatory defence is that because of some excusing condition or characteristic the defendant is relieved of responsibility and blame for his wrongful act.

However, the excusing condition need not be such as to provide full relief from responsibility. It might simply be a *partial excuse* which results in a reduction of blame but not complete exculpation. Blame is not an absolute "all or nothing" concept. There are degrees of blame. We will generally blame the intentional wrongdoer more than the negligent one. So, too, we might blame certain actors less because they have some excuse for their actions (but not a sufficient excuse to render them blameless).

Provocation is a good example of a partial excuse. It is a partial excuse to murder only, reducing the defendant's liability to manslaughter. (Other crimes do not have fixed penalties and so provocation can be taken into account as a mitigating factor at the sentencing stage.) The essence of provocation is that the defendant must have been so provoked as to lose self-control and the provocation must have been sufficient to make a reasonable man in the defendant's situation do as he did (Homicide Act 1957, section 3, as interpreted by *Camplin*, 1978 and *Smith*, 2000).

The provocative actions can come from any source. In *Doughty* (1986) it was held that the persistent crying of a small baby could be enough to trigger the defence. The focus is on the defendant and whether he or she has a plausible excuse. It is irrelevant that the victim is blameless.

However, the law has been careful to place strict limits on the defence. We all get angry at times. Much violence in pubs, clubs and in the home is the product of such anger. One cannot simply excuse all such violence on the ground that the defendant was angry. Accordingly, the law has insisted that the defendant be so angry as to have "lost self-control". This does not, of course, mean that the defendant must have been in a frenzy and unaware of his actions, but, rather, he must be so angry as to be unable to restrain himself (*Richens*, 1994). Flowing from this, the law has adopted a "male typology of anger" (O'Donovan, 1991) that the loss of self-control must be "sudden and temporary" (*Duffy*, 1949). The stereotype portrayed here is that of the male whose honour (or whatever) has been affronted: he "snaps" and lashes out in anger. The problem with this approach is that it excludes from the possible ambit of the defence of provocation persons who do not react in such an immediate manner. This issue has been high-lighted in recent years by a series of cases dealing with battered women who have been subjected to years of violence by their husbands or partners and who suffer "slow-burn" anger whereby anger and despair builds up and finally erupts into the killing of the man. In *Ahluwalia* (1992) the wife had been beaten, raped and subjected to humiliation by her husband for years. Finally, one night she poured petrol over him while he was sleeping and ignited it. He died from his burns. While the defence of provocation was denied her (her conviction for murder was quashed on appeal and a retrial ordered to enable her to plead diminished responsibility, the court took a significant step in holding that the defence of provocation *could* be available in such cases where there was a delayed reaction although "the longer the delay and the stronger the evidence of deliberation on the part of the defendant, the more likely it will be that the prosecution will negative provocation." Thus, while difficult to establish, the defence of provocation is now a possibility for battered women suffering from slow-burn anger.

The other safeguard the law imposes on the defence of provocation to avoid excusing all angry outbursts is that the provocation must be of such a magnitude that a reasonable person would have reacted similarly. Under section 3 of the Homicide Act 1957 (which qualified the common law) where is evidence of loss of self-control, "the question whether the provocation was enough to make a reasonable man do as he did shall be left to be determined by the jury; and in determining that question the jury shall take into account everything both done and said according to the effect which, in their opinion, it would have on a reasonable man."

A central issue over the past half-century has been one of determining what is meant by the "reasonable man" in this context. In *Bedder* (1954) (a case prior to the 1957 Act) it was held that the reasonable man could not be endowed with any of the characteristics of the defendant. In this case a man killed a prostitute after she had mocked him because of his impotence. The House of Lords ruled that the jury should disregard the defendant's impotence when applying the reasonable man test. The reasonable man had no peculiarities or imperfections. In short, he was the perfect man. (Quite why such a perfect man would lose his self-control and kill when provoked rather than exercise restraint was never explained.) In *Camplin* (1978) the door to flexibility was opened. In this case the defendant, a 15 year-old boy, was forcibly buggered by a man. When the man started to laugh and gloat over his sexual triumph, the defendant lost his self-control and beat the man to death with a chapati pan. The House of Lords held that account should be taken of the age of the defendant; the question was whether a reasonable 15 year-old, who had just been buggered, would have responded in a similar way.

After *Camplin* (1978) the law started to draw a distinction between characteristics affecting the gravity of the provocation and characteristics affecting the power of self-control (*Newell*, 1980; *Morhall*, 1996). With regard to the former the jury could take into account any factor bearing on the gravity of the provocation. If a person has a particular characteristic and is taunted about it, the provocation will be more grave than it would be for other people without that characteristic. In such cases the law allowed the jury to consider how a reasonable man with that characteristic would have reacted. For example, in *Morhall* (1996) the defendant was taunted about his addiction to glue-sniffing. He lost his temper and stabbed the taunter to death. It was held that the defendant being an addict affected the gravity of the provocation to him and therefore the jury could take this into account.

When dealing with characteristics affecting the defendant's power of self-control, two lines of authority emerged. On the one hand, there was a view that only the age and sex of the defendant could be permitted to vary the strict reasonable man standard. In *Luc Thiet Thuan* (1997) the defendant was suffering from brain damage which could have made it difficult for him to control his impulses and temper. His ex-girlfriend taunted him about her new lover. The Privy Council held that the jury was not entitled to take his brain damage into account. If he had been provoked about his mental infirmity, that would have been relevant as affecting the gravity of the provocation to him. But, as he was taunted about something else, his brain damage could not be considered. In short, while age and sex do affect the reasonable man standard because we have all been fifteen and are all either male or female, to endow the reasonable man with a characteristic such as brain damage would be to destroy the reasonable man test. The defence of diminished responsibility (p. 103), which allows mental abnormality to reduce murder to manslaughter, is the appropriate defence for such persons.

On the other hand, a line of Court of Appeal decisions rejected this *Luc Thiet Thuan* (1997) approach and ruled that a wide array of characteristics of the defendant could be taken into account by the jury as affecting the defendant's power of self-control. This line of authority has approved the case of *Raven* (1982) where the jury was asked to consider how a reasonable man with a physical age of 22 but a mental age of only nine years would have responded. In *Humphries* (1995) it was held that the abnormal immaturity and attention-seeking characteristics of the defendant could be taken into account. In *Ahluwalia* (1992) it was indicated, *obiter*, that, with appropriate medical evidence, it could be relevant to consider how a reasonable woman suffering from "battered woman syndrome" would have reacted. In *Dryden* (1995) the defendant had developed an obsession about his planning problems and killed a planning officer who was engaged in demolishing his bungalow pursuant to an enforcement notice. It was held that his obsessiveness and eccentricity should have been left to the jury as mental characteristics to be taken into account.

The result of all this was confused and incoherent law. The distinction between characteristics affecting the gravity of the provocation and those affecting self-control was not an easy one for juries to grasp. The defendant in *Morhall* (1996) was provoked about his glue-sniffing addiction; the jury could take that into account. If he had been provoked about something else (say, his impotence caused by the addiction) the jury (on the *Luc* line of authority) had to ignore his condition. On the other hand, following the Court of Appeal line of authority attributing a wide range of characteristics to the defendant produced "monsters" (*Smith*, 2000) such as the reasonable obsessive or the reasonable abnormally immature and attention-seeking person.

In a long-awaited judgment the House of Lords in *Smith* (2000) attempted to resolve these difficulties. Arguing that the law had descended into something out of "wonderland", the majority sought a return to the real world. Whether they found the right way back through the looking-glass is, however, debatable.

The defendant in this case suffered serious clinical depression and killed his friend in a flaming row over stolen tools. The issue was whether his depressive illness could be taken into account by the jury in deciding whether a reasonable man would have lost his self-control. The majority held that section 3 had left the entire task to the jury to take into account "everything" to determine the effect it would have on the reasonable man. It would be contrary to section 3 for a judge to direct them to ignore the characteristics of the defendant. Accordingly, the jury should be allowed to consider whether there was some characteristic of the defendant which "affected the degree of control which society could reasonably have expected of *him*" (Lord Hoffman). The issue for the jury is: "what could reasonably be expected of a person with the accused's characteristics?" (Lord Slynn). Realizing that attributing characteristics to the reasonable man had produced "monsters" such as the reasonable glue-sniffer, the majority held that the "reasonable man" in section 3 was but an "image" or an "opaque formula" to convey the "standard of reasonable behaviour expected of a person in the situation of and with the characteristics of the accused" (Lord Clyde). Accordingly, judges need not refer to the reasonable man in every case. What should be explained to the jury is that it is necessary that the defendant have exercised "a reasonable level of self-control for someone with her history, her experience and her state of mind" (Lord Clyde). The majority rejected the distinction between characteristics affecting the gravity of the provocation and those affecting self-control. They further confirmed that there is a clear overlap between provocation and diminished responsibility. However, the overlap is not complete: there will be some cases, for example battered women, where the person is not abnormal but has undergone experiences affecting their powers of self-control.

The problem with this approach is that it comes close to a complete obliteration of the objective reasonable man test specified in section 3. The defendant did lose self-control and kill. Why did this happen? If one takes her history, experience and state of mind into account that simply shows that she a person liable to lose self-control and kill in such circumstances. As Lord Hobhouse (dissenting) put it: "if one adds all the characteristics of the defendant to the notional reasonable man, the reasonable man becomes 'reincarnated' in the defendant".

Conscious of the dangers of such an approach which would basically allow anger as a partial excuse to murder in all cases (and amount to a complete rejection of section 3), the majority stressed that certain characteristics should be ignored in order to preserve the objective test in section 3. The following were listed as appropriate for exclusion: male possessiveness and jealousy, obsession, a tendency to violent rages or childish tantrums, violent disposition (Lord Hoffman); quarrelsome or choleric temperament; drunkenness or other self-induced lack of control; exceptional pugnacity or excitability (Lord Clyde).

Most of these characteristics seem to be directly related to a propensity to anger and losing one's temper and self-control.

Lord Hoffman described them as "defects of character rather than an excuse". There are problems with this approach. There are often reasons why people have, say, a choleric temperament. It might be, for example, because they are impotent or mentally ill. Under this test the underlying cause can be taken into consideration but what is the point if the symptoms of this (choleric temperament) must be ignored? Some of the other characteristics listed do not, however, appear to relate directly to anger and temper and self-control. Male possessiveness, jealousy and obsession are not necessarily connected to the lack of ability to exercise self-control. Rather, it seems that they are disapproved-of characteristics. But, why should they be rejected as defects of character while addiction to glue-sniffing is still a permissible characteristic to be taken into account? Lord Clyde approved *Dryden* (1995) that obsessiveness with regard to planning permission was an acceptable characteristic to take into account yet Lord Hoffman rejected male obsessiveness as being relevant. This approach invites trial judges to reflect their individual values and prejudices in determining which characteristics are relevant or not.

Further, drunkenness cannot be taken into account. For policy reasons this is understandable and there are special rules on the effect of intoxication on criminal liability (p. 107). But there are also special rules on the effect of mental abnormality in murder cases (diminished responsibility: p. 103). Yet mental abnormality is a factor for the jury's consideration in provocation cases.

In short, despite Lord Clyde stating that his aim was "to clothe [the reasonable man] with a reasonable degree of reality", it appears in truth that the law is still in Wonderland. Alice, who has been subjected to violent abuse, can have her history and experience taken into account. But the obsessively jealous Alice must be judged by the standard of the reasonably calm woman with her obsessiveness ignored. What they would make of that at the Mad Hatter's tea party is a matter of conjecture.

The real problem here is that the law has been cut loose from its theoretical moorings. The law has been unable to grasp the nettle and decide whether anger ought (partially) to excuse liability. Section 3 has gone for the messy compromise of qualifying the conditions when anger should excuse: only when it is reasonable to lose one's self-control and kill. In some cases we might accept that a reasonable person without any unusual characteristics could be provoked to kill. A reasonable woman discovering her husband having just raped her daughter could well lose her self-control and kill. But if such conduct is felt to be reasonable, blame of any degree seems inappropriate. The law can and should set a standard to try to make people behave reasonably. If a person conforms to this standard, it seems harsh to convict him or her of manslaughter. On the other hand, if the real explanation of the loss of self-control is some characteristic (battered woman syndrome, mental disability, etc.), a defence ought to be provided that is aimed at that condition: diminished responsibility or a new defence. If a person loses self-control because of their disability and kills, it is mislabelling to term the defence provocation rather than labelling it something that addresses the disability. There will, however, be cases that do not come within either of the above situations: where someone does lose their temper: the reasonable person would not have killed in response but because of their condition or history or situation it is felt that their loss of self-control is sufficiently excusable for murder to be reduced to manslaughter.

In the United States the Model Penal Code provides a partial defence of "extreme mental or emotional disturbance . . . for which there is a reasonable excuse" (section 210.3.1(b)). This is designed to cover provocation, as well as mental abnormality and duress. For fair labelling reasons such a provision is too broad; the current defences of diminished responsibility and duress should continue their work here. However, an adaptation of this provision to allow a partial defence of "extreme emotional disturbance for which there is a reasonable explanation or excuse" could serve to allow murder to be reduced to manslaughter in cases where, although the killing is unreasonable, some compassion to human infirmity is clearly appropriate.

(iii) Blame and Inchoate Offences
The discussion of blameworthiness so far has concentrated on the paradigm of the blameworthy actor who commits the prohibited harm, for example, the actor who kills or injures another. However, as seen earlier, some crimes are "inchoate" (above, pp. 21–28). With attempt, conspiracy and incitement the prohibited harm need not occur. Liability is based on the defendant trying to commit, planning or encouraging the full offence. In such cases one does not have a corpse or an injury from which to "work backwards" and infer the defendant's level of culpability. What type or degree of blameworthiness is required here?

The paradigmatic crime is one where the actor has intentionally caused the prohibited harm. One can have departures from the paradigm, for example, crimes of recklessness but, to avoid the danger of over-criminalisation, such departures need to be justified and need to be marked by the imposition of less liability and/or punishment to emphasise that this is a departure. Thus manslaughter, a crime that can be committed recklessly, is labelled differently and carries a lesser penalty (a maximum of life imprisonment as opposed to mandatory life imprisonment which is the penalty for murder). Further, in certain activities the risks involved are so great, universal and well known that a double-departure from the paradigm can be justified to try to prevent persons performing those activities dangerously. Examples include the offences of dangerous driving and careless driving (Road Traffic Act 1988, sections 2 and 3) and failing to ensure the health and safety of employees at work (Health and Safety at Work Act 1974, section 2). These offences are similar to what are called in the United States "offences of reckless endangerment". However, because they involve such a major departure from paradigmatic crimes, these offences carry greatly reduced penalties. For example, if someone is killed by dangerous driving, the maximum penalty is either life imprisonment (motor manslaughter) or ten years' imprisonment (causing death by dangerous driving). On the other hand, the offences of dangerous driving and careless driving carry maximum penalties of two years' and six months' imprisonment respectively. The double-departure from the paradigm is clearly marked.

The inchoate offences of attempt, conspiracy and incitement all involve departures from the paradigm: the ultimate harm is not committed. One could also depart from the paradigm of blameworthiness, intention, and allow these crimes to be committed recklessly. There are, however, two important reasons why this should not be permitted.

First, the creation of criminal liability in any field involves the suppression of human activity and the restriction of our freedom. Accordingly, criminal offences need to be justified and their reach limited to what is necessary to prevent the harmful activity (see below pp. 252–256). One should not dilute the special symbolic and stigmatic significance of criminal liability by "criminalising everything in sight". Accordingly, using the law of attempt as an example, one needs to ask whether the double-departure from the paradigm that would be involved in criminalising reckless attempts would be justifiable. Do we really want to punish someone who does not mean (intend) to commit a crime and who in fact causes no harm? Apart from the linguistic distortion involved in saying that someone is attempting to commit a crime when he or she is not trying to commit that offence, are such persons sufficiently blameworthy to warrant the imposition of criminal liability? Would the creation of such offences have a deterrent effect? Are such persons so dangerous that criminal liability and punishment is necessary to exercise restraint over them? The answers to these questions are not easy but suffice it to say for present purposes that *generally* the case for inchoate liability in such situations is far from proven and, accordingly, given the presumption in favour of liberty and non-criminalisation, criminal liability for the crime of attempt, etc., would not be justifiable in these circumstances.

Secondly, while the risk-creation offences cited above carry significantly reduced penalties, the same is not true of the crimes of attempt, conspiracy and incitement. An attempt to commit a crime is punishable to the same extent as the complete offence (Criminal Attempts Act 1981, section 4(1)). The same is generally true of conspiracy (Criminal Justice Act 1987, section 12). Incitement is an offence punishable entirely at the discretion of the court. Accordingly, as these inchoate offences are regarded at the legislative level as being of equal seriousness to the completed offence, only a minimum departure from the paradigm should be tolerated and so, as no actual harm has been caused in such cases, the "fullest" possible species of blameworthiness, namely, intention, should be required for these offences.

The law has largely followed this reasoning. For an attempt the defendant must act "with intent to commit an offence" (Criminal Attempts Act 1981, section 1(1)). For example, in *O'Toole* (1987) it was held that while arson was an offence that could be committed recklessly, for attempted arson the defendant had to intend to cause criminal damage by fire. However, there has been a relaxation of this rule with regard to "surrounding circumstances". In *Khan* (1990) it was held, on a charge of attempted rape, that while the defendant had to intend to have sexual intercourse, recklessness as to whether the woman was consenting sufficed. The defendant must intend to "achieve that which was missing from the full offence" (*Attorney General's Reference* (*No. 3 of 1992*), 1994). What was missing was sexual intercourse. In respect to the remaining elements, only the same *mens rea* as for the full crime need be proved.

With conspiracy the position is not entirely clear. In principle, each conspirator should intend that the offence be carried out (Criminal Law Act 1977, section 1(2)). This simple proposition was, however, disapproved by the House of Lords in *Anderson* (1986) where it was held that it was not necessary to prove that the defendant intended that the crime be committed. What was required was that he enter into an agreement that it be committed and intend to play some part in the agreed course of conduct in furtherance of the criminal plot. Fortunately, however, subsequent cases seem to be ignoring this decision and insisting on proof of an intention that the crime be committed (*Edwards*, 1991; *McPhillips*, 1989). In *Yip Chiu-cheung* (1994) an undercover drug enforcement officer agreed with the defendant to smuggle heroin from Thailand to Hong Kong and Australia. This was done with the connivance of the authorities in the latter two countries in the hope of breaking up a drug ring. When the plan was not carried out the defendant was charged in Hong Kong with conspiracy to traffic in heroin. He claimed that there was no conspiracy as his alleged co-conspirator lacked the necessary *mens rea*. The Privy Council was emphatic in rejecting this argument holding that conspiracy necessitated proof of an intention that the agreement be carried out and that the undercover agent had such an intention. The fact that he never expected to be prosecuted and was "acting courageously and with the best of motives" was irrelevant.

This approach is consistent with principle and preferable to that adopted in *Anderson* (1986). The correct solution to the problem posed in *Anderson* (1986), where a person agrees to commit a crime but intends to withdraw from the enterprise and does not expect the crime to be carried out, is to convict such a person of aiding and abetting a conspiracy.

The position with incitement is reasonably clear. The inciter must intend that the person incited will commit the offence. This, of course, means the inciter must believe that person will have the *mens rea* necessary for that crime. Accordingly, if I encourage you to accept, either as a gift or at a very cheap price, goods that are in fact stolen, I am not guilty of incitement if I believe you are unaware of this fact. However, if I do believe you have the *mens rea* of the crime, I am liable for incitement even if in fact you lack the requisite *mens rea*. In *Armstrong* (2000) the defendant encouraged a man who, unknown to him, was really a police officer, to supply him with pornography involving young girls. It was held that as long as the defendant believed the other would have *mens rea* in doing what he was asked, there could be liability for incitement. It was not necessary that there be "parity of *mens rea*" between the two. The fact that the police officer never had any intention of supplying the pornographic material was immaterial.

(iv) Blame and Accessories

We saw earlier that a person who assists or encourages another to commit a crime can be liable for the full offence committed. In some situations mere words of encouragement have been held to suffice. But what type of blameworthiness is required in such cases?

It will be recalled that there were different categories of accessories: aiders and abettors, counsellors and procurers but, with the exception of procuring, these terms are effective synonyms and what is more important is the mode of participation in the offence (see pp. 28–33). Procuring presents little problem because the procurer, like many principal offenders, "produces by endeavour" (*Attorney-General's Reference (No. 1 of 1975)*, 1975); it must be established that the procurer caused the prohibited harm and that this result was intended. For example, in *Blakey and Sutton* (1991) the defendants laced the principal's tonic water with vodka. They intended to tell him before he left to drive home so that he would spend the night with one of them. In short, they gave him alcohol so that he would not drive. Unfortunately, he left before they could tell him his drinks had been laced and he was stopped and subsequently convicted of driving with excess alcohol. The defendants, also convicted of this offence on the basis of procuring its commission, had their appeals allowed because for procuring it is necessary to prove an intention to bring about the crime.

But with the remaining cases of aiding and counselling there is a problem here in that the normal cognitive culpability requirements (intention and recklessness) refer to intention or recklessness in relation to *one's own* actions and their consequences. When the principal deliberately shoots a victim he can clearly be said to have intended death as a result of his actions over which he had control. The question is whether the accessory, who has merely shouted encouragement, needs to have *mens rea* with regard to *the consequence* (intending that the victim be killed by the principal offender) or whether he simply needs to intend to *help or encourage*. If it is the latter, *what* must he intend to help or encourage? There should clearly be a difference between encouraging the principal to fire his gun in the general direction of the victim and encouraging him to fire the gun with the intention of killing the victim. In other words, we might need to investigate the mental attitude of the accessory *to the mental state of the principal offender*. Following this latter view the accessory would only be guilty of murder if he realised that the principal would fire at the victim intending to kill or cause grievous bodily harm.

This issue has caused most difficulty in two groups of cases: those involving a "joint unlawful enterprise" and those where encouragement is provided before the commission of the crime. A typical case of "joint unlawful enterprise" was *Slack* (1989) where the accessory and the principal offender burgled a flat with the intention of robbing the occupant. While they were in the flat but the accessory was out of the room, the principal offender murdered the victim. Murder had not been part of their plan but the accessory had foreseen that the principal offender might intentionally cause death or grievous bodily harm. On the basis of such knowledge Slack, the accessory, was himself found guilty of murder. This approach has since been confirmed by the House of Lords in *Powell; English* (1998). All that is required is that the accessory foresee or realise that there is a risk that the principal offender will commit the crime with the *mens rea* of the crime. So, on a murder charge it must be established that the accessory realised as a "possible incident" of the activity that the principal offender might kill with intent to kill or cause grievous bodily harm (the *mens rea* of murder).

A good example of encouragement prior to the crime (where the same rules apply—*Reardon*, 1999) is to be found in *Rook* (1993) where the defendant planned a murder with others but never turned up on the agreed day having simply wanted to get his money and then disappear. It was held, consistent with the above cases, that he would be guilty of murder if he foresaw that there was a real risk that the others would, with appropriate *mens rea*, commit the murder.

Although the point has not been finally settled, it would appear that this *Powell; English* (1998) principle applies in all cases (with the possible exception of those involving procuring) and that many of the leading cases need to be reread in the light of the new principle. It was common to state that the accessory had to have knowledge of the circumstances rendering the conduct criminal (*NCB v. Gamble*, 1959) or, more modernly, be reckless as to the possibility of the consequence occurring. Under *Powell; English* (1998) recklessness as to the result is not enough. The accessory must foresee the principal offender bringing about the result with the *mens rea* of the crime in question. A similar approach should be adopted with respect to the extent the accessory must know the details of the principal offender's intended offence. For example, in *Bainbridge* (1960) the defendant sold oxy-acetylene equipment to the principal offender thinking it was going to be used to cut up stolen property; it was in fact used to break into a bank. It was held that the defendant could be liable for the offence (which would now be burglary) if he knew that a crime of the *same type* as that finally committed was intended by the principal offender. The problem with this approach is that one is convicting a person of burglary when it has never entered his head that a burglary could be committed. The policy here seems to be that the accessory was prepared to help in the commission of a crime and therefore he will be liable for any broadly comparable crime that is ultimately committed. A better approach (although *Bainbridge* has never been overruled) was adopted in *DPP for Northern Ireland v. Maxwell* (1979) that the defendant would be liable if the crime committed was one on a "shopping list" of crimes that he had foreseen might be committed. Here the defendant is blameworthy in relation to the offence committed and therefore liability for that offence can be justified. After *Powell; English* (1998) foresight of the crime on the shopping list must mean foresight of the principal offender committing that crime with the appropriate *mens rea*.

This whole approach adopted in *Powell; English* (1998) raises a dilemma. A principal offender can only be guilty of murder if he *intends* to kill or cause grievous bodily harm. Yet an accessory can be liable for murder purely on the basis of being *reckless* as to whether the principal offender will, with *mens rea*, commit murder. The policy of the law is clear. Joint or gang ventures are extremely dangerous. If a gang of burglars sets out each realising that one of them might well murder the householder, they are all displaying a willingness to kill. They have become participants in an intentional offence (Smith, 1998). It might be chance that it was the principal offender rather than the accessory that actually did the killing. Maximum deterrence needs to be directed against such enterprises and where one of them deliberately kills a murder conviction for each is appropriate.

On the other hand, the better view is that it is highly anomalous that the person who does not actually kill should be guilty of murder on the basis of mere recklessness. A principal offender who kills recklessly reveals a willingness to kill but that will not suffice. Why should such a mental state be enough for the accessory who is further removed from the crime in terms of causation and who has not broken through the psychological barrier of actually killing? Such accessories should be convicted and punished for what they have done. Reckless killings are the traditional territory of manslaughter. Criminal responsibility and liability should be calibrated to culpability. The accessory who merely foresees the risk of the principal offender killing with the *mens rea* of murder should only be liable for manslaughter. Since *Powell; English* (1998), however, this is not the law. Such an accessory is guilty of murder.

But, what is the position if an accessory, acting within the scope of the joint enterprise, does not consider the possibility of the principal offender killing with the *mens rea* of murder? A strict interpretation of *Powell; English* (1998) is that the accessory must be guilty of the same offence as the principal offender or nothing (other than separate offences he might have committed). Under this approach Slack could still be guilty of burglary or robbery as a co-principal but, in relation to the murder charge, he must either be guilty of murder along with the principal or not liable for any homicide offence. However, a different approach was adopted in *Gilmour* (2000) where an accessory drove the principal offenders to the scene of the crime knowing that a petrol bomb attack was to take place but not realising the principal offenders intended death or grievous bodily harm. It was held that the defendant should be guilty of "the degree of offence appropriate to the intent with which he so acted" and a verdict of manslaughter was substituted. Such an approach is to be welcomed although whether it is consistent with *Powell; English* (1998) and whether it will be followed is an open question.

The approach adopted in *Powell; English* (1998) is, of course, consistent with the principle of derivative liability underlying the law of complicity. A crime has been committed (say, murder); the issue is whether other participants can be derivatively liable for that crime. Taken to its logical conclusion this would mean that an accessory could never be guilty of a more or less serious offence than the principal offender and, of course, the principal must be liable for the crime: if she escapes liability there is no crime and therefore there is nothing from which accessorial liability can derive.

However, the English courts prior to *Powell; English* (1998) had been gradually loosening the tie of derivative liability. In *Howe* (1987) the House of Lords held that an accessory could be convicted of murder even if the principal offender was only liable for manslaughter. If the accessory intended death, his liability should be linked to his culpability (murder) and not constrained by the offence committed by the principal offender. A further group of cases (all on procuring) have concluded that an accessory may be liable even though the principal offender escapes all liability because of lack of *mens rea* or because of a defence—provided the *actus reus* of the crime was committed. For example, in *K and B* (1997) two young girls procured a boy to rape another girl. Under the law as it then stood if the boy was under 14 years of age he could have escaped liability. It was nevertheless held that as the *actus reus* of rape had been committed, the girls who had *mens rea* could be liable. Similarly, in *Cogan and Leak* (1976), Leak forced his wife to have sexual intercourse with Cogan. Cogan believed she was consenting and accordingly his conviction was quashed. The procurer, Leak, was nevertheless found liable.

It is difficult to reconcile these cases with the *Powell; English* (1998) principle that the accessory must realise that there is a risk the principal offender will commit the offence with the *mens rea* of the offence. The defendants in the above two cases did not have such a realisation. Accordingly, either all these cases will need to be reconsidered in the light of *Powell; English* (1998) or, alternatively, it could be argued that these were procuring cases and, because procuring involves causation and not consensus, different rules should apply. (This latter view does not explain *Howe* (1987) or the subsequent decision of *Gilmour* (2000) which did not involve procuring.)

Perhaps, as already argued, the best way forward would be to reject the whole *Powell; English* (1998) approach. Two possibilities present themselves. First, one could continue with a flexible form of derivative liability. In all the above cases the *actus reus* of the crime was committed; the "wrong" of homicide or rape had occurred. Other participants" liability can derive from that wrong, their precise liability being calibrated to their *mens rea* as was done in *Gilmour* (2000). The second, and more radical, alternative would be to abandon derivative liability completely and, following the Law Commission's recommendation, create two new inchoate offences of assisting and encouraging crime (see pp. 35–36).

5. STRICT LIABILITY

While the general rule insists upon proof of blame as a prerequisite to the imposition of criminal liability, there is an "exceptional" category of crimes for which no such blame need be established. The defendant can be convicted even though he or she had no *mens rea* and was not blameworthy in any other way. These are called crimes of strict liability. Whether such crimes can truly be described as "exceptional" is somewhat doubtful as more than half the 8,000 crimes in English law are strict liability offences (Justice, 1980; Ashworth, 2000a).

Take, for instance, the House of Lords case of *Alphacell Ltd v. Woodward* (1972). The defendant company was a paper manufacturer whose premises were adjacent to a river. Its manufacturing process produced effluents that were run into filtration equipment designed to prevent the effluents entering the river. The equipment was regularly examined and well maintained. Nevertheless, due to a pump becoming blocked on one occasion, effluent was discharged into the river. The company's conviction for causing polluted matter to enter the river contrary to section 2(1)(a) of the Rivers (Prevention of Pollution) Act 1951 was upheld by the House of Lords. The fact that it had not known, and had no reason to believe, that the pollution was taking place was irrelevant. The offence was one of strict liability.

The development of most strict liability offences dates from the nineteenth century. In the aftermath of the industrial revolution a great deal of legislation was enacted dealing with the new areas of public health, safety and welfare. The trend increased in the twentieth century as an increasingly complex society demanded social regulation. Legislation dealing with traffic regulation, consumer protection, control of impure food and drugs, health and safety at work, protection of the environment and so on was steadily passed.

Much of this developing regulation could have been placed under administrative control without involving the criminal law. For instance, local authorities could have been given powers to close down or in some other way to restrict the operations of companies causing polluted matter to enter rivers. Indeed, most of the enforcement agencies in these fields are given powers of this nature. For example, the Health and Safety Executive commonly employs prohibition and improvement notices and regards its main function as being one of advising and helping employers to make their workplaces safer. However, it was felt that such procedures alone could be insufficient to deal with the recalcitrant company or other employer. Enforcement agencies could employ a compliance strategy but employers would more readily comply if there were a threat of criminal sanctions. Such laws would best stimulate the required diligence and cause persons engaged in such activities to police their enterprises to ensure compliance with the law. Also, of course, many of these activities do cause real and serious harms: causing polluted matter to enter rivers clearly harms the environment. The criminal law has always been one of the traditional mechanisms of social control and prevention of harms.

While these traditional principles of the criminal law not incorporated into these offences? Why was the requirement of blame or fault dispensed with? Norrie (1993) argues that one of the main reasons for the introduction of strict liability at this time was that this was the only way in which magistrates could be persuaded to convict "their own kind", the factory owners. In other words, strict liability emerged out of the "ambiguity of policing respectable men". Further, proof of blame would have raised problems of law enforcement and could have undermined the efficacy of the law. Take, for instance, offences relating to the sale of impure or adulterated food or drugs. Advances in chemical analysis meant that adulteration became easier to detect but the huge increase in the standard of products, and the increased complexity of their component ingredients made it extremely difficult to prove that a manufacturer or merchant knew that the goods did not conform to standards (Leigh, 1982). If *mens rea* needed to be proved, the law would become a dead letter.

While these practical considerations of enforcement were the main reason for the proliferation of strict liability offences, other justifications were soon added. Strict liability promotes increased care and efficiency. Knowledge of strict liability is a cost to be weighed when setting up a trade or business. It encourages enterprises to appoint experts, say chemists or bacteriologists, to ensure that their products are safe. It is preferable to place the burden on such enterprises who are in a position to prevent the harm than on the innocent public.

Another line of justification is that no injustice is caused as strict liability offences are not "real crimes". They are only quasi-criminal offences, or "violations". Conviction does not entail the same stigma as for real crimes. The penalties are usually slight and generally in the form of fines. Research has revealed that in fact prosecutions are only brought against those who are at fault, at least in the sense of being negligent (Richardson, 1987). If, in any case, the truly blameless were to be prosecuted and convicted, a minimal sentence such as an absolute discharge would be appropriate.

And, finally, it is argued that the sheer volume of these offences necessitates dispensing with *mens rea* or other indicators of blameworthiness. It would be too time-consuming if blameworthiness had to be proved in every case involving, say, parking on a double-yellow line.

Despite such claims (the validity of which will be explored shortly), the courts have been cautious about interpreting offences as imposing strict liability. Most crimes of strict liability are statutory and it is for the courts to interpret these statutes to ascertain whether an offence of strict liability has been created. The relevant statutory provision in *Alphacell Ltd v. Woodward* (1972) imposed criminal liability "if he causes . . . to enter a stream any poisonous, noxious or polluting matter". No word pointing to *mens rea* or blame was used—but that did not necessarily mean the offence was one of strict liability. The provision needed to be interpreted according to established principles of statutory interpretation to ascertain whether Parliament intended the offence to be one of strict liability.

The most important of these principles is the now well-established presumption in favour of *mens rea*. Lord Reid in the leading case of *Sweet v. Parsley* (1970) stressed that there was a clear presumption that Parliament did not intend to make criminals of persons who were in no way blameworthy in what they did. This presumption is particularly strong where the offence is "truly criminal" in character *(Gammon Ltd v. Att.-Gen. of Hong Kong,* 1984). In *B v. DPP* (2000) a 15 year-old boy invited a 13 year-old girl on a bus to perform oral sex with him. He believed she was over 14 years of age. The House of Lords, in quashing his conviction for inciting a child under 14 to commit an act of gross indecency contrary to section 1(1) of the

Indecency with Children Act 1960, emphasised the importance of the *Sweet v. Parsley* (1970) presumption of *mens rea* and that the more serious the offence and its level of punishment, the graver the stigma and so the stronger the presumption.

On the other hand, the presumption in favour of *mens rea* can be rebutted if it is clear that Parliament has "expressly or by necessary implication" provided to the contrary (*B v. DPP*, 2000). This, of course, involves a close examination of the relevant statutory provision and how it compares with other similar provisions in the statute. For example, if a statute creates 10 criminal offences dealing with similar subject-matter and nine of those provisions contain a *mens rea* word, the necessary implication of the omission of such a word from the tenth offence could be that it was deliberately meant to be a strict liability offence.

An important factor in assessing whether the presumption in favour of *mens rea* should be rebutted is the subject-matter of the crime. Where the offence is of a "public welfare" nature lacking social obloquy, or concerned with issues of "social concern" such as "public safety" (*Gammon Ltd v. Att.-Gen. of Hong Kong*, 1985), there will be a greater readiness to rebut the presumption in favour of *mens rea*. If the offence has been introduced within the framework of a regulatory scheme and enforced by regulatory agencies, there is a greater likelihood of the offence being regarded as relating to "public welfare". However, beyond these areas and road traffic offences it is difficult to determine whether an offence relates to matters of public welfare. Statements such those in *Gammon Ltd v. Att.-Gen. of Hong Kong* (1985) are particularly unhelpful as most of the criminal law is devoted to matters of "social concern" and "public safety".

One factor that tends to incline the courts towards rebutting the presumption in favour of *mens rea* is the vulnerability of the potential victims. This applies particularly in fields of activities in which the public has little choice whether to participate (for example, buying food and drink or breathing the air). Also, where children are vulnerable to exploitation by older persons, the courts seem more willing to impose strict liability. For example, In *Land* (1998) it was held that the offence of possessing indecent photographs of children was an offence of strict liability in that it was not necessary to prove that the defendant knew the child photographed was under the age of 16. In *Harrow LBC v. Shah* (1999) it was similarly held that the offence of selling National Lottery tickets to persons under the age of 16 was a strict liability offence. On the other hand, in *B v. DPP* (2000) the presumption of *mens rea* was held to be applicable to the offence of inciting a child under 14 to commit an act of gross indecency. While recognising that the object of this statute is the protection of children from the actions and solicitations of predatory, older paedophiles, the practical effects of the imposition of strict liability in such a case needed consideration. The offence was so broad as to cover mere verbal invitations in private ("relatively innocuous behaviour") between teenagers if one of them was under the age of 14. In short, while the offence in *B v. DPP* (2000) could well be committed by experimenting teenagers of roughly the same age, it is unlikely that the offence of possession of indecent photographs (or the prior taking of the photographs) would be committed by anyone other than an older person and the object of that legislation was to "protect children from exploitation and degradation" (*Land*, 1998), so justifying the imposition of strict liability.

Even where it is concluded that the subject-matter of the offence falls within the territory of strict liability offences, the presumption can only be rebutted if it can be shown that the imposition of strict liability will be effective to promote the objectives of the statute by encouraging greater vigilance to prevent the activity in question (*Gammon Ltd v. Att.-Gen. of Hong Kong*, 1984). If the creation of a strict liability offence would not help promote observance of the law because, say, the defendant could not have done anything to avoid breaking the law, then there is no point in imposing strict liability (*Lim Chin Aik*, 1963).

Finally, it is sometimes asserted that the less severe the penalty, the more likely it is that Parliament intended to impose liability without fault. Such a view, however, must be treated with caution. Certain offences of strict liability carry severe penalties including terms of imprisonment. Lord Scarman pointed out in *Gammon Ltd v. Att.-Gen. of Hong Kong* (1984) that there is not necessarily anything inconsistent in such an approach especially where the rationale of those offences is their deterrent effect: a severe penalty will be a more significant deterrent. Indeed, research has revealed that about half the offences triable in the Crown Court (the more serious offences) do not require *mens rea* in relation to an *actus reus* element (Ashworth and Blake, 1996).

Despite this judicial emphasis on the presumption of *mens rea* and caution in allowing its displacement, the fact nevertheless remains that there are several thousand offences of strict liability in English law raising crucial questions. Can one justify the use of strict liability in the criminal law on moral or utilitarian grounds? If not, could the same degree of regulation of the various activities involved be achieved without the invocation of the criminal law by, say, administrative processes?

The justifications of strict liability were considered above. The traditional case against strict liability is that it is unjust and morally indefensible to punish the blameless. A person who does not know she is doing wrong and who has taken all reasonable precautions to avoid harm (*i.e.* was not negligent) does not deserve criminal conviction and punishment. Describing such offences as "quasi-criminal" or "violations" is no more than a semantic evasion which "seems rather like saying that it is all right to be unjust so long as you are not too unjust" (Brett, 1963). No matter how trivial, a strict liability offence is still a crime that can result in prosecution and conviction in the criminal courts. Such moral condemnation is unjustifiable in the absence of blame.

Further, it is simply not true to assert that all offences of strict liability are minor offences carrying lesser penalties. In *Hussain* (1981) the defendant was convicted of unlawful possession of a firearm contrary to section 1 of the Firearms Act 1968 even though he believed it was merely a toy used by his son. The court held that this offence, carrying a maximum penalty of three years' imprisonment, was one of strict liability. Such an offence can hardly be described as a "mere violation". While supporters of the strict liability doctrine could point to the fact that Hussain was only fined £100 (presumably because of his lack of blameworthiness), it nevertheless remains the case that he was convicted of a criminal offence clearly involving stigma and he was made to forfeit a significant sum of money—hardly a "just" solution.

Finally, it is often asserted that no injustice occurs in reality as in most cases prosecutions are only brought against those who are in fact blameworthy. For instance, Viscount Dilhorne, who participated in *Alphacell Ltd v. Woodward* (1972), has declared that in his opinion the company was at fault in installing their infiltration system where they did (Leigh, 1982). Opponents of strict liability reject this argument. A criminal conviction carries with it the moral condemnation of the community; this cannot be made dependent on the private judgment of prosecutors. Further, the assertion cannot be true of all cases. The defendant company in *Alphacell Ltd v. Woodward* (1972) was fined £20 and ordered to pay £24 costs—hardly the sort of penalty that would have been imposed had the justices felt it was to blame for polluting the river.

Turning to the utilitarian arguments, there appears to be little evidence that the imposition of strict liability makes people more careful. Some persons involved in the sorts of activities generally regulated by strict liability offences will simply regard any fines incurred (the typical penalty) as a licence fee for operating as they do. Others, if they are to retain their competitiveness in the market, will generally only be able to afford to take such precautions as are *reasonable*. In other words, the imposition of strict liability achieves nothing in deterrent terms that could not be achieved by making all such crimes ones of negligence. Further, a blameless operator does not need rehabilitation or incapacitation (the other two established objectives of the criminal sanction)—or if he did, this could be better achieved by administrative control and sanction (see below, p. 142).

What, finally, of the arguments of expediency—that it would be too difficult and time-consuming to have to prove *mens rea* or other blame in each case? Clearly, administrative convenience cannot be allowed to dictate the contours of the criminal law: no one would suggest making theft an offence of strict liability simply because of the vast number of prosecutions that are regularly brought and the difficulty of establishing *mens rea*. Also, it is doubtful whether the existence of strict liability saves that much time and money in many cases as after conviction there needs to be some enquiry (albeit not subject to the same burden of proof) as to blameworthiness in order to fix the appropriate sentence. If the defendant company in *Alphacell Ltd v. Woodward* (1972) had been deliberately dumping effluent in the river, the punishment would have exceeded the £20 fine that was imposed.

Despite the weight of such arguments, it is submitted that it would be naive and inappropriate to contemplate the decriminalisation of all offences of strict liability or their wholesale conversion into offences involving fault. As already seen, many strict liability offences exist as part of regulatory schemes aimed at ensuring compliance with set standards in fields such as health and safety and pollution. Such legislative schemes are aimed at corporate defendants and not at private individuals. In these areas administrative procedures are extensively used.

Factory inspectors, health and safety officers and other such persons regularly inspect premises and often seek improvement by co-operation and persuasion. Other administrative remedies are at their disposal: planning permissions can be revoked or modified, enforcement and stop notices issued and so on. For example, as a result of the enforcement scheme created by the Health and Safety at Work Act 1974, in 1996–97 there were 8812 improvement and prohibition notices issued, compared with only 1654 prosecutions being commenced (Health and Safety Commission, 1998). Such non-criminal alternatives could be far more effective than prosecutions. Faced with the threat of closure of their premises, for example, companies will quickly effect the necessary improvements—and far sooner than if they merely had to pay a fine as the cost of their infraction.

However, as already observed, there is a strong case in such fields for allowing these compliance strategies to be operated against a backdrop of criminal sanctions as the ultimate threat. A compliance strategy involves "bargaining and negotiation" (Gunningham, 1987). It is easier to bargain with a gun in one's hand. The threat of criminal prosecution in the background can only facilitate the negotiation process. Further, to insist on proof of blame with corporate defendants would render such laws ineffective. Companies would simply use their complex organisational structures as a shield against prosecution. Often, it will be impossible to attribute blame to any individual within the company. The pollution (or whatever) will be the result of a failure to implement or enforce a safety or prevention policy (see below, p. 145). Only by imposing strict liability on the company itself can the law be enforced. Further, "some corporations operate in spheres of such potential social danger, and wield such power (in terms of economic resources and influence), that there is no social unfairness in holding them to higher standards than individuals when it comes to criminal liability" (Ashworth, 1999). Finally, there is the danger that decriminalisation of such activities would only serve further to marginalise them and undermine the seriousness of the harms involved.

On the other hand, when it comes to the punishment of individuals such as Hussain, the objections to offences of strict liability carry more weight. Whether the legislation in question is aimed at individuals or companies would appear to be a factor influencing the courts in their construction of the offence as strict or otherwise (compare *Sweet v. Parsley*, 1970 with

Alphacell Ltd v. Woodward, 1972). However, even in such cases the elimination of all offences of strict liability is simply not realistic. Some minor crimes, such as parking offences that are widely perceived as not being "truly criminal" and that carry a minimal penalty, must clearly remain as offences of strict liability. For the remainder, there is an alternative and that is to convert such strict liability offences into ones requiring some degree of blame—most probably negligence. Such an approach has already been adopted in relation to many former strict liability offences by the introduction of "due diligence" defences. The crime remains *prima facie* one of strict liability, thus not increasing the prosecutor's burden—but if the defendant can show that he was not negligent, he will escape liability. Thus the crime effectively becomes one of negligence—except in relation to the burden of proof. Canadian and Australian law have developed general due diligence defences applicable to all crimes of strict liability. English law, on the other hand, has preferred a more selective use of such defences with notable examples to be found in such important legislation as the Trade Description Act 1968 and the Misuse of Drugs Act 1971.

Clearly there is room for further expansion along such lines. What is needed is a conscious re-appraisal of all strict liability offences with a view to determining at whom they are targeted. Where the object of the legislation is corporate enterprises, any accompanying regulatory scheme needs examination to ensure that criminalisation (on a strict liability basis) is necessary to back up a compliance strategy. One cannot adopt a knee-jerk response of making an offence one of strict liability simply because it is mainly committed by companies. Equally, one cannot simply accept that a compliance strategy is necessarily appropriate in all cases of corporate undertakings. As will be seen in the next section, where companies are engaged in dangerous activities that result in death or injury to their employees or the public, there is a strong case for saying that such compliance strategies have contributed to the marginalisation of the offences committed in such cases.

Where the legislation is aimed at individuals (for example, drugs and offensive weapons), there needs to be a careful consideration of the type of offence and degree of stigma and punishment carried on conviction to determine whether they need to remain as criminal offences but with due diligence defences added, or, whether, if they are truly minor offences, they can be retained as pure strict liability offences.

6. CORPORATE WRONGDOING

As seen in the preceding section, one might be justified in more readily dispensing with the blameworthiness requirement when dealing with offences aimed at corporate wrongdoing. With such strict liability offences the company can be held vicariously liable for the actions of its employees without fault on anyone's part having to be proved (see above, pp. 47–49).

In recent years, however, a great deal of attention has been focused on companies whose dangerous operations have caused death or serious injury and whether such companies can be liable for offences involving blameworthiness, such as manslaughter.

In 1987 the ferry, Herald of Free Enterprise, left Zeebrugge with its bow doors open. Water flooded into the vehicle deck and the vessel capsized killing 192 people. The doors should have been closed by the assistant bo'sun but he, not aware that he should have been doing this, was asleep in his cabin. The first officer should have checked that the doors were closed but as the company who owned and operated the ferry, P. & O. European Ferries (originally Townsend Car Ferries Ltd), was operating with one officer less than the full compliment, this first officer was effectively required to be in two places at once; he was on the bridge and did not check whether the doors had been shut. There had previously been five or six other "open door" incidents. No person was assigned responsibility within the company for collating such information. When a master from a sister ferry requested warning lights to indicate whether the doors were shut, the response from the boardroom at P. & O. was a series of facetious comments, such as "Nice, but don't we already pay someone" and "Do they need indicator lights to tell them whether the assistant boatswain is awake and sober?" The predicament of the ferry was further exacerbated by the fact that the captain had no idea how much ballast had been taken on board; despite repeated requests, the management of the company had not fitted ballast gauges. Accurate passenger lists were not kept and complaints about overloading were ignored. The Sheen Report which investigated the causes of the disaster concluded that the company failed to operate any proper safety system: "the underlying or cardinal faults lay higher up in the company. The Board of Directors did not appreciate their responsibility for the safe management of their ships . . . All concerned in management . . . were guilty of fault . . . From top to bottom the body corporate was infected with the disease of sloppiness" (Sheen Report, 1988). Eventually a prosecution for manslaughter was brought against the company itself (as well as against certain individuals in the company). A company is a "legal person" and can be convicted of manslaughter (*P. & O. European Ferries (Dover) Ltd*, 1991). However, the problem was, and is: how can the blameworthiness requirement, developed to apply to individuals, be adapted to deal with corporations?

The law, instead of trying to look at the problem of corporate wrongdoing with fresh eyes, has tried to superimpose its individualistic constructs on to companies. It has reasoned that only human beings can "actually" commit crimes and therefore it has tried to find a senior individual within the company who committed the *actus reus* and *mens rea* of the crime. Where such a person, who must be regarded as part of the "brains" as opposed to the "hands" of the company (*Bolton Engineering v. Graham & Sons*, 1957, approved in *Tesco v. Nattrass*, 1972), was acting in the course of the company business, his actions can be attributed to the company and the company held liable. This is known as the "identification doctrine" (*Tesco v. Nattrass*, 1972).

The problem with this approach is that in many instances, particularly with the larger corporations with complex management structures, it will be impossible to identify any one individual who committed the requisite elements of the crime. In *P. & O. European Ferries (Dover) Ltd* (1991) there was no one senior individual whose actions and blameworthiness could amount to the crime of manslaughter. It had been argued that the law should adopt the "aggregation doctrine" whereby the cumulative actions of the various persons within P. & O. would be aggregated so that in their totality they might amount to the requisite degree of blameworthiness for the crime of manslaughter. This approach was rejected (*H.M. Coroner for East Kent, Ex Parte Spooner*, 1989; *Stanley and others*, 1990) meaning that the company could not be held liable. Under present law it is thus extremely difficult to impose criminal liability on companies for such offences as it will usually be the absence of a safety system resulting from failures in management strategies that is the real cause of the resultant deaths or injuries.

However, it is not only problems associated with the identification doctrine that have led to the dearth of prosecutions against companies for these serious offences. Over the past decade 3,759 persons (employees and members of the public) have been killed in workplace incidents (Bergman, 2000). In

1997–98 there were 430 persons killed (about double the number convicted of manslaughter, excluding diminished responsibility cases) and 57,000 persons seriously injured in workplace incidents. The Health and Safety Executive has itself stated that 90 per cent of the deaths could have been prevented and that "in 70 per cent of cases positive action by management could have saved lives" (Blackspot Construction, 1988). In many of these cases prosecutions for serious offences could have been brought but were not. Why?

In an attempt to regulate and improve safety at work the Health and Safety at Work etc Act 1974 creates special criminal offences for employers who fail to ensure the health and safety of their workers and members of the public. This legislation is enforced by the Health and Safety Executive (HSE) (although since 1998 the police are involved when a death has been caused). The HSE openly adopts a compliance strategy and regards advice and assistance to companies as being more important than prosecution. As a result the HSE only brings a prosecution in some 20 per cent of cases where death has occurred at work and in 1 per cent of cases after a major injury has been reported (Bergman, 2000). These prosecutions normally relate to relatively minor offences under the Health and Safety at Work etc. Act 1974 and are usually brought in the magistrates' court where the fines imposed on convictions are relatively small. The result of these different procedures and enforcement policies has been to marginalise corporate crime—a trend, until recently, reinforced by the media. Deaths at work are seen as "accidents"; deaths in situations such as the capsize of the Herald of Free Enterprise are "disasters".

Over the last few years, however, the tide has been turning. The deaths on the Herald of Free Enterprise and the collapse of the manslaughter prosecution against P. & O. precipitated intense academic and media coverage of corporate killings. We no longer think of deaths on the road as a result of very dangerous driving as being "accidents". Prosecutions can be brought for motor manslaughter or the serious offence of causing death by dangerous driving punishable by a maximum of ten years' imprisonment. Attitudes are similarly changing to deaths in the workplace caused by dangerous machinery and conditions and where there has been a minimum regard for safety. The result has been a greater willingness to commence prosecutions against companies and in 1994 a company was convicted for the first time of manslaughter in a case where the gross negligence of an activity centre caused the deaths of four teenagers on a canoeing trip in Lyme Bay (*Kite*, 1994). This conviction was facilitated by the fact that OLL Ltd, owners of the centre that organised activity holidays, was a small company that could easily be identified with the managing director (who was also convicted of manslaughter). Further, there is controversy as to whether such activity centres were covered by the Health and Safety at Work etc. Act 1974 (*The Independent*, December 9, 1994). The fact that the (private) activity centre industry was not regulated and inspected made it less easy for blame to be deflected and rendered the company more vulnerable to conviction. It will still be difficult to obtain convictions against larger companies with complex organisational structures whose activities are policed by bodies such as the HSE. For example, in 1999 the manslaughter prosecution against Great Western Trains Company Ltd, following the Southall train crash in which seven people were killed and 151 injured, collapsed because no company director had been identified as personally liable (*Attorney General's Reference* (*No. 2 of 1999*), 2000).

The Law Commission (1996) and a Home Office Consultation Paper (2000) have recommended the creation of a new offence of corporate killing. The new offence would abandon the identification doctrine and would instead be committed where there was a management failure: where the company's "conduct in causing the death falls far below what could reasonably be expected" and the death is "caused by a failure, in the way in which the corporation's activities are managed or organised, to ensure the health and safety of persons employed in or affected by those activities".

There are dangers with the creation of such a special offence. It could lead to marginalisation, in that it would not be regarded as seriously as the normal offence of manslaughter and, further, it could send out a message that companies will only be held responsible for serious offences if employees or members of the public are killed. As seen, far greater numbers of persons are seriously injured in workplace incidents and such cases, where appropriate, should be prosecuted as offences against the person. Nevertheless, overall, this proposal is to be welcomed. Concentrating on the company's management failures (the company's policies and organisational practices that fail to ensure the health and safety of others), as opposed to trying to find a culpable senior individual as required under the identification doctrine, will greatly facilitate the securing of a conviction in cases such as P. & O. European Ferries and Great Western Trains. Further, the creation of a special offence (as opposed to simply abolishing the identification doctrine for the purposes of manslaughter) is appropriate. In fair labelling terms there is something distinctive about the context in which such killings occur. Companies are engaged in lawful activities that would generally be regarded as socially beneficial were they safely performed. A primary lawful motivation drives the actions. Unlike acts of violence, running a train company, for example, does not have harm of any degree to the victim as part of its rationale in acting. While it has become fashionable to talk of "corporate violence", such killings, like causing death by dangerous driving, belong to a different family of offence. It is thus right that these killings be removed from the general offence of manslaughter and be dealt with separately as "corporate killings".

Another issue needs consideration. Companies have "no soul to damn and no body to kick" (Coffee, 1981). Why do we want to punish them? Why do we not rest content with punishing the individuals in the company? Does not the true blame lie with them and, as human beings, are they not the most amenable to deterrence?

There are several reasons for prosecuting and punishing companies. First, in many instances it is truly the company that committed the offence and not the individuals within the company. As in the P. & O. prosecution, there will often be insufficient evidence to bring a prosecution against any individual person. Many of these offences are the result of organisational policies or the lack of them. Individuals are expendable. If the individuals were punished and replaced by new ones in the company the same criminal offences could still be committed because the same policies (or lack thereof) would be in place. Further, punishment, and the threat thereof, can force companies to exercise the proper care to prevent the deaths or injuries. It is companies, and not individuals, who have the resources to collate information and implement safety procedures. It was P. & O., and only P. & O., that could have installed the warning lights. Further, modern companies now often promote themselves as distinct identifiable entities. Such advertising "designed to humanise the company" (Dunford and Ridley, 1996) has led to public perceptions that companies are entities that can be blamed. In the aftermath of the P. & O. capsize the relatives of the victims who died were primarily interested in a prosecution of P. & O. and not of the individuals (Wells, 1989).

It is crucial, however, to emphasise that while prosecution of companies is often appropriate, in many cases there are individual directors or managers who have committed the wrongful act and should themselves be prosecuted. One of the dangers of the Law Commission's proposed new offence of corporate killing is that it could deflect attention away from blameworthy individuals enabling them to escape prosecution. Over the past 10 years only six company directors have been convicted of manslaughter in relation to 3,759 workplace deaths. The simple point that must not be lost sight of is that often it is individuals, either alone or jointly with their companies, who should be prosecuted and held criminally liable.

Finally, it is often alleged that imposing criminal liability on companies is pointless as even when they are convicted, they can only be fined and even then the fines are generally small. Such assertions cannot be accepted. With regard to fines, there is no reason why the amounts should necessarily be small. Indeed, the average fine imposed on companies for breaches of the health and safety legislation has been steadily increasing over the past decade and in some cases very large fines have been imposed. For example, Great Western Trains were fined £1.5 million following the Southall train crash. Further, the Court of Appeal in *Howe and Son (Engineers) Ltd* (1999) stressed that in future fines should reflect the seriousness of the offences and that this was particularly true when a death had resulted. In response to the argument that large fines could create a risk of bankruptcy and consequent redundancy, the court responded that "there may be cases where the offences are so serious that the defendant ought not to be in business". The Sentencing Advisory Panel (2000) (which provides sentencing advice to the Court of Appeal) has similarly concluded, in relation to environmental offences, that fines should be large enough to have a real economic impact on companies so as to create "pressure on management and shareholders to tighten regulatory compliance and change company policy". An alternative approach would be to fine companies a percentage of their turnover. For example, the European Commission attempted to fine British Steel £28.8 million for engaging in anti-competitive practices. If penalties of this magnitude can be imposed in such circumstances, surely comparable punishments would be justifiable when blameworthy companies have caused the death of their workers or innocent members of the public or seriously polluted the environment.

While the fine is the only penalty currently employed against companies in England, there is no reason why other penalties could not be introduced. Such possible sentences could include corporate probation whereby the company would be forced to change those policies and procedures that allowed the offence to be committed or community service whereby companies could be required, for example, to engage in various projects such as cleaning up rivers they have polluted. The Law Commission has proposed, in relation to its suggested new offence of corporate killing, that, in addition to fines, courts should have powers to make remedial orders under which the company would be obliged to remedy the harm caused and eliminate the cause of the harm.

Higher levels of fines and a wider range of sentencing options would greatly help persuade the media and the population at large that corporate crime is a serious matter that needs to be treated seriously with rigorous enforcement and punishment and not marginalised as "accidents".

7. CAUSATION

We have seen that for "result crimes" criminal liability can only be imposed upon a blameworthy actor whose conduct has caused the forbidden harm. Without this causative link being established the defendant must escape liability. In *White* (1910) the defendant tried to murder his mother and gave her a drink containing poison. The mother had a taste of the drink and then, quite by chance, had a heart attack and died. White could not be convicted of murder because it was not his conduct that had caused her death. (He was, however, convicted of attempted murder.)

The problem faced by the law here is one of defining the necessary circumstances for the establishment of causation. When is the causal link between an act and an event established? In what circumstances will it be broken? In *Lewis* (1970) a wife locked herself in her third-floor flat and refused to admit her husband, claiming he had previously inflicted great violence upon her. He shouted threats including a threat to kill her and she heard the sound of breaking glass. She was in another room but, terrified of what he might do, she jumped from the window and broke both her legs. It was held that the husband's actions had caused her injuries. They had not been "self-inflicted". Is it possible to discern any principle or policy behind such an approach? What would have been the position if, instead of throwing herself from the window, the wife had committed suicide by shooting herself? Would it have been held that the husband had caused her death?

It is interesting (and instructive) to note how little interest has been paid by English law to the issue of causation. Attention, both judicial and otherwise, has focused primarily on the notion of blameworthiness. The irony is that much of blameworthiness is established by proof of mental elements that are in reality elusive and incapable of precise proof. Causation, on the other hand, need not be linked to mental elements and could be capable of purely objective (and thus realistic) ascertainment. Indeed, it could be argued that the way forward for the criminal law would be to tighten up and clarify the rules on causation: this could lead to a diminution of the importance of the doctrine of *mens rea* in particular. However, the law has eschewed such an approach and rarely tried to develop any coherent principles, with the result that "the entire field of causation in criminal law is utterly bankrupt" (Schulhofer, 1974).

The problem of causation can be approached in several ways. One view is that there are no underlying general principles at all. The courts simply resort to considerations of "policy" to determine whether a particular defendant has caused a specified harm. Whether or not causation is established is no more than a "moral reaction" or a "value-judgment" (Williams, 1983). While many of the cases appear to be explicable only in terms of such a policy-oriented analysis, such an approach is fraught with problems and opens the door not only to inconsistency in verdicts, but also to inconsistency in prosecutions as prosecutors, too, will only be guided by "policy" or their "moral reactions" in deciding whether to prosecute. Also, while "policy" might explain why a defendant, say Lewis, was prosecuted and convicted of an offence, it is not at all clear that the policy considerations dictate liability for the offence charged. Why was Lewis found guilty of inflicting grievous bodily harm? If "policy" dictates he be liable for a crime, why not for an assault—which seems to be what he really did? If his wife had shot herself, would "policy" dictate he be liable for a homicide offence? Answers to such questions are not possible once one has abandoned principle for an *ad hoc* approach.

Another view is that an analysis of causation cannot proceed independently of the criterion of blameworthiness and, going further, is dependent on it. Causation cannot be judged in purely objective physical terms. It must be assessed in terms of blameworthiness and responsibility. According to this view, if blame can be established, the result cannot be that remote and therefore causation is deemed to be established. If a defendant has *mens rea*, he will usually expect or foresee the result. Causation will almost certainly be established where the defendant has reason to expect or foresee the consequence (Gross, 1979).

While such an approach certainly goes some way towards explaining the criminal law's relative lack of interest in causation, it cannot be accepted as a true explanation of the issue of causation (and certainly can be no explanation for the rules of causation in strict liability offences). According to this view, once it had been established that Lewis was blameworthy this automatically resolved the problem of causation. But again the question becomes: blameworthy in relation to what crime? Lewis was clearly blameworthy in relation to a common assault but it was only on a somewhat technical basis that he was adjudged to have *mens rea* in relation to inflicting grievous bodily harm (see p. 179). And what if Lewis had been insane? Insanity would have relieved him of responsibility and blameworthiness. Must one then conclude that an insane person cannot cause a harm? And, conversely, it is obviously not true that a finding of causation must necessarily flow from a finding of blameworthiness. Let us alter the facts of *Lewis* (1970) and assume that he wanted to kill his wife. He knew she was neurotic and would leap from the window. He expected her to die from the fall. Mrs Lewis did jump but, by chance, landed unhurt. Unfortunately for her she landed at the feet of a sadistic mugger who shot and killed her. In this altered situation Lewis had the *mens rea* of murder; his actions have led to a chain of events that ultimately resulted in the death of his wife. But nobody would seriously suggest that Lewis caused the death of his wife. She was killed by the mugger. So all the "real work" cannot be left to be done by the concept of blame or *mens rea*. Some principles or rules on causation are necessary and it is to a summary of these principles, crude as they are, that we now turn.

It is generally stated that there are two main principles of causation in English criminal law. First, the defendant's actions must be a "but for" cause of the result (a *causa sine qua non*). "But for" Lewis shouting his threats and breaking the window, his wife would not have jumped from the window. This insistence upon factual causation is natural. It would be an intolerable violation of any principle of personal responsibility to hold a person liable for a harm he did not cause at all. But as the altered facts of *Lewis* (1970) above indicate, a "but for" cause is not sufficient to attribute causal responsibility. "But for" Lewis's actions, his wife would not have been shot by our hypothetical mugger. His actions were, therefore, in a sense, a cause of her death—but merely being a "but for" cause is not enough. A second requirement must be satisfied. The defendant's actions must be the "significant", "operative" or "proximate" cause of the result. These words mean no more than that the defendant's actions must be the *legal* cause of the prohibited result as well as being the factual cause.

This second requirement of legal causation is satisfied where the defendant's actions are a sufficiently direct cause of the result. One way of determining this is to ask whether some other cause of sufficient significance "intervened" to break the causal chain. Many events or causes can "intervene" or contribute towards the ultimate harm. But not all will break the chain of causation. Suppose Lewis had broken into the room and struck his wife. Being thrust backwards by the blow she tripped over a chair and fell out of the open window. This tripping and falling is a contributory or "intervening" cause of her ultimate injury—but it is a *dependent intervening cause*; its occurrence was dependent on and closely connected to Lewis's blow. Such dependent intervening causes are of insufficient significance to break the causal link. But in our earlier *Lewis* (1970) and the mugger variant, the act of the mugger shooting Mrs Lewis was an *independent intervening cause* (a *novus actus interveniens*); its occurrence was independent of and not immediately connected to Lewis's actions. Such an independent intervening cause will break the causal link and exempt Lewis from responsibility for his wife's death.

These two examples are of course extreme and thus "easy" ones. The real problem arises when faced with the exact facts of *Lewis* (1970). Mr Lewis was outside the matrimonial flat. On hearing his threats and the breaking window, Mrs Lewis jumped and sustained injuries from that fall. Her act of jumping was clearly a contributory or "intervening" cause of her injuries. How does the law determine whether it was a dependent or an independent intervening cause?

While the answer to this question is by no means clear, some broad principles can be extracted from the authorities. The Law

Commission in its Draft Criminal Code Bill 1989 (Law Commission, 1989) argues that its proposal represents the present law. Clause 17 provides that: "a person causes a result . . . when . . . he does an act which makes a more than negligible contribution to its occurrence . . . (but) does not cause a result where, after he does such an act . . ., an act or event occurs—(a) which is the immediate and sufficient cause of the result; (b) which he did not foresee, and (c) which could not in the circumstances reasonably have been foreseen."

This is based on the test adopted in *Roberts* (1971) where a girl leapt out of a moving car in order to avoid the sexual advances of the defendant. It was held that if the girl's actions were reasonably foreseeable causation was established. However, if her jumping from the car was "daft" or "unexpected', the causal link would be broken. So, according to this analysis it must have been regarded as reasonably foreseeable that Mrs Lewis would try to escape by jumping from the window. On this basis while it might (at most) be reasonably foreseeable that she would try to escape by jumping and injure herself, it would not be reasonably foreseeable that she would shoot herself. Such an action would be unforeseen and "the immediate and sufficient cause of the result"; Lewis would therefore not be responsible for his wife's death had she shot herself. This test of reasonable foresight is purely objective with no account being taken of the age or any other characteristic of the defendant (*Marjoram*, 2000).

Related to this central principle is the commonly stated proposition that a voluntary intervention by a third party, who is not acting in concert with the defendant, will break the causal chain (Hart and Honoré, 1985). The mugger in our earlier *Lewis* (1970) variant was an independent third party acting voluntarily. His actions would break the chain of causation. Another way of stating this same proposition is that it was completely unexpected and unforeseeable that he would be there and would kill Mrs Lewis. This point was raised in *Pagett* (1983). The defendant, holding a girl as hostage and shield, opened fire on police attempting to arrest him. The police officers returned the fire and their bullets hit and killed the girl. It was held that the defendant's acts had caused the death of the girl. The "intervention" of the police was in effect involuntary; they were acting in reasonable self-defence. Goff L.J. declared that there was no distinction between a reasonable attempt to escape violence and a reasonable attempt to resist violence by defending oneself.

Thus the morally involuntary conduct of the police was reasonably foreseeable; it was a dependent intervening cause which did not exempt the defendant from liability.

While the courts have thus developed some broad principles of causation, it is nevertheless clear that the contours of these principles have been largely shaped by policy considerations. The defendant in *Pagett* (1983) was engaged in a morally reprehensible activity. The police were acting in the exercise of their duty. This context influenced the courts to hold that the police response was merely a dependent intervening cause so that the defendant could be held liable. (It is interesting that in a subsequent civil case the police were found to have been negligent in their handling of the operation and were liable in damages to the girl's parents.) Equally, where the third party intervention is by doctors trying to administer medical treatment to an injured victim, it will only be in the "most extraordinary and unusual case" that the treatment will be so "independent of the acts of the accused" (*Cheshire*, 1991) that the chain of causation will be broken. The policy considerations here are clear. The National Health Service resources are stretched. The courts are unlikely to exempt violent assailants from liability because their victims did not receive the best treatment.

Much the same policy-driven approach has been adopted in pollution cases. In the leading House of Lords' decision of *Empress Car Co. (Abertillery) Ltd v. National Rivers Authority* (1998) a company maintained a diesel oil tank on its premises. An outlet from the tank was governed by a tap that had no lock. An unknown person (probably a vandal) opened the tap allowing the oil to run into the river. This was clearly a "voluntary intervention by a third party" which under the above principles should have broken the causal chain. However, Lord Hoffman stressed that one needs to understand the "purpose and scope of the rule" before deciding whether causation is established. With pollution offences "strict liability is imposed in the interests of protecting controlled waters from pollution". Given that objective it was necessary to ensure that anyone who had any role in the resultant pollution be held a causer. The causal chain would only be broken if the act of the third party were "abnormal and extraordinary". Just as violent assailants can only escape liability if their victims received extraordinarily bad medical treatment, so too companies who run operations that can pollute the environment will only escape liability if something amounting to an "extraordinary coincidence" occurs.

What is the position if the alleged intervening act is by the victim herself? Will this break the causal link? For instance, in *Kennedy* (1999) the defendant supplied a heroin-filled syringe to another who injected it immediately and died within an hour. It was argued that the decision to inject himself amounted to a voluntary intervening act breaking the chain of causation. This view was however rejected. The Court of Appeal distinguished two situations: if drugs were supplied but it was "entirely a matter for the recipient whether he injected himself or not" (as in the earlier case of *Dalby*, 1982) the causal chain would be broken. However, where heroin was supplied for immediate injection (as in the present case), this amounted to encouragement and so the causal chain was not broken. This distinction is untenable and would result in all suppliers of weapons for immediate use being held to have caused the results of the use of the weapons. Adopting this approach would collapse much of the distinction between counsellors and procurers on the one hand, and principal offenders on the other. The better view is that the normal principle should apply and this voluntary action by the drug-user should break the causal chain. Further, there are no strong policy reasons for insisting that the actions of the victim be "extraordinary" (which they certainly are not) before breaking the causal chain. Indeed, the fact that the defendant is engaged in committing an offence within one family of offence (drugs) dictates that policy should not be invoked to hold him liable for an offence within a completely unrelated family of offence (violence) (see p. 208).

There is one final well-established proposition developed by the courts that is not easy to reconcile with the above "principles". It is commonly stated that the defendant must take his victim as he finds her. This causes no problem with regard to the physical condition of the victim. If the victim has a thin skull or a weak heart and a single blow from the defendant kills her, causation is clearly established. There is no intervening act, even of a dependent nature. An existing condition cannot be regarded as an "intervening" event. But problems arise when this proposition is extended to psychological conditions or beliefs. In *Blaue* (1975) the defendant stabbed a Jehovah's Witness, piercing her lung. It was established that with a blood transfusion she would have survived. Because of her religious beliefs, however, she refused the transfusion and died. The Court of Appeal expressly rejected the argument that an unreasonable refusal to have a blood transfusion would break the chain of causation. Instead, it ruled that the defendant must take his victim as he finds him and this "means the whole man, not just the physical man". Thus it makes no difference whether the victim has a thin skull, a religious belief that forbids her medical attention or is a neurotic liable to leap out of the window for little cause. The defendant must take his victim as he finds her in mind and in body.

An interesting extension of this principle and one where policy considerations were again clearly decisive is to be found in *McKechnie* (1992). The defendant hit the victim on the head with a television set causing serious head injuries. In hospital it was discovered that the victim had a duodenal ulcer. The doctors decided that because of the head injuries it would be dangerous to anaesthetise him and operate on the ulcer (apparently, a somewhat questionable decision). The victim later died of bleeding from the duodenal ulcer. The defendant was held to have caused the death of the victim and was convicted of manslaughter. Here, unlike in *Blaue* (1975), the victim did not die from the blows inflicted by the defendant. He died from a burst duodenal ulcer. At first sight this decision seems surprising. If the victim had not been attacked he might simply have gone home where the ulcer could have burst and he could have died. The attack by the defendant seems almost coincidental and unconnected to the death. However, viewed from a different perspective, the decision can be supported. The defendant's actions prevented the victim obtaining the necessary medical treatment. If a victim with a duodenal ulcer were kidnapped and while being held prisoner the ulcer burst causing death, there can be little doubt that the kidnapper would be held to have caused the death of the victim. The situation in *McKechnie* (1992) is analogous. The severe head blows rendering medical treatment impossible (allegedly) made the victim (metaphorically) still the "prisoner" of the assailant. The latter's actions were thus the legal cause of the death.

With this last principle in mind let us consider a final variant of *Lewis* (1970) and his defenestrating wife. Suppose now that Lewis is a generally non-violent man who lives on the twentieth floor of an apartment-block. He and his wife are having an argument in the course of which he threatens her with minor violence—say, a light slap. Unknown to her husband, Mrs Lewis is in fact neurotic and pathologically terrified of any physical force. She runs into the next room and leaps from the window (or takes out a revolver and shoots herself). Under *Roberts* (1971) such action is plainly "daft" and "unexpected" and would constitute an *independent intervening cause*. But, under the *Blaue* (1975) qualification, Lewis must take his wife as he finds her, neuroses and all; he has caused her injuries.

The best way of reconciling these tensions within the law would be as follows. The central principle of reasonable foresight or expectation as established in *Roberts* (1971) should prevail. However, in ascertaining whether the victim's response was reasonable, account must be taken of particular idiosyncrasies of the victim. In *Roberts* (1971) the girl was "normal". The question is simply whether her response was reasonable. In *Blaue* (1975) the question becomes one of ascertaining whether it was reasonably foreseeable that a Jehovah's Witness would refuse a blood transfusion, and in our final *Lewis* (1970) variant the issue is whether one could reasonably foresee or anticipate that a neurotic wife might act as Mrs Lewis did. Such an approach was adopted in *Williams and Davis* (1992) where it was held that, in assessing whether the reaction of a man who jumped out of a moving car was reasonably foreseeable, the jury should bear in mind the particular characteristics of the victim. This test has the advantage of taking account of the victim's condition but limiting the chain of causation to reasonable responses from such a victim. It is surely right that we be held causatively responsible for all the reasonably predictable consequences that flow from our actions—but not responsible for the outlandish or occasionally totally unpredictable consequences that can follow therefrom.

8. THE FORBIDDEN HARM

The final element in the general construction of paradigmatic criminal liability is that the blameworthy actor's conduct should have caused the forbidden harm.

The nature of the requisite forbidden harm, of course, varies from crime to crime. For homicide offences the victim must have been killed; for rape the victim's vagina or anus must have been penetrated by the defendant's penis; for theft the victim must have been deprived of property or some interest therein—and so on.

(i) The importance of harm

An obvious question raises itself at this point. Why does the criminal law for its paradigmatic offences insist upon proof of such direct harm? If an assassin aims a gun and fires at the intended victim, why should it matter whether the bullet kills, wounds or misses the victim? The conduct and degree of blameworthiness are the same whatever the outcome. If criminal liability, or the extent of that liability, is to depend upon the result, is this not reducing the criminal law to a lottery? Why should chance (whether the bullet hit or missed) be relevant in our moral assessment of the actions? In *Krawec* (1985) the defendant killed an elderly pedestrian by carelessly driving his motorcycle. He was convicted of driving without due care and attention. The Court of Appeal, reviewing his sentence, stressed that the primary consideration was the quality of the driving. The fact that he had happened to kill someone was not relevant.

In much the same vein many commentators (for example, Ashworth, 1999) argue that "the principle of correspondence" is a fundamental precondition to the imposition of criminal liability. Respecting the autonomy of persons involves only holding them criminally liable and subjecting them to censure for those consequences they know they are bringing about or risking. The defendant in *Krawec* (1985) should only be held liable and punished for causing death if he knew or realised that there was a chance his careless driving could cause death. Such writers condemn constructive liability as breaching this principle of correspondence. Under constructive liability (employed in some crimes in English law) persons are held accountable for more serious consequences than they expected. For example, if a person assaults another (say, by hitting her) he commits the offence of common assault punishable by a maximum penalty of six months' imprisonment. If, however, as in *Williams* (1996), the victim reels from the blow, falls backwards and hits her head on a wall-mounted heater and dies, the defendant is liable for constructive manslaughter carrying a maximum penalty of life imprisonment (see p. 207). The argument of the correspondence proponents is that this is allowing the extent of liability to be determined by luck. The defendant should be liable only for assault with the resultant chance death being ignored. There was no correspondence between the defendant's culpability and the death.

However, an opposing approach can be adopted which rejects this strict principle of correspondence and allows some constructive liability to be supported. This view regards the significance of resulting harm to be critical (in at least some cases) in the construction of appropriate levels of criminal liability. Let us first consider the *generalised* case that the level of harm caused is significant and that the approach taken in *Krawec* (1985) is ill-conceived. The argument can then be fine-tuned to assess whether this harm is *always* important.

There are several related reasons for condemning the stance taken in *Krawec* (1985). The fact is that we do judge people by the results of their actions and not simply on the basis of the quality of their actions and their exertions (Robinson and Darley, 1998). If a student makes a spectacular effort to hand in a good essay that is assessed for examination purposes but sadly the resultant product is appalling nonsense, his tutor might, in recognition of his endeavours, treat him sympathetically in private—but the essay must ultimately be judged on its objective merits. He will get an appropriate low mark, reflecting the result and not the quality of his efforts. This is the mark he deserves and in fairness to him (in according him the respect and dignity owed to a responsible human being) and in fairness to his fellow students (who will make comparative judgments in relation to their essays and marks) this is the mark he must receive. And the converse is equally true. If the most idle and cavalier student puts in a minimal effort but fortuitously spots all the relevant points and turns in an excellent essay, she must get an excellent mark. Her essay must again be judged by its results and not on the basis of how hard she tried.

This same approach is surely appropriate to the defendant in *Krawec* (1985). Of course, we can and must judge the quality of his actions (his careless driving in itself) but the fact that his actions have resulted in the death of a human being totally alters our moral judgment. His actually killing someone arouses resentment in society (quite apart from the bitterness and pain caused to the relatives and friends of the deceased). Imagine ourselves as observers. We see Krawec riding his motorcycle and going through red traffic lights. He does not see an elderly pedestrian but misses him by inches. Our response is one of momentary fright: "Did you see that? How can people drive like that?" we exclaim indignantly, but, thankful that no harm occurred, we forget the incident and return to our routines. But if we, as observers, witness these same events but this time the elderly pedestrian is in Krawec's path and is knocked over and killed, we do *not* simply respond: "How can people drive like that? And what bad luck that the old man was in his way", as the Court of Appeal in *Krawec* (1985) seems to feel we ought to respond. Our reaction is now one of horror. He has *killed* the pedestrian. His driving was not just dangerous, that is, likely to cause danger. The danger has materialised and someone lies dead. We do not simply forget the incident and return to our lives. The resultant harm makes its mark; it leaves a lasting impression. If Krawec tries to drive away we will chase him or ensure we have his registration number. In short, our entire reaction to the event is profoundly affected by the *results* of the dangerous driving. Such condemnation and resentment is relevant in determining the level of Krawec's criminal liability and punishment, and suggestions to the contrary by the Court of Appeal in that case ignore clear moral distinctions drawn in everyday life. If one took the *Krawec* (1985) approach that the causing of death was "pure luck" to its logical conclusion, one should abolish the crime of murder and convict those who kill and those who attempt to kill of the same core offence. Indeed, one should dispense with all result crimes and concentrate instead on defining all offences with reference to the defendant's endeavours and/or risk-taking conduct. Such an approach is totally counter-intuitive and takes no account of the important principle of fair labelling under which the moral significance attached to killing a person is such that the fact of death needs marking by the existence of a separate offence category.

This approach is reinforced if we view the events from Krawec's or any other defendant's own point of view. Those who cause harm feel greater remorse than those who have "close calls" (Fletcher, 1978). If we had been driving and had narrowly missed the pedestrian, our prime reaction would be relief—not guilt. But if we had knocked him over we would know that our actions had now had a permanent and concrete impact on the lives of others. Feelings of guilt and remorse are truly appropriate when harm has been caused—again, a natural response that ought to be reflected by the law.

There is a further reason why the law should attribute weight to the causing of harm. It has already been argued (above, pp. 14, 158) that the paradigmatic crime is the intentional causing of the prohibited harm. Departures from this paradigm should be marked by less liability and/or punishment to emphasise that this is a departure. Consequently, it was there argued that with attempts (where there is no direct harm) the law should insist on proof of *intention* rather than allowing a "double-departure" from the paradigm. Similarly, where no harm or less harm is caused this is equally a departure from the paradigm which deserves recognition. For example, killing someone should be regarded as a more serious offence, carrying a higher level of punishment, than injuring someone.

The above arguments challenge the principle of correspondence in suggesting that there need not be an exact correlation between the defendant's culpability and the resultant harm. But this is not necessarily to suggest there need be absolutely no relationship between the two. In some situations a defendant can do something culpably wrong which could have completely unconnected harmful results. For example, a defendant could be stealing another's property; the owner of the property sees this and in rushing to the scene of the crime, trips and kills herself. Here it would be inappropriate to hold the defendant liable for the death. This death would be pure (bad) luck. This raises the question: when should a person be held liable for the unforeseen consequences of actions or when should these consequences be disregarded as pure bad luck.

Horder (1995) distinguishes between "pure luck" and "making one's own luck". The former covers situations where a fortuitous result unconnected to one's endeavours occurs while in the latter case the consequence is directly connected to one's endeavours. He uses the example of the university fundraiser who is approaching alumni for money for their former university. If he asks an alumnus for £100 but is unexpectedly given £500, this is not pure luck. Obtaining the £500 was directly connected to the endeavour of fundraising. He has made his own luck and deserves some credit for his achievement. On the other hand, if a complete stranger came up to the fundraiser and, unsolicited, handed over £500, this would be pure luck unconnected to the endeavours of the fundraiser.

How can this distinction between "making one's own luck" (where one should receive praise or blame for the outcome) and "pure luck" (where praise or blame for the outcome is not deserved) be applied in the criminal law? We saw earlier (p. 11) that the criminal law is divided into various "families" of offence (Gardner, 1994). There are offences of violence, offences against property, offences against public order, driving offences and so on. Each of these families is (or should be) distinct and each has its own paradigm. For example, the paradigmatic offence of violence is intentionally killing another. If one's endeavours and the result are both within the same family, the defendant can be regarded as making her own luck. There is a sufficient connection between culpability and result to justify criminal liability—although the level of liability will depend, as seen, on the extent of the departure from the paradigm. On this basis, the defendant in *Williams* (1996), by hitting the woman who died, made his own bad luck and liability in respect of the death was justifiable (see p. 159). But if, as in the earlier example of the woman tripping and dying when rushing to prevent the theft of her property, the defendant's endeavours are within one family of offences (offence against property) but the unexpected result falls within a different family of offences (violence), the result is pure bad luck and criminal liability in relation to the resultant death is inappropriate.

This analysis can be applied to *Krawec* (1985). By driving carelessly the defendant was acting within the family of driving offences. The paradigm or (perhaps better described) the most serious instance thereof is causing death by dangerous driving. (If one used a car to kill intentionally or recklessly one would be within the family of violence using the car as a weapon.) The defendant was not driving dangerously; he was driving carelessly. A departure from the paradigm (on the culpability side of the equation) is necessary and there should be less liability and punishment than for causing death by dangerous driving. But the killing was within the same family of offences and so not pure bad luck. He made his own luck and weight should have been attributed to this fact.

These principles should apply throughout the criminal law; whether they do, and the extent thereof, will be assessed in Chapter 3. At this stage, however, it is appropriate to examine the implications of these principles in cases where there is no apparent harm at all. This is seen most dramatically in the crime of attempt to which we now turn.

(ii) Attempts

Those who argue that punishment should be linked entirely to culpability view attempt as the basic or core offence. Whether one succeeds or fails is beyond one's control and therefore has no effect on one's culpability and level of deserved punishment. As seen above, acceptance of this view would lead to the abolition of all result crimes and the law would concentrate on offences linked to the defendant's endeavours and/or risk-taking conduct. English law has certainly not gone that far and clearly distinguishes completed crimes from attempts to commit such crimes. However, it has endorsed such a view to the extent that it provides that irrespective of the lack of direct harm, attempts to commit crime are punishable to the same extent as the completed offence (Criminal Attempts Act 1981, section 4(1)).

However, in many respects the law does adopt the more harm-oriented conception of crime argued for above. Those who bring about the prohibited harm are found guilty of more serious offences in fair labelling terms. Our initial assassin who fired his gun would be guilty of the most serious offence (murder) if he killed his victim. If he wounded her, he would be guilty of a different (and less serious) offence and if he missed he would be guilty of yet another different offence: attempted murder.

With regard to the punishment of attempts it is submitted that the English approach in section 4(1) is unjustifiable. Despite the obvious case that the attempter is just as dangerous, blameworthy and in need of rehabilitation and deterrence as he who successfully completes the crime, the fact remains that no direct harm has resulted from his actions. It is relatively easy to justify the imposition of some criminal liability for attempts. In addition to the utilitarian case of equal dangerousness, etc., it can be argued that attempts do cause a harm—an indirect or "second order" harm (Gross, 1979). We all have an interest in being secure from harm. Attempts are dangerous and pose a real threat of harm; that threat violates our security interest and right to autonomy; someone has encroached upon our "territory" in a menacing manner. Violations of such interest are "harms". Nevertheless, they are clearly lesser harms than direct or "first order" harms and ought to be treated as such by the law.

This is the approach adopted in other jurisdictions. For example, Californian law provides that an attempt carries a penalty of one half of the penalty available for the full offence (California Penal Code, section 664). Indeed, it does appear that in practice the English courts also accept such reasoning. While section 4(1) permits the same level of punishment for attempters, in reality they tend to receive substantially lesser punishments than are meted out for completed crimes. For instance, in *Foster* (1985) a mother who tried to kill her two children by drugging their Weetabix was put on probation for two years. Had the children died, and had she been convicted of murder, she would have received a sentence of life imprisonment.

(iii) Attempting the impossible

A related problem presents itself. Can there be criminal liability for attempting the impossible? If the direct harm cannot possibly be committed, can there be even a "second order" harm justifying criminal liability? Or are the utilitarian arguments (equal dangerousness, etc.) sufficient in themselves to justify the imposition of criminal liability in the absence of any harm?

Consider the two classic examples of attempting the impossible. First, a pickpocket places her hand in the victim's empty pocket. The crime here is physically impossible; there is nothing for her to steal. Can she be liable for attempted theft? Secondly, the defendant handles goods believing they are stolen but, unknown to him, they are not stolen (the facts of *Haughton v. Smith*, 1975). Here (unlike the first example) the defendant has done all that he means to do but what he has done turns out not to be criminal. The crime is legally impossible as the goods are not stolen. Can he be liable for attempting to handle stolen goods?

The common law answered these questions in the negative (*Partington v. Williams*, 1975; *Haughton v. Smith*, 1975). The crime was impossible and so the defendant's acts could never get close enough to the crime to satisfy the *actus reus* of attempt; one could not get "within striking distance" of nothing (see earlier, pp. 21–25). A conviction in such cases would be a conviction purely on the basis of guilty intentions. Believing that goods were stolen, for instance, did not make them stolen goods. Accordingly, without the possibility of direct harm occurring, there could be no criminal liability for an attempt. One could support such an approach. If the crime were not possible the defendant's actions posed no social danger; they constituted no threat to the interests of others. There was thus no "harm" even of a second-order nature.

Such arguments were, however, unacceptable to those who argued that a person who tried to commit a crime is as morally blameworthy and in need of incapacitation and rehabilitation as he who succeeds; punishment is needed to deter him and others from attempting similar crimes again; whether the crime is possible or impossible could be mere "chance". It was these arguments that finally won the day and resulted in the enactment of the Criminal Attempts Act 1981, section 1(2) of which provides: "A person may be guilty of attempting to commit an offence to which this section applies even though the facts are such that the commission of the offence is impossible."

And section 1(3) confirms the self-evident proposition that where a person believes the facts to be such that he would be committing a crime, he is to be regarded as having the necessary intention to commit the offence. This means that a defendant who intends to handle a particular radio believing it to be stolen when in fact it is not stolen cannot argue that he intended to handle a "non-stolen radio". Section 1(3) makes it plain that if he believed the radio was stolen, he intended to handle a "stolen radio".

However, the House of Lords in *Anderton v. Ryan* (1985) was not prepared to travel such a subjectivist route and, in a quite extraordinary manner, declared that the statute would lead to "asinine" results and proceeded to subvert the legislation from its original purpose. In this case Mrs Ryan had bought a video recorder believing it to be stolen. She had confessed as much to the police who were investigating a burglary at her home. However, there was no actual evidence that the video recorder was stolen and so it had to be treated as though it was not. She was charged with dishonestly attempting to handle a stolen video recorder contrary to section 1(1) of the Criminal Attempts Act 1981.

The House of Lords held that there could be no liability on facts such as these, with Lord Bridge (with whom the majority agreed) drawing a distinction (nowhere to be found in the statute itself) between "acting in a criminal way" and "objectively innocent acts". Only if the defendant were "acting in a criminal way" could there be liability if the commission of the crime turned out to be impossible in the circumstances. For instance, the pickpocket who sticks her hand in another's empty pocket is "acting in a criminal way" and would be liable. But if the defendant's acts were "objectively innocent" (as Mrs Ryan's were) there could be no liability. Mrs Ryan had done all she meant to do by handling the goods, but her completed actions did not in law amount to a crime because the goods were not stolen. Section 1(4) limits the law of attempt "to any offence which, if it were completed, would be triable . . . as an indictable offence". Mrs Ryan's actions "were completed" and did not amount to an indictable offence as required by section 1(4). The same would be true of the man who has consensual sexual intercourse with a girl over 16 believing her to be under that age. His actions are "innocent"; he has done all that there is for him to do but what he has done is not, in law, an indictable offence. To hold him liable for an attempt would be to convict him purely on the basis of his "guilty thoughts". On the other hand, the pickpocket has not completed what she set out to do, but if she had, a criminal offence would have been committed; if she had achieved her objective she would have completed the full indictable offence of theft.

This distinction between "objectively innocent" acts, on the one hand, and "criminal" or "guilty" acts on the other is particularly interesting. It would appear that a "criminal" or "guilty" act is one that looks *manifestly criminal*. (This cannot refer to actual crimes. The defendant stabbing the pillow believing he is stabbing his victim commits no offence if it is his own bedding and pillow that he is damaging. Yet Lord Roskill clearly held that there would be liability for attempt in such a situation.) Fletcher (1978) states that "manifestly criminal" activities must exhibit at least the following essential features. First, the criminal act must manifest, on its face, the actor's criminal purpose. And secondly, the conduct should be "of a type that is unnerving and disturbing to the community as a whole". These requirements are clearly satisfied in the pickpocket and defendant stabbing the pillow cases. The actions manifest the defendant's unlawful purpose and are "unnerving and disturbing" to the community. This requirement of manifest criminality is, of course, one that lays emphasis on *harm*, albeit of a second-order nature. It insists that actions infringe another's security interests; they must seemingly pose real and objective threats of harm.

On the other hand, "objectively innocent" activities such as those of Mrs Ryan or the defendant having sexual intercourse with the 16 year-old girl believing her to be under 16 pose no threat of harm to anyone. Nobody's security interests are being violated thereby. At most, he is manifesting a generalised dangerousness in the sense that he has shown that he could perhaps commit the crime at another time and place. If criminal liability were to be imposed in such cases it would be in the complete absence of any degree of harm, however defined. On this basis it can be suggested that the House of Lords in *Anderton v. Ryan* (1985), despite blatantly ignoring Parliament's intentions and creating confused distinctions, did lend its weight to the view here advanced that the causing of harm is an essential prerequisite in the general formula for the construction of criminal liability.

However, in a remarkable *volte-face*, the House in *Shivpuri* (1986) overruled its decision in *Anderton v. Ryan* (1985) holding that there could be criminal liability in all such cases of attempting the impossible. This case concerned a defendant charged under section 1 of the Criminal Attempts Act 1981 with attempting to commit the offence of being knowingly concerned in dealing with and harbouring prohibited drugs, contrary to section 170(1)(b) of the Customs and Excise Management Act 1979. The defendant had thought he was dealing in prohibited drugs but it transpired that the substance in his possession was only snuff or similarly harmless vegetable matter. Holding that his own distinction between "objectively innocent" and "guilty" actions was "incapable of sensible application", Lord Bridge proceeded to hold that the defendant's actions were more than merely preparatory to the *intended* offence. Because of section 1(2) it was unnecessary to establish that the actions were more than merely preparatory to the *actual* offence.

This decision has introduced certainty and simplicity into the law and has given effect to the legislative intent behind the Criminal Attempts Act 1981. However, one can only feel unease at the manner in which the decision was reached. It is abundantly plain that the House of Lords was faced with a situation in *Anderton v. Ryan* (1985) where they felt that criminal liability was inappropriate. People who purchase cheap videos thinking that they are stolen when in fact they are not have done nothing wrong other than commit a crime in their minds. On the other hand, the House found itself faced with a defendant in *Shivpuri* (1986) whom they felt clearly had done wrong and deserved punishment. He had agreed in India to receive a suitcase of drugs in England that would be delivered to him by a courier. This he did and then, removing one package from the suitcase, he took it, still following instructions, to a railway station to deliver to a third party. He was there arrested. While one can understand the House of Lords' desire to uphold the conviction in such an obvious case of trafficking in "drugs", one nevertheless wonders whether important legal principles ought to be altered so freely to meet the exigencies of the case before the court.

While it is possible to justify the existence of a law of attempt (p. 163) and risk-creating offences (pp. 170–173) despite the absence of a direct harm, such justifications presuppose the potential for causing harm in the real world. If I try to shoot and kill you but my gun is broken or try to steal from your empty pocket, I am attacking your legally protected interests (Duff, 1996) and my actions have a real and observable potential for causing harm. But when I stick pins in a doll believing that it will cause your death, I am not realistically threatening your legally protected interests. Similarly, if I handle goods that are not stolen, whose legally protected interests am I attacking? This is pure thought-crime. The distinction drawn in *Anderton v. Ryan* (1985) between "acting in a criminal way" and "objectively innocent" acts could, with refinement, have been developed into a workable test enabling a distinction to be drawn between those attempt cases involving a realistic attack on a legally protected interest (where liability is appropriate) and other cases that amount to no more than thought-crime (and where no liability should ensue).

Duff (1996) has suggested that attempt liability is only appropriate if there is some apparent prospect of success, or some apparent ability to commit the crime, as measured by a reasonable observer. If I fire my gun at what I believe is my enemy but is in fact a tree stump and any reasonable person would realise I was firing at a tree stump, there should be no liability. But when I stick my hand in your empty pocket, the reasonable observer will not know the pocket is empty; there is an "apparent ability" to commit the crime and attempt liability is appropriate. This test raises the problem: how much knowledge must be attributed to this reasonable observer? Clearly, such an observer must know certain general facts about the world, such as that one cannot kill by witchcraft. But, further, the reasonable observer can only make sense of the defendant's actions if she knows something about the meaning of those actions and, often, neutral actions (such as handling a video recorder) only make sense if there is knowledge of the defendant's dominant intention: the intention that drives and explains the action. Duff (1996) distinguishes between such dominant intentions and incidental but mistaken beliefs (which do not explain the defendant's actions but are simply incidentally held beliefs). Mrs Ryan did not have a dominant intention to handle stolen goods; she was not acting in order to handle stolen goods as she might have been if responding to a bet that she would not have the nerve to handle stolen goods. Her dominant intention was to purchase a video recorder that she incidentally believed was stolen. The reasonable observer should only be endowed with knowledge of dominant intentions and not of this incidental belief. Her actions were therefore "objectively innocent" and she should not be liable. After *Shivpuri* (1986), however, this is not the approach of English law.

The philosophy underlying the Criminal Attempts Act 1981 and the approach adopted by the House in *Shivpuri* (1986) represent "subjectivism" gone mad. It amounts to no more than punishing people for their guilty intentions. The person who takes his or her own umbrella thinking it belongs to another can now be convicted of attempted theft. The Law Commission (1980) anticipated such problems. Conceding that there would be liability in this situation and in the case of a person buying goods at such a low price that he believed them to be stolen when in fact they were not, it concluded that "in neither case would it be realistic to suppose that a complaint would be made or that a prosecution would ensue". This prognosis sadly turned out to be false. *Anderton v. Ryan* (1985) was exactly such a case. A prosecution was brought and under the law as interpreted in *Shivpuri* (1986) criminal liability would ensue. It must surely be a matter of deep regret that English law is now involved in punishing thought-crime.

A further objection is that this extreme lurch into subjectivism is inconsistent with the approach adopted to many other offences where the dictates of fair labelling have ensured that regard be paid to the resulting harm or the realistic prospect of such harm. Some coherence in the approach adopted towards offences is surely desirable. A clearer understanding of the importance of the causing of harm (albeit "second-order" harm) would have ensured some check on unbridled "subjectivism" and would have prevented the present situation arising.

(iv) Endangerment offences

In addition to the inchoate offences, such as attempt discussed above, many offences criminalise conduct that has the potential for causing harm. These are known as risk-creation offences or offences of endangerment. In the United States and Australia many states have general offences of reckless endangerment. In Australia it is common to have separate endangerment offences both in relation to death and to serious injury. This covers all forms of dangerous conduct from firing guns in the direction of another or grappling with a police officer for possession of a loaded gun to risking transmission of HIV during unsafe sexual intercourse (Lanham, 1999).

English law has no such general offences, but instead criminalizes specific dangerous activities that create risks of harms such as injury or death. Examples are dangerous driving, possession of firearms and failing to ensure, as far as reasonably practicable, the health, safety and welfare at work of employees or members of the public. These are "conduct crimes": the activities are not harmful in themselves and might lead to no ulterior harm. It is perfectly possible to possess a firearm without ever using it or injuring another. However, with these offences the risk of serious harm is widely recognized and can, accordingly, be justified in a manner similar to the justification of the inchoate offences as the following examples illustrate. First, the offence of dangerous driving contrary to section 2 of the Road Traffic Act 1988 does in itself constitute a "second-order" harm; it presents a real threat or risk of actual harm to others. But it is indisputably a lesser offence than causing death by dangerous driving contrary to section 1 of the same Act. The direct harm of causing death aggravates the offence. A similar analysis can be applied to speeding laws. Drivers who exceed speed limits may in fact be driving safely and not specifically endangering others. However, there is a statistical expectation that if everyone complied with the speed limit there would be fewer accidents. Drivers have an "obligation to co-operate in a safety-promoting scheme by observing certain speed limits" (von Hirsch, 1996). But, as the harm risked here is even more remote than with dangerous driving, it is a much lesser offence.

Secondly, the offence of possessing a firearm without a firearms certificate contrary to section 1 of the Firearms Act 1968 again constitutes in itself a "second-order" harm. The mere unauthorized possession of such firearms poses a threat of real harm to all of us. Firearms are inherently dangerous and their widespread, unlicensed possession would lead to an increase in their usage in everyday situations: domestic quarrels, children playing with their parents' weapons and so on. Also, the task of the police is made more difficult if householders are permitted their own " 'do-it-yourself' crime-prevention instruments" (Feinberg, 1984). But again, this is a lesser harm (and thus a lesser offence) than using such a gun to injure another.

Whether conduct that could lead to harm is criminalized generally depends on balancing the seriousness of the possible harm and the likelihood of its occurrence against the social value of the conduct. On this basis drunken driving is prohibited while walking drunkenly on the street is not (von Hirsch, 1996). Similarly, possession of firearms is prohibited while possession of other dangerous weapons with greater social value, such as kitchen knives or garden shears, is not unlawful.

Arguably, in some of these areas of activity there is a "middle" (or, at least, different) harm and wrong in cases where the risks start to materialize even if the ultimate harm is not caused. For example, unauthorized usage of a firearm radically alters the normative position of the actor and generates a much greater threat to society than mere possession of the firearm. English law, having no general offence of endangerment, responds in two ways to such cases. First, the defendant can be convicted of the basic conduct offence but receive a more severe punishment. For example, where a defendant charged with unlawful possession of a firearm has actually fired that gun in a blameworthy manner there will generally be an increased punishment (*Hicks*, 1991). Secondly, where a defendant has taken intentional steps towards a crime (but not done enough for an attempt), English law has created certain "crimes of ulterior intent" such as assault with intent to rob or gaining unauthorized access to a computer with intent to commit specified offences (Computer Misuse Act 1990, s.2). Both these examples involve the defendant committing a lesser crime (assault and unauthorized access) but, because there is an intention to commit an ulterior offence, the seriousness of the crime is aggravated. Horder (1996) argues for greater utilization of such offences: acting with the relevant intention changes the moral character of the action and, for fair labelling reasons, should be marked by the existence of a separate offence to fill the gap between, say, the serious offence of attempted murder and the relatively minor offence of possessing an offensive weapon. For instance, he argues that if there were a crime of assault with intent to rape (it is uncertain whether such a crime exists), juries would not be forced to adopt over-expansive interpretations of whether the defendant's actions were sufficiently proximate for attempted rape as in *Attorney-General's Reference (No. 1 of 1992)* (1993, above p. 23), but could instead convict of an offence that accurately describes the nature of the defendant's wrongdoing. This approach is plausible for those ulterior intent crimes that involve defendants having to embark on a threatening course of conduct such as an assault. They have crossed a moral threshold by embarking on criminal activity within the same family of offences. However, Horder's analysis becomes less plausible when applied to other crimes of ulterior intent. For instance, section 3 of the Criminal Damage Act 1971 makes it a criminal offence to possess *anything* (for example, a box of matches) intending to use it to damage the property of another. A person possessing a box of matches intending to set fire to another's property may indeed be said to have "changed the normative character of [the] conduct" (Horder, 1996) but until there is some threatening action towards the commission of a crime it is difficult to see that any relevant moral threshold has been crossed. Such offences run the risk of punishing thought-crime alone.

(v) Conclusion

Harm or clearly risked harm is generally a fundamental component in the construction of criminal liability. Clearly, too, there are degrees of harm: some harms are worse than others. And it is submitted that the causing and degree of harm can be more than pure "chance". The causing or risking of harm is fundamental to our moral assessment of events and so ought to be an integral component in the structuring of levels of criminal liability and punishment.

3

MAJOR CRIMES

1. INTRODUCTION

Having examined how criminal liability is generally con-
structed, we are now in a position to understand the operation
of these general principles in relation to specific crimes.

There is a myriad of offences in English law ranging all the
way from murder to mislabelling a tin of beans. There are
crimes aimed at protecting personal safety (murder, assault,
rape, etc.), protecting interests in property (theft, fraud, criminal
damage, etc.), protecting public order (riot, violent disorder,
etc.), protecting the security of the state (treason, official secrets,
etc.), protecting public morals (bigamy, obscenity, etc.), protecting the administration of justice (perjury, contempt of court, etc.)
and so on. And then there are the countless strict liability
offences aimed at protecting employees, consumers, the
environment—and so the list continues.

It has been estimated that there are some 8,000 criminal
offences in English law (p. 135). It would of course be impossible and quite beyond the function of this book to explore all
these offences. The object here is not to provide a complete
synopsis of the law, but rather to explore the underlying
principles, themes and purposes of the criminal law in our
society today. The best way of achieving this purpose is to focus
only on some of the major crimes—namely, offences against the
person (sexual and non-sexual), homicide and some property
offences.

But even in relation to these chosen offences it must be
stressed that the aim is not to provide a complete summary of
the law. The major interest will be in exploring the structure of
such offences (for example, the relationship of murder to
manslaughter) and how this structure (with concomitant levels
of punishment) reflects the differing weights attached to the
essential components of criminal liability: blame and harm.

2. OFFENCES AGAINST THE PERSON (NON-SEXUAL)

(i) Introduction

Even in the area of non-sexual, non-fatal offences against the person there are numerous criminal offences such as: administering poison, false imprisonment, kidnapping—plus other more esoteric offences such as obstructing or assaulting a clergyman in the discharge of his duties or setting mantraps with intent to inflict grievous bodily harm. Again, selectivity is necessary and the primary focus in this section will be on the main offences covering the infliction of violence upon others.

(ii) The main offences

These offences can be ranked in hierarchical order starting with the least serious and progressing upwards in order of seriousness (and in terms of the penalties attached).

At the bottom of the structure lie technical assault and battery. While these are known generically and somewhat loosely as "common assaults", each is a separate offence (*Taylor; Little,* 1992), charged under section 39 of the Criminal Justice Act 1988, and only triable in the magistrates' court where the maximum penalty is six months' imprisonment.

A *technical* or *psychic assault* is committed when the defendant intentionally or recklessly causes the victim to apprehend imminent force. So if the defendant raises his fist and threatens to punch the victim, a technical assault is committed. The victim has been made to apprehend imminent unlawful personal violence (*actus reus*); the defendant meant to cause such apprehension or was reckless thereto (*mens rea*). While the matter is not entirely beyond doubt, it would appear that the *Cunningham* (1957) recklessness test applies here. The defendant must actually realise there is a risk the victim might apprehend imminent personal violence. A technical assault is thus similar to an attempt in that there is no physical harm caused to the victim. But with a technical assault there is a direct harm: the apprehension of imminent violence. With an attempt, on the other hand, there need be no such fear; the victim could be unaware that the defendant is attempting to inflict violence upon her.

The object of the offence of technical assault is not to protect people from threats of future violence. Indeed, the criminal law does not provide such protection at all unless there is a threat to kill (Offences against the Person Act 1861, section 16). So a defendant may with impunity threaten to cut off his victim's fingers or pull his fingernails out the following day. This is a serious gap in the law. The fear and apprehension caused in such cases could be far greater than with many threats of immediate lesser force. While the time-gap allows the victim an opportunity to seek official protection, such protection will in most cases be inadequate to guarantee the victim's safety. The harm (fear and apprehension) is felt to be so significant in such cases that the Law Commission (1993b) has proposed criminalising such threats to cause serious injury.

Mindful of such considerations and the fact that the essence of (and the harm in) a technical assault is the fear generated by the defendant's threatened violence, the courts have adopted a flexible approach to the requirement that the victim must apprehend imminent violence. In *Smith v. Chief Superintendent, Woking Police Station* (1983) it was held that a woman had been assaulted when she saw the defendant looking through her closed bedsitting room window at 11 p.m. Although he was outside her room and would have had to break or force open her window and climb in before he could actually inflict violence upon her (giving her time to run away), it was held that she had apprehended a sufficiently immediate application of force.

This approach to the requirement of immediacy has been even further extended in a series of cases involving stalking, culminating in the House of Lords' decision of *Ireland; Burstow* (1998). In the first appeal the defendant made repeated silent telephone calls (although sometimes resorting to heavy breathing), mostly at night, to three women. It was held that the immediacy requirement was satisfied because of "the fear that the caller's arrival at her door may be imminent. She may fear the *possibility* of immediate personal violence". A similar approach was adopted in *Constanza* (1997) where a stalker had made repeated silent telephone calls and sent 800 letters culminating in two letters which the victim interpreted as clear threats. It was held that there had been an assault when the victim read these latter letters as there was a "fear of violence at some time not excluding the immediate future". While one can understand this judicial response to the appalling plight of the victims concerned who suffered serious psychiatric illness as a consequence, this is surely stretching the immediacy requirement too far. Research suggests that the general frequency of violence among stalkers is low (Tjaden *et al.*, 1998) although, of course, what matters is not the empirical facts but what the victim apprehends. However, it seems inconceivable that, having received 800 letters without ensuing violence, a victim should apprehend the possibility of immediate violence upon receipt and reading a particular letter when the stalker could not possibly know when the letter was being read. A better solution to the problem was that adopted by the Court of Appeal in *Ireland* (1996) (but rejected by the House of Lords) that upon receipt of letters or telephone calls from stalkers what the victim apprehends is not immediate physical violence but rather psychological violence in the sense that the calls or letters would cause immediate trauma (tension, anxiety, sweating, etc.).

In response to media clamour for more effective criminal laws against stalking, the Protection from Harassment Act 1997 creates two criminal offences of harassment. For the lesser offence, carrying a maximum sentence of six months' imprisonment (section 1), the defendant must pursue a course of conduct (on at least two occasions) which amounts to harassment of another and which the defendant knows or ought to know amounts to harassment. For the more serious offence, carrying a maximum sentence of five years' imprisonment (section 4(1)), the defendant must pursue a course of conduct (on at least two occasions) which causes another to fear that violence will be used against her. In fair labelling terms these offences are more appropriate in most cases of stalking as the essence of the wrongdoing is causing distress and anxiety rather than a specific fear of physical violence. However, in some of the more extreme instances of stalking where the victim suffers serious illness, utilisation of the traditional offences of violence could be appropriate and could be achieved without a gross distortion of the law by following the (rejected) approach adopted by the Court of Appeal in *Ireland* (1996).

The other species of "common assault" is a *battery*. A battery is the intentional or reckless infliction of unlawful personal force by one person upon another. Again, *Cunningham* (1957) recklessness probably suffices. Here the force must actually be inflicted as opposed to being merely threatened. The term "force" is somewhat misleading. All that is required for a battery is that the defendant touch the victim without consent or without any other lawful excuse. While the issue is somewhat controversial, the better view is that such a touching must be hostile, rude or threatening (*Wilson v. Pringle*, 1986). We all have a right to personal integrity but if one were simply touched in a non-sexual, non-threatening and non-hostile manner, such invasion of an interest could hardly be sufficiently important to warrant protection via the criminal law. Further, while the issue is not entirely settled, it appears that the force may be applied indirectly (*Haystead*, 2000). Charging Guidelines for the Crown Prosecution Service have been introduced (Crown Prosecution Service, 1996) and indicate that a prosecution under section 39 is appropriate where the following type of injuries have been caused: grazes; scratches; abrasions; minor bruising; swellings; reddening of the skin; superficial cuts; black eyes. So, while a battery can, in theory, be committed by any hostile touching, in practice a prosecution is most unlikely unless some injury of this sort has been caused.

The touching must be without consent. The law, not surprisingly, implies consent in a whole range of everyday activities: when we run for buses, stand in queues, walk in the street, we all accept that there will be a certain degree of bodily contact and accordingly are deemed to consent thereto. This effectively means we are deemed to submit to all touchings that could be regarded as generally acceptable in the ordinary course of daily life (*Collins v. Wilcock*, 1984). Whether one can lawfully consent to more serious injuries has been discussed above at pp. 81–85.

Moving up the hierarchy, we next find the more serious offence of *assault occasioning actual bodily harm* punishable by a maximum of five years' imprisonment (Offences against the Person Act 1861, section 47). In view of the potential penalty, one would naturally expect that both the degree of harm and culpability necessary for this offence would be considerably greater than that required for a common assault. Such expectations are, however, not fulfilled.

The harm required is actual bodily harm. While this is more serious than mere apprehension of violence or a mere touching, in *Chan-Fook* (1994) it was held that any injury could suffice as long as it was not "so trivial as to be wholly insignificant". This includes psychiatric injuries as long as they amount to an identifiable clinical condition supported by psychiatric evidence; mere "emotions" such as fear, distress or panic do not qualify (*Ireland; Burstow*, 1998).

Such a broad definition leaves maximum scope to the prosecution to charge either common assault or section 47 in a large number of cases. This naturally leads to inconsistency in practice in different areas of the country. In order to try to introduce some consistency and control over prosecutorial discretion, the Charging Guidelines for the Crown Prosecution Service (Crown Prosecution Service, 1996) list the following as examples of injuries that should lead to a prosecution under section 47: loss or breaking of a tooth; temporary loss of sensory functions (includes loss of consciousness); extensive or multiple bruising; displaced broken nose; minor fractures; minor (but not merely superficial) cuts of a sort probably requiring medical treatment (*e.g.* stitches); and psychiatric injury as specified in *Chan-Fook*, (1994) and *Ireland; Burstow* (1998).

The blame required for this offence is identical to that required for a common assault. All that is required is that the defendant have the *mens rea* of a common assault, *i.e.* the *mens rea* of either a technical assault or a battery (*Savage; Parmenter*, 1992). In *Roberts* (1971) (see earlier, p. 154) the defendant tried to pull a coat off his female passenger in his moving car (a common assault). The girl jumped from the car and sustained actual bodily harm. The defendant's argument that he had not intended or foreseen actual bodily harm was rejected. He had the *mens rea* of a common assault and that was all that was necessary.

At first sight it seems odd that where the blame is constant a much more serious offence and liability to so much greater punishment can result from such a slight increase in harm. This is a classic example of constructive crime where there is no correspondence between the harm caused and the *mens rea* of the defendant. We have already seen (p. 15) that many commentators argue that this is incoherent and that there should be a connection between the twin components of criminal liability, blame and harm. The defendant should need to intend or foresee the risk of actual bodily harm. The strength of this argument and whether English criminal law should be entirely driven by this principle of correspondence was discussed at pp. 15 and 162.

The next offence in the structure is *malicious wounding or inflicting grievous bodily harm* (Offences against the Person Act 1861, section 20). The defendant's conduct must result in a wound (the inner and outer skin must be broken) or the infliction of grievous bodily harm ("really serious bodily harm"—*Smith*, 1961), which can include a serious recognisable psychiatric illness (*Ireland; Burstow*, 1998). In some cases, of course, a wound need not be very serious. Particularly with the advances of modern medical science one can only wonder at the significance of "wounding" in itself. A wound can be medically either serious or not serious and ought logically to be treated as such without any special significance. However, many wounds and certainly all forms of grievous bodily harm do constitute more serious harms than those required for actual bodily harm. The Crown Prosecution Service Charging Standard (1996) gives the following as examples of grievous bodily harm: injury resulting in permanent disability or permanent loss of sensory function; injury which results in more than minor permanent, visible disfigurement; broken or displaced limbs or bones, including fractured skull, compound fractures, broken cheek bone, jaw, ribs, etc.; injuries which cause substantial loss of blood, usually necessitating a transfusion; and injuries resulting in lengthy treatment or incapacity.

A higher degree of blame is also required for section 20. The defendant must act "maliciously", which has been interpreted to mean that he must himself foresee the risk of *some* harm occurring; he need not foresee serious harm resulting (*Mowatt*, 1967; *Savage; Parmenter*, 1992). The courts have eschewed the idea that "maliciously" should be interpreted in the light of *Caldwell* (1982). Subjective foresight of some harm is necessary (*Savage; Parmenter*, 1992).

Section 20 is thus clearly meant to be a more serious offence than section 47: a greater level of harm and a higher degree of blame is required, yet the maximum penalty for section 20 is five years' imprisonment—exactly the same maximum as for section 47. This absurdity highlights the basic incoherence and confusion underlying the structure of offences against the person.

All three of the offences discussed so far (common assault, section 47 and section 20) become more serious offences if they are *racially aggravated*. Concern over increasing levels of racial violence (fuelled by intense publicity in a few high-profile cases such as arose following the death of Stephen Lawrence) led to the creation of the new racially aggravated offences in the Crime and Disorder Act 1998. A racially aggravated common assault is punishable by a maximum sentence of two years' imprisonment; section 47 and section 20, when racially aggravated, both carry a maximum penalty of seven years' imprisonment (s.29). Under section 28 an offence is racially aggravated if the offender demonstrates or is motivated (wholly or partly) by racial hostility.

While one has natural sympathy with the policy objectives underlying the creation of these racially aggravated offences, one has to doubt whether they will be effective in affording greater protection to members of ethnic minorities for the following reasons. First, it will be necessary for the police to record and the CPS to process the incident as a racial crime. The evidence suggests that at present there is a failure by both bodies to identify crimes as racial (Brennan, 1999)—although it is possible that the existence of these offences could prompt these agencies into greater vigilance in the classification of offences. Second, there is the danger that plea-bargaining will result in offenders charged with the racially aggravated offences pleading guilty to the lesser unaggravated offences and it then becomes questionable whether the racially aggravating features of the attack can be taken into account at the sentencing stage. Finally, evidence from the United States, where similar "hate-crimes" have been introduced, suggests that these offences could end up being used mainly against members of ethnic minorities when white victims have been attacked (Jacobs and Potter, 1998) thus subverting the policy underlying the introduction of the new offences. Whether there are sufficient fair labelling reasons to trump these concerns and justify the introduction of the new offences is discussed later (p. 184).

At the apex of the hierarchy lies *wounding or causing grievous bodily harm with intent* (Offences against the Person Act 1861, section 18). This is a serious offence punishable with a maximum of life imprisonment. With such a high potential penalty it was though unnecessary to introduce a racially aggravated category of the crime. The harm that needs to be caused under section 18 is identical to that necessary for section 20, namely, a wounding or grievous bodily harm. What distinguishes the two offences is their differing *mens rea* requirements. For section 18 the defendant must actually *intend* to cause grievous bodily harm or, alternatively, must intend to resist or prevent the lawful apprehension or detainer of any person.

Research has indicated that only 23 per cent of offenders indicted under section 18 are eventually convicted of that offence with most of the remainder being convicted of (or having the charge reduced to) lesser offences of violence, such as section 20 (Genders, 1999). While there are many possible explanations for this (for example, selecting a higher charge to facilitate later plea-bargaining), one clear reason is the difficulty of proving the requisite intention for section 18. The cases in which the offenders were finally convicted under section 18 were those where there was some objective evidence of premeditation such as when a weapon had been deliberately taken to the scene of the crime or when the offender initiated the attack by first demanding money, property or sex from the victim (Genders, 1999). Indeed, the Charging Standard (Crown Prosecution Service, 1996) specifies the type of factors that are indicative of the requisite intention: "a repeated or planned attack; deliberate selection of a weapon or adaptation of an article to cause injury, such as breaking a glass before an attack; making prior threats; and using an offensive weapon against, or kicking, the victim's head".

Clearly, causing grievous bodily harm intentionally renders the offence more serious than section 20 which only requires recklessness. However, given that both offences require the same degree of injury (although research suggests that the graver the injury the more likely the offender is to be convicted under section 18: Genders, 1999), it is somewhat doubtful that the differing culpability requirements for the two offences justifies such an enormous differential in terms of available punishments.

(iii) Conclusion

The picture that emerges is one of chaos. There is wide agreement that these offences need to be reconstructed completely so as to represent a true hierarchy of seriousness with appropriate levels of punishment attached to each offence. Drawing on the work of the Law Commission (1993b) the Government in 1998 published a Consultation Document containing a Draft Bill (Home Office, 1998a) which proposed an overhaul of the main offences of violence as follows:

(i) intentionally causing serious injury (maximum of life imprisonment);

(ii) recklessly causing serious injury (maximum of seven years' imprisonment);

(iii) intentionally or recklessly causing injury (maximum of five years' imprisonment);

(iv) intentionally or recklessly applying force to or causing an impact on the body of another or intentionally or recklessly causing the other to believe that such force or impact is imminent (maximum of six months' imprisonment).

Such a proposal is clearly an improvement on the present law, but is one that pays insufficient attention to the varying degrees of harm and blame. There are obviously more levels of injury than the above proposal suggests. Is a broken nose (clearly serious bodily harm—*Saunders*, 1985) which is straightened, leaving no lasting disfigurement or impairment of function, really on a par with serious injuries from which a victim never recovers consciousness (but does not die) or cases where the victim is permanently disabled and confined to bed or only mobile in a wheelchair for the rest of her life? It has been suggested that offence seriousness should be measured by ranking harms according to the impact they have on a person's standard of living (von Hirsch and Jareborg, 1991). Permanently disabling injuries have a greater impact on such living standards than transitory injuries. Accordingly, the argument seems strong that a more subtle restructuring of these offences in terms of harm is required, involving, in order of seriousness: serious injury which is permanently crippling or disfiguring; serious injury of a temporary nature; injury; aggressive force (*i.e.* "touchings" of a hostile or threatening nature) and apprehension of immediate force. Alternatively, if it were felt that this would over-complicate the law "serious injury" should be defined so as only to include the very serious injuries having a major impact on living standards. Either of these approaches would have significant "fair labelling" advantages in communicating that there are clear moral distinctions between serious and less serious offences.

Again, more precise fine-tuning is required with regard to the blame component. The Draft Bill 1998 distinguishes intentionally causing serious injury from recklessly causing serious injury (with a huge differential in maximum penalty), yet does not distinguish intentionally causing injury from recklessly causing injury. Such an approach is indefensible. It is widely accepted that it is worse (in moral terms) to cause a harm intentionally than to cause it recklessly. The law simply cannot afford to ignore such basic moral distinctions.

The Draft Bill 1998 assigns recklessness its subjective *Cunningham* (1957) meaning (cl.14(2)). The defendant must actually foresee the injury or serious injury. But what of the other indicators of blame—particularly recklessness as defined by *Caldwell* (1982)? If acting in such a manner is indicative of blame for many other offences, there seems little case for excluding personal injuries. A person who fails to consider an obvious risk and thereby causes criminal damage is liable. On this basis a person who fails to consider an obvious risk and thereby causes injuries to the victim surely ought to be liable also. As seen earlier (p. 69) a failure to consider obvious and serious risks (which one is capable of considering) expresses an attitude towards those risks, an attitude of indifference. If one does not care whether consequences occur, it is difficult to see why it should matter whether any particular result is contemplated. The culpability resides in acting without caring.

The Draft Bill 1998, and the above criticisms of it, accept the premise that the offences of violence must be structured in a hierarchy of seriousness to reflect the culpability of the defendant (intention or recklessness) and the degree of harm caused (seriousness of injury). There is, however, a different way of thinking about and structuring offences of violence. According to this view, for fair labelling reasons crimes should be categorised and defined to capture the essence of the wrongdoing involved. What matters is the *wrong* involved and not just the harm caused or the culpability of the offender. For example, theft and blackmail involve the same harm (loss of property) and the same culpability (intentionally extracting property from another). But the essence of the wrongdoing is so different that they are retained as separate offences. Indeed, the present English law relating to violence contains a host of specific offences, other than those discussed above, aimed at marking different forms of wrongdoing. As already seen, there are the racially aggravated offences of violence. Under section 51 of the Police Act 1964 there is a separate offence of assaulting a police officer in the execution of his duties. Under section 38 of the 1861 Act there is the offence of assault with intent to resist arrest or to prevent a lawful arrest. Sections 23 and 24 of the same Act deal with the administration of poisons. Section 134 of the Criminal Justice Act 1988 creates the offence of torture by an official. The Public Order Act 1986 contains several offences of violence (riot, violent disorder, affray) aimed at group offending. Gardner (1994), discussing some of these and other specific offences in the 1861 Act (such as choking, burning and maiming) concludes that they are "notable for the moral clarity with which they are differentiated" and for similar reasons Horder (1994b) rejects the Draft Bill as "a slide into the vice of moral vacuity".

Taking this thinking to its logical conclusion the following factors (in addition to culpability and level of injury caused) could be identified as important in capturing the essence of the wrongdoing in cases of non-fatal injuries: (i) the method of causing injury (for example, using a dangerous weapon, torture, poisoning); (ii) the context in which injury is caused (for example, public group violence, assault while resisting arrest, injuries caused through a business operation or while driving a vehicle on the road, terrorist attacks); (iii) the identity of the victim (for example, a police officer in the execution of his duties; racial attacks; the vulnerable: children or elderly persons); (iv) the identity or status of the defendant (for example, a parent or public official abusing a position of trust).

It is not difficult to see that each of these involves a different wrong. For example, using a dangerous weapon puts the victim at a great disadvantage and generates extra fear and increases the likelihood of more serious injury or death. The torturer is deliberately inflicting usually prolonged pain and suffering and will often be asserting power and causing degradation to the victim. Poisoning is normally the product of sly planning and premeditated execution over a hapless victim who has no opportunity to defend herself or extricate herself from the situation. Public group violence can generate fear and a threat to public order and group pressure (egging each other on) can lead to excessive and prolonged violence. There are special deterrent reasons for seeking to protect police officers acting in the execution of their duties; an attack on them is also an attack on the authority of the law and the legal system. Racial attacks involve more than injury to an individual; they are an expression of hatred and contempt of an entire racial group and the victim, not being attacked as an individual but as a member of a racial group, is particularly vulnerable. And so on.

There is undoubtedly something morally interesting and different about each of these forms of wrongdoing. However, the issue is whether these differences are sufficiently *significant* to warrant the creation or retention of such a host of separate offences bearing in mind that this could lead to over-specificity or the vice of "particularism" (Horder, 1994b: see p. 11). The significance of the moral distinctions between the above forms of wrongdoing can be challenged. For example, repeatedly kicking someone on the head can be just as dangerous, injurious and painful as stabbing or poisoning them. The identity of the victim should be ignored: all persons have equal rights and interests in bodily integrity. Justice should be colour and status blind. And so on.

There are two further problems with the proposals to mark out the different wrongs in all these cases. First, identifying each wrong by a different label fails to distinguish the offences in terms of seriousness. It was argued earlier (pp. 11–12) that different families of offences need not all be structured according to the same criteria. With property offences, for example, our understanding of particular crimes largely depends on the essence of the wrong involved (contrast theft with blackmail) rather than the harm involved which is always property deprivation (or the threat thereof). However, with offences of violence the level of harm (injury) caused has great significance. Within this latter family of offences part of the fair labelling process is not only to capture the essence of the wrongdoing involved but also to convey the level of rejection of the activity involved. Different scales of punishment should usually be imposed to reflect this degree of rejection. To some extent, of course, this is already done; for example, a racially aggravated assault carries a higher maximum penalty than other assaults. However, it is perhaps not imperative that every offence be ranked at a different level in a hierarchy of seriousness. For example, one could conclude that the moral difference between torture and poisoning is sufficiently significant to warrant separate crime status but that they are equally serious and should be punished to the same extent. However, concluding that offences are of equal seriousness—especially when the level of injury caused is the same—is perhaps a partial admission that the moral difference between the two wrongs might not be sufficiently significant to justify separate offence status.

Secondly, the case for greater offence specificity assumes that these distinctions should be made at the substantive stage (that is, incorporated into a reformed structure of offences against the person). However, these differences could instead be reflected at the sentencing stage. For example, section 82 of the Crime and Disorder Act 1998 provides that if an offence is racially aggravated, this is to be treated as a factor increasing the seriousness of the offence for sentencing purposes. Similarly, more severe sentences could be imposed for attacks on the particularly vulnerable and so on. Of course, whether such matters are dealt with at a substantive or sentencing (or prosecutorial) stage depends largely on the degree of control exercised over sentencing (and prosecutorial) discretionary powers. For instance, if one employed a guideline model of sentencing, some of the factors, such as abuse of trust, could be incorporated into the guidelines without alteration to the substantive law. These matters are considered in the final chapter.

One thing emerges from the above discussion. While the Draft Bill 1998 has much in terms of its simplicity to commend it, it is over-blunt in its exclusion of other morally significant factors that could mark the essence of the wrong in an offence. Before reform is introduced there needs to be a much fuller discussion of these different wrongs and, bearing in mind the need to avoid over-specificity, careful analysis as to whether the differing wrongs are sufficiently significant to justify separate offence status.

3. SEXUAL OFFENCES

(i) Introduction

Many of the non-sexual offences against the person discussed in the previous section could have been committed with a sexual motive and could have involved a variety of harms other than purely physical ones. The victim in *Roberts* (1971), for instance, sustained her injuries in trying to escape from a sexual attack and would almost certainly have suffered mental anguish in addition to her physical injuries. However, the main emphasis there was on physical harm (or a clinically diagnosable psychiatric condition). Such harm is easily capable of ascertainment and gradation in terms of seriousness.

With "sexual offences", on the other hand, the focus is on the unacceptable conduct of the defendant and not on any physical injury that might be caused. Further, while many sexual offences are certainly physically and psychologically damaging to the victim (and this might be the ultimate rationale of some of them), it is unnecessary to prove such injury. If the defendant committed the prohibited act with the requisite degree of blameworthiness, he is liable. (Such offences are thus "conduct crimes".)

The harm involved in these offences varies enormously, making it difficult to develop a coherent structure here; comparisons between them are not always easily made. Broadly, sexual offences can be grouped into three classes.

First, there is non-consensual sexual aggression that covers offences such as rape and indecent assault. The harm here is the violation of another's interests in bodily security, autonomy and privacy. In addition, such offences can involve degradation, humiliation and psychological trauma.

Secondly, there are offences aimed at protecting the vulnerable: children and the mentally subnormal. For instance, girls under 16 cannot consent to sexual intercourse. The law is here concerned with protecting the immature from the risks of psychological harm that are believed to result from sexual intercourse before attaining a sufficient degree of sexual maturity.

Thirdly, there is an alarming array of sexual offences whose main rationale is primarily to preserve "accepted standards of morality". Such offences include incest and gross indecency between men in circumstances where the Sexual Offences Act 1967, section 1, does not apply (this Act "legalised" private homosexual activities between consenting men over the age of 21; the age has since been reduced to 16: Sexual Offences (Amendment) Act 2000, section 1). There are also various criminal offences relating to prostitution and indecent exposure at common law (there is arguably no need to prove the exposure was actually witnessed by anyone, indicating that offensiveness is not the essence of the offence). The crime of bigamy can possibly be added to this list; there is a direct harm to a victim here: the bigamist's first spouse and the new "spouse", if the latter is unaware of the bigamy, have certainly been harmed. However, the law's primary concern here seems to be protection of the institution of marriage as a basic unit in society; the offence involves "an outrage on public decency and morals" (*Allen*, 1872). Finally, the law relating to consent illustrates the law's concern with morality in this field. In *Brown* (1993) it was held that one could not consent to the infliction of bodily harm if the purpose for which the force was inflicted were disapproved of—in this case, injuries inflicted by consenting sado-masochists. On this basis, flagellation and all other sado-masochistic activities are unlawful if they result in the infliction of any physical harm. In these cases the victim is consenting. While, arguably, the law here is protecting such persons from themselves, the more obvious and generally accepted rationale of such law is that it is aimed at upholding morality in society.

Such "victimless" or consensual offences raise their own particular problems—in particular, whether they ought to be criminalized at all and whether such laws breach the European Convention on Human Rights. For instance, the European Court of Human Rights has ruled in *ADT v. U.K.* (2000) that the offence of gross indecency between men amounts to a violation of Article 8 (right to respect for private life). On the other hand, in *Laskey, Jaggard and Brown* (1997) it was held that there had been no violation of Article 8 in *Brown* (1994). Until 1994, consensual heterosexual buggery was an offence punishable by a maximum of life imprisonment. Such conduct has now been decriminalized if it takes place in private and both parties have attained the age of 16. Whether the other offences in this category should also be decriminalized will be considered later (pp. 244–256). Selectivity again being necessary in order to sharpen the focus, the remainder of this section will be devoted mainly to the first category of sexual offences mentioned above, namely, offences of sexual aggression or violence directed at non-consenting adults.

(ii) The main offences

Three such offences will be considered: indecent exposure under the Vagrancy Act 1824, indecent assault, and rape. Indecent exposure can only be committed against women. The victim of an indecent assault or rape may be either male or female.

Under section 4 of the Vagrancy Act 1824 the offence of *indecent exposure* is committed when a man wilfully and indecently exposes his penis with the intention of insulting any female. The exposure need not be in a public place. The offence is triable only summarily and punishable with a maximum of three months' imprisonment. This can be regarded as an offence of sexual aggression against women. The underlying "harm" is the fear, apprehension and disgust felt by a woman so accosted. While a woman might be offended by the exposure of a backside, such exposure presents a far lesser threat of further sexual aggression and so does not fall within the ambit of the offence (although such an exposure in public could well constitute the common law offence of indecent exposure which is aimed at upholding standards of decency). The Sexual Offences Review (2000) has proposed extending this offence to include exposure to males but would limit the offence in all cases to exposures that the defendant knew, or should have known, would cause fear, alarm or distress to any person.

An *indecent assault* is an assault or a battery committed in circumstances of indecency. The maximum penalty for this offence used to be two years' imprisonment where the victim was a woman but 10 years' imprisonment where it was a man. This absurd position which seemed to regard an invasion of a male's autonomy over his body as far worse than a comparable

invasion of a woman's autonomy was remedied and the maximum penalty is now 10 years' imprisonment irrespective of the
gender of the victim (Sexual Offences Act 1985, section 3(3)).

As the offence may be committed by either a technical assault
or a battery, it is clear that there need be no actual touching
provided the victim apprehends an unlawful touching (*Rolfe*,
1952). Thus the distinction between indecent exposure and
indecent assault can be a fine one. If the defendant exposes his
penis to a woman it will be an indecent exposure if she does not
apprehend being touched, but indecent assault if she does
apprehend a touching. The *mens rea* distinction can be even finer
in such cases. For indecent exposure the defendant must intend
to insult the woman; for indecent assault he must intend to
make her apprehend an indecent touching or be reckless
thereto.

The assault or battery must be committed in circumstances of
indecency, which means that in the circumstances it is "capable
of being considered by right-minded persons as indecent"
(*Court*, 1988). Even if the defendant's motive is indecent, there is
no indecent assault if the circumstances of the assault are in no
way objectively indecent. For example, in *George* (1956) the
defendant attempted to remove a girl's shoe; being a "shoe
fetishist", he obtained sexual gratification from such activities. It
was held that this was not an indecent assault as the actions
were not overtly indecent. On the other hand, where the
circumstances of the assault are ambiguous and *could* be indecent, the defendant's purpose and motive become decisive. In
Court (1989) a shop assistant pulled a girl aged 12 across his
knee and spanked her on the bottom; she was fully clothed.
Because the circumstances of the assault were ambiguous (his
motive could have been disciplinary), his motivation became
relevant and because he had a "buttock fetish" this was an
indecent assault. However, most indecent assaults are overtly
"sexual" and usually involve some form of touching of the
genitals. In these cases all that is required is that the defendant
have the *mens rea* of the assault; it is not necessary to establish
an indecent motive. The same would be true in "lesser" cases of
clear objective indecency, for example, bottom-pinching.

The sexual offence that has attracted by far the most public
attention is that of rape, an offence punishable by a maximum of
life imprisonment. Until 1994 this was an offence that could only
be committed against women: it was limited to vaginal intercourse without consent. However, the Criminal Justice and

Public Order Act 1994 expanded the definition of rape to cover any sexual intercourse (penetration of the vagina or the anus with the penis) with a person (male or female) who does not consent to it. The defendant must know the victim is not consenting to the intercourse or be reckless as to whether there is consent (Sexual Offences Act 1956, section 1, as amended).

The sexual intercourse used to have to be "outside marriage". Unless there was a relevant court order, for example a decree of judicial separation, a husband could not be convicted of an offence of rape against his wife. This rule, a monstrous relic from an earlier era when wives were effectively regarded as the property and playthings of the husband, was overturned by the House of Lords in *R* (1992). This decision was subsequently confirmed by the Criminal Justice and Public Order Act 1994, section 142, amending the Sexual Offences Act 1956, section 1. While to many persons (particularly male) the paradigmatic rape is "stranger rape", the reality is otherwise with only some 30 per cent of rapes actually involving strangers while 35 per cent of rapes are committed by men well-known to the victim (Grace, Lloyd and Smith, 1992). The position is now clear. Not only boyfriends and cohabitants, but also husbands, can be convicted of rape.

The sexual intercourse must be without consent. This gives rise to enormous evidential problems as defendants commonly claim that the other person was consenting and it can be extremely difficult to establish this point one way or the other in court. This can result in humiliating and distressing cross-examination in court (and similarly distressing interrogation prior to that). Nevertheless, establishing lack of consent is crucial: it is what transforms the lawful activity of sexual intercourse into the very serious crime of rape.

Consent refers to voluntary agreement by a person in control of his or her actions. If there is intercourse without such voluntary consent, the *actus reus* of rape is committed. The lack of consent does not have to be demonstrated or communicated (*Malone*, 1998) but, of course, without any such demonstration or communication there would be major evidential problems establishing the lack of consent and the defendant's *mens rea*. Case law has established that there is no consent in the following situations: if the victim is incapable of consenting because she is asleep or unconscious through, say, drink or drugs, or so mentally impaired as not to be able to understand what is happening; if there is a fundamental mistake as to the identity of the defendant with the complainant being deceived into thinking it is her husband (Sexual Offences Act 1956, section 1(3)) or boyfriend (*Elbekkay*, 1995); if the complainant has been deceived as to the nature of the act (for example, thinking the sexual intercourse is a surgical operation: *Flattery*, 1877); if the complainant submits to intercourse because of threats of serious violence. On the other hand, the law regards consent as being validly given even though the complainant is drunk and would never have consented if sober as long as he or she still understands what is happening. Also, minor pressure persuading the complainant to agree to sexual intercourse will not invalidate consent even though the sex was not truly wanted, for example, agreeing to have sex to keep the man in a good mood.

However, between the above extremes are the more difficult cases such as where there is an implicit threat of lesser violence or unpleasant consequences such as being sacked from one's job unless one agrees to intercourse. In *Olugboja* (1981) it was held that there was a distinction between consent and submission to intercourse. There is a line to be drawn: some submissions do involve consent (as in the above example of keeping the man happy); other submissions do not involve consent (fear that the man will get violent). It was held that it was for the jury to decide which side of the line a particular case fell. The problem with this approach is that it is inherently vague and uncertain. Every case has to be decided on its facts and there is no clear indication of which submissions amount to consent and which involve rape. The obvious danger is that different juries can reach different conclusions on similar facts. While this is always a problem when juries are left to interpret concepts, as opposed to being restricted to facts, it is unacceptable when dealing with a crime as serious as rape: probably the most serious crime in the criminal calendar after murder and some manslaughters.

It is, however, no easy matter to determine where the boundaries of consent should be drawn. Some feminists have argued that the definition of rape should be expanded to include "unwanted sex" as opposed to merely non-consensual intercourse. There are many reasons why a woman might consent to unwanted sex, for example, to continue a relationship, to avoid rejection, sulking or ill-temper by the man, economic dependence or to avoid violence against herself or her children. Chamallas (1988) would replace the requirement of consent by one of mutuality: "whether the target would have initiated the encounter if she had been given the choice". The problem with this view is that it would make the line between lawful sexual intercourse and rape almost impossible to draw. We all often consent to things we do not want and this is probably particularly true of women who are in an unequal position in a sexist society. The reality is that "all human co-operation . . . is caused by unequal pressures" (Dripps, 1992) and invocation of the criminal law cannot solve all these social evils. The criminal law should be reserved for violation of a person's interests in the exclusive control of their bodies. Consenting to unwanted sex, in certain circumstances, is exercising control. If a person only consents because he or she depends on the security and comforts of home-life, this must count as real consent for the purposes of the criminal law. However, the concept of consent needs re-evaluation to make explicit the circumstances in which various threats will negate consent. In doing this account must be taken of the need for "parity of status" (Sexual Offences Review, 2000) between the parties that must involve a recognition of the relative powerlessness of many woman, in particular. The Sex Offences Review (2000) has proposed that consent be redefined as "free agreement" and that a statutory list of examples be provided indicating situations where there is no free agreement. Most of these examples are uncontroversial and in accordance with the present law outlined above. However, one problematic example given is that the law should specify there is no free agreement if a person submits because of threats of "serious detriment of any type" to themselves or another. This could cover many situations where threats are made: losing a job or killing the family pet or failing an exam. The Review is careful to limit its recommendations to threats of a coercive nature and therefore promising rewards for sex—as in the classic "casting couch" scenario—would not prevent free agreement. What this whole approach boils down to is shifting the focus away from the reality of "consent" to an evaluation of the conduct of the defendant. Some threats (losing a job or denying access to children) are to be regarded as so reprehensible that the defendant deserves to be labelled a rapist. Other threats (promotion denied or not getting a job) are also reprehensible but not sufficiently so for the crime of rape. Instead the defendant can be convicted of the lesser offence of procuring sex by threats (Sexual Offences Act 1956, section 2(1), punishable by a maximum of two years' imprisonment. Whether there is a clear moral distinction that can sensibly be drawn here is a moot point. To some persons who are struggling to survive economically the prospect of not getting a promotion may be an extremely serious detriment. Indeed, it is questionable whether any of these threats (other than ones of death or serious injury) should be regarded as negating consent for the purpose of the law of rape. If the essence of the crime of rape is that it is non-consensual intercourse, perhaps rape should be limited to the clearer cases of lack of consent and the other threats of detriment (apart from threats of death or serious injury) should be dealt with by the separate offence of procuring sex by threats and the maximum punishment for that offence could be increased significantly to reflect the gravity of such conduct on the part of the defendant.

It used to be thought that what was necessary was that the woman did not consent to the penetration of the penis. However, in *Kaitamaki* (1984) it was held that rape was committed if the woman was not consenting at any time during intercourse. So, even though she consented to penetration, if during the intercourse she revoked her consent and advised the man thereof but he persisted in the intercourse, this would be rape. This is a difficult decision. Clearly, a person by consenting initially to intercourse cannot be "estopped" from later revoking the consent; the intercourse could be causing great pain and distress. Nevertheless, one cannot help feeling that while such a man should clearly be guilty of a serious offence, it should not be rape. The person has consented to the man inserting his penis into the vagina or anus. The degree of emotional and psychological trauma is not the same as for other people who never so consented. The crime and label "rape" should be reserved for these worst cases where consent to penetration was never given.

As indicated earlier, the requisite degree of blameworthiness, in the form of *mens rea*, for rape is spelled out by the Sexual Offences Act 1956, section 1. The defendant must *know* the person is not consenting or must be *reckless* as to whether there is consent. Case law has tended to interpret recklessness here as either realising the person might not be consenting or as having a "couldn't care less" attitude and pressing on regardless (*Satnam and Kewal*, 1984). This covers cases not only where the defendant is indifferent as to consent but also situations where he may have failed to address his mind to the question of consent. Despite judicial claims that the *Caldwell* (1982) test of recklessness has no application here (*Satnam and Kewal*, 1984), a test of recklessness based on a failure to consider risks bears all the hallmarks of *Caldwell* (1982) recklessness. However, if the defendant genuinely believes the person is consenting, section 1(2) of the Sexual Offences (Amendment) Act 1976 comes into operation. This section endorses a subjective test: the question is whether the defendant actually believes the other person is consenting; the reasonableness of his belief is only important in evidential terms. No matter how absurd the defendant's mistake, if he honestly believed the complainant was consenting (and if the jury believe him) he will not be guilty of rape. Again, the wisdom of such an approach can be queried. In the "date rape" cases it becomes all too easy for the man to contend that because the woman consented to return to his flat he believed she was consenting to intercourse and in a "phallocentric culture . . . [where] women's rejection of sex is . . . always ambiguous" (Smart, 1989) he is likely to be believed and escape liability. The point here surely is that such a mistake can easily be avoided. If there is the slightest doubt as to whether the woman is consenting, he should ask her. He will, after all, be close enough to do so easily. And, it must be emphasised, that "no means no". If a man fails to make such an enquiry, this indicates a lack of concern for a woman's bodily integrity. It is the "man who is responsible for what he does with his penis" (Henderson, 1992). Failure to take the requisite care when it could so easily be taken is surely blameworthy—and when it results in such a major harm as a violation of a person's autonomy over his or her own body then this is surely sufficient to justify the moral condemnation of the criminal law. In line with this thinking the Sexual Offences Review (2000) has recommended that a "defence of honest belief in free agreement should not be available where there was self induced intoxication, recklessness as to consent, or if the accused did not take all reasonable steps in the circumstances to ascertain free agreement at the time".

(iii) Conclusion

As with the non-sexual offences against the person, the structure of the above sexual offences could be seen to be incoherent. Is rape (maximum of life imprisonment) always that much more serious than indecent assault (maximum of 10 years' imprisonment)? Is penetration of the vagina or anus by the penis necessarily so much more reprehensible than prolonged and painful penetration of the vagina or anus by an object or than forcible fellatio? Is it always so much worse than many of the other humiliating and degrading indecent assaults than can include defecating or urinating upon a person?

Is there a common denominator to the main sexual offences? It is often asserted that these offences are not committed through a desire for sexual gratification, but rather that they represent an assertion of power by a man wanting dominance and humiliation over his victim. Rape and indecent assault, in particular, are offences of violence. With or without penetration, the man is using the other as his object without any respect for the autonomy of the victim. Acceptance of this view leads one to question whether it is necessary to retain the distinction between these two offences. Why not abolish both these crimes and substitute a single broad offence of unlawful sexual assault? The judge would then be able to tailor the sentence to fit the individual facts of the case and so take account of the reality that these offences vary enormously in terms of seriousness. As such a offence, ranging from bottom-pinching to penetrative sex, would be far too broad and would lead to an unacceptable increase in judicial discretion in sentencing, a more feasible proposal would be subdivision of the new offence into degrees, each degree representing a different level of seriousness and carrying its own penalty. This approach has been adopted in several jurisdictions. For example, in Canada three sexual offences have been introduced: sexual assault; sexual assault with a weapon/threats to a third party/causing bodily harm; and aggravated sexual assault (Criminal Law Amendment Act, S.C. 1983, c.127). This gradation of offences emphasises the level of violence inflicted with penetration being irrelevant.

The main objection to this approach, which subsumes rape as simply another form of sexual violence, is that it amounts to the "desexualisation of rape" (Tempkin, 2000). Modern feminist critique has started challenging the focus on violence in sexual offences. While the older view enabled men to understand the seriousness of the crime (because men can understand violence), it also enabled many men to distinguish what they were doing (for example, non-consensual intercourse on a "date" where the motive was sexual) from rape. If rape was a vicious, violent attack, they could not be rapists (Henderson, 1992). The rape-is-violence view might be true of "stranger-rapes" but it fails to encompass many "date-rapes" and rapes by husbands. Accordingly, such feminists have begun redefining rape, in particular, as a crime of sex that is not gender-free (MacKinnon, 1989). It is an offence which causes terror, pain and the psychological degradation of being treated as an "object" to be used at the whim of the man (Queen's Bench Foundation, 1976). As Gardner and Shute (2000) say: the wrong in rape is "the sheer use of a person, and in that sense the objectification of a person, is a denial of their personhood. It is literally dehumanising."

In order to emphasise these features most commentators now accept that penetrative sex needs to be distinguished from other forms of sexual assault. Minnesota has replaced the individual sexual offences with a single offence of "criminal sexual conduct", but this offence has been sub-divided into four degrees, each degree representing a different level of seriousness and carrying its own penalty. Several factors are utilised in distinguishing between the four degrees—such as causing personal injury to the victim or being armed with a dangerous weapon. But the most important distinguishing feature is that drawn between "sexual penetration" and "sexual contact"—the former aggravating the offence. "Sexual penetration" is defined as including any intrusion into the victim's "genital or anal openings" by any part of the defendant's body (penis or hand etc.) or by any object. Thus there is no distinction drawn between vaginal and anal penetration and it does not matter whether the penetration is by the defendant's penis or other object. "Sexual contact", on the other hand, is touching the victim's "intimate parts" for the purpose of satisfying the defendant's "sexual or aggressive impulses" (Minn.Stat.Ann., sections 609.341–609.345).

This approach is still open to the fundamental objection that abolishing the crime of "rape" as such could lead to a downgrading in the perceived seriousness of penetrative sex. The category and label "rape" (with its severe penalty) is used to emphasise the utter reprehensibility of such conduct; it is employed to convey the symbolic message to the public that such activity is the "worst" form of sexual misconduct. Absorbing rape within a hierarchy of sexual assault offences, even a hierarchy dependant on the presence or absence of penetration, would convey a distorted message as to the degree of societal rejection of the activity involved.

However, assuming retention of the crime of rape, the question of how penetration should be defined still remains. English law has expanded the definition of rape to include non-consensual anal intercourse with a woman or a man and the Sexual Offences Review (2000) has proposed that rape be extended to include oral penetration by the penis. However, there is a case for not going further and for limiting rape to penetration by the penis. There are several reasons for regarding penetration by the penis as warranting distinctive offence status. The non-consensual intrusion of a man's penis into the vagina or anus (or mouth) represents one of the most extreme forms of invasion of a person's privacy and autonomy. Rape involves an intrusion into the most private domains by the very symbol of male aggressiveness, the penis. While the physical pain might be greater with the insertion of a bottle or other such object, it is penis penetration that is regarded as specially significant: it is the ultimate assertion of male power. The victim is having to suffer the most intimate proximity possible between him or herself and the assailant—a proximity not only degrading in itself, but one that creates a fear of venereal disease, AIDS and, with vaginal intercourse, of pregnancy. And finally, there are the traumatising after-effects of such penetration that can make people fearful of sexual intercourse for years, if not forever.

For all these related reasons it would appear that the case for retaining rape as a special offence, and limiting it to penis penetration, is overwhelming. The public understands what "rape" is. Indeed, it was through a desire to make people take non-consensual male buggery more seriously that the crime of male rape was introduced. The special label and higher punishment was deemed important to communicate the utter reprehensibility of the conduct. The law should not stray too far from reflecting such common understanding.

One final possibility deserves brief mention. If we are going to retain rape and indecent assault as separate offences, are not these offences too broad? One possible approach would be to subdivide both these offences. The Sexual Offences Review (2000) considered the creation of a lesser offence of "date rape". Particularly in cases where there has been an existing sexual relationship between the parties "in some instances the violation of the person and defilement that are inevitable features where a stranger rapes a woman are not always present to the same degree" (*Berry*, 1988). Further, the existence of the lesser offence might encourage victims to report offences and juries might be more willing to convict. There are, however, strong objections to this proposal to create a lesser rape offence. The Sexual Offences Review (2000) pointed out that rape by an acquaintance/friend/husband could be even worse than stranger rape. These victims suffer feelings of betrayal of trust and guilt for being in the situation. The attack is directed at them personally as opposed to being a chance attack by a stranger. Research suggests that such victims suffer greater long-term effects including a fear of future attacks (Rumney, 1999). Such a separate offence would further encourage the stereotypical view of rape as a crime of violence committed by strangers enabling many men to excuse their conduct on a "date" on the basis that their motive was sexual and it was not a vicious violent attack (Henderson, 1992). Indeed, Rumney (1999) argues that the breach of trust involved in such cases can be so psychologically devastating that the existence of a prior relationship between the parties should be regarded as an aggravating factor in sentencing.

With indecent assault (or sexual assault as the Sex Offences Review (2000) would rename the offence), however, the case for subdividing the offence into degrees, each with its own maximum penalty, is much stronger. At present, the offence is so broad as to cover conduct from bottom-pinching to vaginal penetration with an object. The main problem is achieving agreement on the criteria for distinguishing between the different degrees of such an offence. One approach, adopted by the Australian State of Victoria, is that the more serious offence is only established if the indecent assault is accompanied by an aggravating circumstance from a specified list, for example, inflicting serious personal violence upon the victim or doing an act which seriously degrades or humiliates the victim (Crimes (Sexual Offences) Act 1980, section 46(1)).

However, the better approach, advocated by the Sex Offences Review (2000), is that a new offence of sexual assault by penetration should be introduced. This would cover non-consensual penetration of the anus, vagina or the external genitalia by objects or parts of the body other than the penis. While it was argued above that the label rape, involving penetration by the penis, should be retained for fair labelling reasons, it is clear that the fear, degradation and pain involved in the insertion of objects into the vagina or the anus is in many respects comparable to that involved in rape. This offence, while being "different" from rape, would be regarded as equally serious and would carry the same maximum penalty as rape (life imprisonment). All other non-penetrative sexual touchings would be covered by the basic offence of sexual assault. While the seriousness of such touchings can vary considerably, further subdivision of the offence could lead to the danger of over-specificity (p. 11).

4. HOMICIDE

(i) Introduction

There are four categories of homicide in English law: murder, manslaughter, vehicular homicide and infanticide.

When a person has been unlawfully killed it is often assumed that, if a prosecution is brought, it will be for one of these four offences. Empirically, this is not true. The context in which the killing takes place has a strong influence on the law's response. Many more people are killed as a result of bad driving or unsafe work practices than are killed by violent attacks. In these cases the most common response is for a prosecution to be brought in relation to the underlying dangerous activity: persons will more usually be charged with careless or dangerous driving or with breaches of the Health and Safety at Work etc. Act 1974 (see p. 146) and the fact that death has resulted will be considered, if at all, at the sentencing stage. However, in all cases of unlawful killing a homicide prosecution is an option. While this is statistically rarer in cases where death has resulted from driving or dangerous business operations, this is the most likely outcome in cases involving violent attacks.

In structuring offences against the person and sexual offences we saw that the law was concerned to capture the essence of the wrongdoing by, *inter alia*, balancing the various harms that could occur with the differing degrees of blameworthiness that could accompany the defendant's actions. With homicide offences, on the other hand, one is dealing with a constant harm, namely, the death of the victim. Accordingly, homicide offences have been graded primarily in terms of blameworthiness. Take, for instance, the distinction between the two main homicide offences, murder and manslaughter. The *actus reus* of these two offences is identical: the defendant must unlawfully kill the victim. But what distinguishes them is the different level of blameworthiness required for each. Murder is committed when the defendant unlawfully and without excuse kills his victim with malice aforethought. Manslaughter is an unlawful killing without malice aforethought, but with a different and lesser degree of blameworthiness.

However, while blameworthiness is the central criterion for distinguishing murder from manslaughter, the context in which the killing takes place is regarded as being sufficiently significant at the substantive level to justify the existence of the separate offences of vehicular homicide. Whether this approach of treating such killings differently (in most cases) is justifiable is a matter to which we shall return.

(ii) The offences

The most serious of the homicide offences is *murder*. The very word "murder" encapsulates all our moral beliefs as to the dreadful and terrible nature of the crime. Murderers are immortalised in our museums and literature; their trials are publicised and dramatised in our daily press; they have committed the ultimate and irreversible harm of taking away another's life; they have committed a "crime like no other"; the maximum wrath of society is visited upon them: previously the death penalty and now the fixed sentence of life imprisonment, a sentence that must be imposed upon all murderers.

Such emotive "reasoning" causes little dissent when dealing with the paradigmatic cases of murder, such as those of Fred and Rosemary West or Peter Sutcliffe, the notorious Yorkshire Ripper. Their horrendous crimes are rightly stigmatised as murder. The real problem, as far as the law is concerned, arises in those cases where the defendant has killed but claims that he did not mean to do so. The defendant in *Hyam* (1975) (p. 57) realised that her actions could cause serious injuries or death to her victims but she was not trying to kill. In *Moloney* (1985) the defendant and his stepfather, who had both been drinking fairly heavily, engaged in a "ridiculous challenge" to ascertain who was quicker on the draw with a shotgun. The defendant claimed that he did not aim the gun but simply pulled the trigger. The stepfather was killed. Here his purpose was to be quickest on the draw and at firing the gun. Death or serous injury was, however, a very likely consequence of such actions. In *Hancock* (1986) two striking miners pushed a large lump of concrete from a bridge on to the convoy of cars below carrying a miner to work. The concrete struck a taxi's windscreen and killed the driver. The defendants claimed they had not meant to kill or cause serious injury. Their plan was to drop the concrete in the middle lane of the carriageway (the convoy being in the nearside lane). Their aim had been to block the road and frighten the miner in order to prevent him getting to work. In *Woollin* (1998) a father lost his temper and threw his baby son across the room causing the child to hit his head on something hard and die. He admitted that he had realised there was a risk of serious injury, but claimed he had not meant to kill or cause serious injury to the child.

The defendants in these cases were all found guilty of murder at their trials. On appeal, the House of Lords ultimately affirmed the murder conviction in *Hyam* (1975) but reduced the defendants' liability to manslaughter in the other three cases. It is, however, by no means clear that Mrs Hyam was indeed sufficiently blameworthy to be classified as a murderess—or, alternatively, that the defendants in the other three cases deserved to escape liability for murder.

Leaving aside, for the moment, cases of vehicular killings and infanticide, the central problem for the law has thus been one of devising a criterion for distinguishing the worst cases as murder from the remaining unlawful homicides which are classified as manslaughter and carry the lesser stigma and punishment of a maximum of life imprisonment (as opposed to mandatory life imprisonment for murder). To effect this classification the law has developed the concept of *malice aforethought*. Only if a defendant kills with this malice aforethought is he sufficiently blameworthy to be classified as a murderer. But what does "malice aforethought" mean?

Originally the term bore its literal meaning. There had to be "malice" in the sense of spite or ill-will and the killing has to be "aforethought" in that it must have been planned or premeditated. However, it was soon realised that this was too narrow a definition for murder and the term "malice aforethought" was expanded to become a mere technical label, describing those perceived to be sufficiently blameworthy to deserve hanging (or, since 1965, the fixed mandatory penalty of life imprisonment for murder). The degree of expansion of the concept has varied over the years, such inconsistency meaning that a "murderer" of one year might only be guilty of manslaughter in another year, or vice versa. Mrs Hyam, for instance, was convicted of murder in 1974; today she would almost certainly only be convicted of manslaughter.

Nevertheless, despite such variations in precise meaning, it is clear that for the last century, at least, the crime of murder has not been limited to those who kill intentionally. The law has also sought to embrace within the category "murder" those who have acted with extreme recklessness on the basis that such gross recklessness evidences indifference to the value of human life and a willingness to kill which can be as reprehensible as most intentional killings. In the United States there has been an open articulation of such a view with the Model Penal Code (1962) stating that it is murder to kill another "recklessly under circumstances manifesting extreme indifference to the value of human life" (section 210.1(1)(b)) but only manslaughter when a criminal homicide is "committed recklessly" (section 210.3).

In England, however, malice aforethought, the dividing line between murder and manslaughter, has never been openly and honestly defined in such a manner but the law has adopted a variety of devices to try to achieve the same result. Thus it has long been the law than an *intention to cause grievous bodily harm* suffices for the *mens rea* of murder. The most acceptable rationale of this rule is that a defendant who intends really serious bodily harm is running a grave risk that death might result from his actions; such excessive risk-taking deserves to be punished as murder. Secondly, until 1957, if one killed while engaged in committing a felony which was "known to be dangerous to life, and likely in itself to cause death" *(Serné, 1887)* one became guilty of murder under the "felony-murder rule". This, of course, was simply another way of punishing extreme recklessness. Indeed, under the Model Penal Code's formulation the commission of a listed dangerous felony raises a presumption of the requisite high degree of recklessness required for murder. Thirdly, the law achieved its desired result of punishing gross recklessness as murder by some rather unsubtle semantic trickery. The House of Lords in *Smith* (1961) and two of their Lordships in *Hyam* (1975) stated that murder was a "crime of intention" and then proceeded to give the word "intention" a meaning broad enough to encompass cases of extreme recklessness. However, two other members of the House of Lords in *Hyam* (1975) (Lords Cross and Kilbrandon) were prepared to rise above such sophistry and admit openly that murder could be committed by gross recklessness and without an intention to kill. The majority in *Hyam* (1975) held that this requisite degree of extreme recklessness for malice aforethought (whatever its formal nomenclature) was satisfied when the defendant foresaw death or grievous bodily harm as a highly probable result of her actions.

Such an approach has been subjected to fierce criticism on two fronts. First, it is argued that intentional killings are morally more reprehensible than killings by gross recklessness and that the special label "murder" should be reserved for the very worst killings, the intentional killings. Secondly, if the distinction between murder and manslaughter is one between extreme recklessness and recklessness, one is forced to draw very fine lines on the continuum of risk-taking. It is rather like distinguishing between a long piece of string and a very long piece of string. No clear principled basis for the distinction exists. The result is a blurring at the edges of both murder and manslaughter and in this "grey area" it becomes impossible to predict with any certainty whether defendants like those in *Hyam* (1975) *Moloney* (1985), *Hancock* (1986) and *Woollin* (1998) are guilty of murder or manslaughter.

The House of Lords has partially responded to these criticisms. In *Moloney* (1985) the House firmly ruled that murder was a crime of intention. Gross recklessness in the form of foresight would not suffice. The *mens rea* of murder requires proof of either an intention to kill or an intention to cause grievous bodily harm. Nothing less will suffice. At first sight such an approach seems attractive and to have simplified the law greatly. However, one is still left with the central problem of defining intention with sufficient precision to enable murder to be distinguished clearly from manslaughter. As was seen earlier (pp. 58–65) *Moloney* (1985), *Hancock* (1986) and *Woollin* (1998) have left the law on this point in a state of some confusion. There is arguably now no general definition of intention, its meaning being entirely a matter for the jury to determine. The result is that the line between murder and manslaughter is more blurred than ever before; it has become even more difficult to predict whether defendants, such as those in the leading cases, are guilty of murder or manslaughter. Reading between the lines, the House of Lords appears determined to have its cake and eat it. Murder is a "crime of intention" but maximum flexibility is retained by not defining intention to ensure that juries can still legitimately convict of murder those felt to be deserving of that label even if such persons did not actually mean to kill or cause grievous bodily harm. This is an intolerable position. If murder is to be reserved as a crime of intention, intention should be defined so as to demarcate murder from manslaughter. On the other hand, if those who act with gross recklessness are felt to deserve the label "murder", then this should be stated explicitly. Despite the efforts of the Court of Appeal in *Nedrick* (1986) and the House of Lords in *Woollin* (1998), it is clear that the House of Lords is not going to adopt either course. It is therefore incumbent upon Parliament to take the initiative in this regard.

A final criticism relating to the *mens rea* of murder must be mentioned. If the crime and label "murder" is to be reserved for the "worst" killings and if these worst killings are intentional killings, then there is a strong case for arguing that the *mens rea* of murder should be limited to an intention to kill or, at the very least, an intention "to cause serious personal harm and being aware that he may cause death" (Law Commission, Draft Criminal Code, 1989). Yet it is clear that a mere intention to cause grievous bodily harm will suffice for murder (*Cunningham*, 1982). There seems little justification for such an approach. It is difficult to see that this species of risk-taking is any worse or more dangerous than the other forms of risk-taking. Under the present law, if one intends to break one's victim's leg (grievous bodily harm) but instead she is killed, one is guilty of murder. But if one sets fire to a house foreseeing the *death* of the occupants as *likely*, one is only guilty of manslaughter. This is plainly absurd. Either all forms of extreme risk-taking should constitute murder, or none should. One cannot pick and choose between categories of risk-taking in such an indiscriminate manner.

Finally, a brief word needs to be said about the punishment for murder for adults. While all convicted murderers must be sentenced to life imprisonment, they seldom actually remain in prison for their whole lives. The judge, in imposing life imprisonment, can recommend a minimum period which in his or her view should elapse before the offender can be released. Thus when in *Sutcliffe* (1981) the "Yorkshire Ripper" was sentenced to life imprisonment for murder, the trial judge recommended that he spend at least 30 years before being considered for release. In all other cases the trial judge will still specify a tariff period: an indication to the Home Secretary how long he or she feels the offender should serve. The usual length of the tariff is 14 years' imprisonment which may be increased or reduced to allow for aggravating and mitigating features (*Practice Statement (Juveniles: Murder)*, 2000). Thereafter, the real sentencing power passes to the Home Secretary who can, at any stage after a recommendation by the Parole Board and the Lord Chief Justice, release the offender. Such advice is not binding. For instance, the Home Secretary recently increased the tariff on Myra Hindley, the notorious "Moors" murderess who had already served 33 years in prison, to a "whole life tariff". Indeed, a whole life tariff has been imposed on 30 occasions since 1988 and the House of Lords has upheld the legality of such discretionary power by the Home Secretary (*Secretary of State for the Home Dept, Ex Parte Hindley*, 2000). It is surely inappropriate for such a decision which involves "assum[ing] a quasi-judicial role by reviewing the offender's criminal desert as distinct from any risk presented by his or her release on parole" (Blom-Cooper and Morris, 1999) to be made in private by a member of the Executive. Despite these objections the European Court of Human Rights has declared that the mandatory sentence for adult murderers is not in breach of Article 5 or Article 6 of the Convention *(Wynne v. United Kingdom,* 1994). Even when released by the Home Secretary such an offender is never entirely free: for the remainder of his life he is "on licence", that is, he is subject to supervision by a probation officer and may be recalled to prison at any stage should his conduct give cause for concern and suggest that he might be a threat to society.

Because murders vary considerably—from deliberate cold-blooded killings to "mercy killings"—it has been argued that the automatic sentence of life imprisonment for all murderers is inappropriate; the judge ought to be able to impose any sentence which would accurately reflect the gravity of the crime. Such a proposal would mean, however, that for most practical purposes there would be little distinction between murder and manslaughter. Whether these two crimes should in fact be merged into one single offence will be considered at the end of this section, after the crime of manslaughter has been examined.

While the crime of murder is meant to be limited to the most reprehensible killings, the crime of *manslaughter* is an extremely broad "dustbin category" covering most unlawful killings that are not murder. There are several categories of manslaughter each with its own technical rules but all sharing the same common premise that the defendant is blameworthy in some way, but not sufficiently blameworthy to be classified as a murderer. The degree of blameworthiness can vary enormously: the killing might only just fall short of murder or, alternatively, it might be little more than an accidental killing and only just criminal. These differing degrees of culpability can be reflected by the sentence imposed. The judge may impose any sentence up to a maximum of life imprisonment.

Manslaughters are traditionally classified as being either "voluntary" or "involuntary". Voluntary manslaughter is committed where the defendant does possess the necessary "malice aforethought" for murder but is regarded as having a reduced level of blameworthiness because of the existence of a specified excuse, namely, provocation, diminished responsibility, or because the killing was pursuant to a suicide pact (see earlier, pp. 103–107, 119–126).

Involuntary manslaughter, on the other hand, is regarded as less serious than murder because the defendant does not act with malice aforethought. He or she has a less blameworthy state of mind—but there must nevertheless be some blame. This requisite blame can be established in one of three ways:

First, there is *reckless manslaughter*. Where the defendant subjectively foresees a risk of death or serious injury (but the degree of foresight fails to come within the *Woollin* (1998) test of intention required for murder), there will be liability for manslaughter. As the law of murder has been progressively narrowed with tighter tests of intention, so this category of manslaughter has been correspondingly broadened. The existence and parameters of this basis of liability are uncontroversial. Such killings are the near-neighbours of murder and should be treated and punished as such. Research suggests that this species is the most common route to a manslaughter conviction. Apart from cases where subjective manslaughter is proved at trial, it covers situations where the defendant is charged with murder but the jury convict of manslaughter or the appellate courts substitute a verdict of manslaughter or where the defendant pleads guilty to manslaughter having a plea of not guilty to murder accepted (Clarkson, 2000).

Secondly, under the doctrine of *constructive manslaughter*, if the defendant is engaged in committing an unlawful act (for example, a common assault) from which death results, the law will readily impose liability insisting only that the unlawful act be slightly dangerous in that it must expose the victim to the (objective) risk of some physical harm. This is the successor to the old "misdemeanour-manslaughter rule" which was the correlative of the old "felony-murder rule" (see p. 203). However, any type of criminal unlawful act will now suffice as long as it is criminal *per se*; it must be criminal for some independent reason—and not simply that it is a *prima facie* lawful act (for example, driving) being performed in a negligent manner (*Andrews v. DPP*, 1937). The defendant is blamed for engaging in such a dangerous unlawful act in the first place. If no death resulted he would be blamed and punished for that unlawful act itself. But if his actions have additionally caused the death of another, then this blame, coupled with the aggravated harm, leads to liability for the more serious offence of manslaughter. For instance, in *Larkin* (1943) the defendant brandished a razor at a man in order to terrify him. His drunk mistress fell against the razor, cut her throat and died. Here there was an unlawful act (an assault by intentionally terrifying the man); it was dangerous in that it exposed the victim to a risk of some physical harm (brandishing razors at persons who have been drinking heavily must always be dangerous); the defendant was accordingly liable for manslaughter.

Constructive manslaughter has been strongly criticised in that there need be no correspondence between the defendant's culpability and the resultant death which might be entirely fortuitous. It is argued that Larkin, for example, only meant to assault his victim and so should only be liable for the crime of assault. The fact that someone died is "pure chance" for which Larkin should not have been held responsible. On the other hand, constructive manslaughter can be defended. Such defendants have chosen to engage in criminal, dangerous activity: usually a violent attack. They have changed their "normative position *vis-à-vis* the risk of adverse consequences of that wrongdoing" (Horder, 1995). They have deliberately engaged in a morally different course of action compared to those who act lawfully and inadvertently cause death. The resultant death is not "pure luck". By committing an unlawful act and risking injury, they have "made their own luck" (Horder, 1995) and should be held responsible for any injuries—even death—that result (see p. 162). While the defendant's culpability does not "correspond" with the death, there is "relevant culpability". It is arguable, however, that as manslaughter is largely a crime of violence, there can only be relevant culpability if the defendant has chosen to engage in a violent attack on the victim—in the sense of attacking them intending or foreseeing some injury. In so acting, defendants bring themselves within this family of violence and should be held responsible for the luck they have created (Clarkson, 2000). On this basis, perhaps, constructive manslaughter should be narrowed to exclude cases, such as those where the unlawful act involves the supply or injection of drugs (for example, *Cato*, 1976), that do not involve a violent attack. For instance, in *England* (1995) the defendant set fire to a car in the middle of the night being completely unaware that a young man was asleep in the back of the car. The young man was burnt to death and the defendant convicted of manslaughter. However, this could be regarded as a case where there was no relevant culpability (for constructive manslaughter) and the death was "pure luck". The unlawful act was an attack on property and not a violent attack upon a person. The fortuitous death should not have been permitted retrospectively to alter the characterisation of the moral quality of the defendant's actions so as to bring him within the family of violence.

The third species of involuntary manslaughter is *gross negligence manslaughter*. If the defendant is engaged in a *prima facie* lawful activity, such as treating a patient or taking care of an aged aunt, from which death results (and legal causation is established), liability for manslaughter will ensue only if it is established that he or she was grossly negligent. This had long been the law (*Bateman*, 1925; *Andrews v. DPP*, 1937) but in *Seymour* (1983) it was held that the *Lawrence* (1982) recklessness test applied here. However, *Seymour* (1983) was overruled in *Adomako* (1995) and the gross negligence test restored. Under this test where the defendant owes a duty of care to the victim and breaches that duty in a grossly negligent manner causing death, there can be liability for manslaughter. Whether there has been gross negligence is "supremely a jury question" and the essence of the matter is whether "having regard to the risk of death involved, the conduct of the defendant was so bad in all the circumstances as to amount in their judgment to a criminal act or omission". This test is both broader and narrower than the *Lawrence* (1982) recklessness test that applied for a decade. It is broader in that a defendant who "rules out a risk" (above pp. 67–68) can nevertheless still be convicted of gross negligence manslaughter. It is narrower in that it appears there must be gross negligence as to death, whereas under the *Lawrence* (1982) recklessness test, as applied to manslaughter, it was sufficient that there was an obvious and serious risk of causing physical injury. The House of Lords in *Adomako* (1995) was clearly concerned that the *Lawrence* (1982) test was too elaborate and complex for juries to comprehend and apply. In its place we now have no standards at all other than whether the jury thinks the defendant's conduct was "so bad" as to justify a conviction for manslaughter. This approach is circular in that the jury is invited to convict of a crime if they think the defendant's conduct was criminal. This amounts to juries deciding questions of law and leads to problems with prosecutors being uncertain whether to prosecute and creates the danger of inconsistent verdicts. We saw with murder that the approach of the courts in interpreting "intention" was to allow maximum flexibility to the jury. The same is now true of gross negligence manslaughter.

Many commentators are critical of gross negligence man-slaughter on the basis that criminal liability and punishment should be linked to moral guilt which they perceive as involving only blaming those who have chosen to cause a harm in the sense of intending or knowing that the harm could occur. However, as argued earlier (p. 69), moral guilt need not neces-sarily be linked to cognition. We can blame people for making choices even when the possibility of that harm is not in the forefront of their minds. By not considering an obvious risk of death, they are demonstrating an attitude of indifference (Duff, 1990). For example, the builder who absent-mindedly tosses a brick on to a crowded street below and causes the death of a passer-by has prioritised his own interests. Whether he is upset, angry or day-dreaming, he has allowed his own concerns to prevail over the safety-interests of others. Their safety is not sufficiently important to him. Whether there should be liability in all cases of such inadvertence (irrespective of the degree of injury caused) is controversial (see p. 69), but where the harm risked and caused is as serious as death, the prevailing view now is that there is sufficient culpability to justify a manslaugh-ter conviction (Law Commission, 1996).

Gross negligence manslaughter is the category utilised in cases of "motor manslaughter" and "corporate manslaughter". Whether this is the most appropriate way of dealing with such killings is discussed below.

Finally, in relation to involuntary manslaughter, it should be stressed that this is a single broad offence that can be committed in one of the three ways discussed, but the prosecution does not have to specify which category is being charged; different jurors can convict on different bases—and, of course, in cases where the defendant has pleaded guilty, the species will remain unknown. This is particularly problematic in that the sentencing judge (and the Court of Appeal when reviewing the sentence) will not necessarily know the factual basis of the conviction or the guilty plea. The implications of this uncertainty will be assessed shortly (p. 217).

The next category of homicide is *vehicular homicide* of which there are two species: causing death by dangerous driving (Road Traffic Act 1988, section 1, as amended) and causing death by careless driving when under the influence of drink or drugs (Road Traffic Act 1988, section 3A, as amended). Pre-viously drivers who killed with their motor vehicles were simply charged with manslaughter. Juries, however, were extremely loath to convict for this offence with its serious stigma. They could relate to such defendants in a way that they could not emphasise with defendants in other manslaughter cases such as *Larkin* (1943); most jurors drive cars (or are driven by family and friends) but they do not brandish razors in a threatening manner. To combat this "there but for the grace of God, go I" thinking, the two separate offences with different labels were introduced. Originally, these crimes carried a maximum sentence of five years' imprisonment. Since then there has been a hardening of public opinion against dangerous motorists who cause death and in 1993 the maximum sentence was increased to 10 years' imprisonment which has resulted in a general increase in the severity of sentences imposed as all sentences "must take their colour" from what the maximum sentence is (*Attorney-General's Reference* (*No. 1 of 1994*) (*Day*), 1995).

In "very grave cases" (*Jennings*, 1982) it is still possible to charge a defendant with "motor manslaughter", governed by the *Adomako* (1995) test of gross negligence although such prosecutions have become relatively rare. However, the shift in public attitudes towards road deaths has led to calls for the abolition of the special offences, the argument being that these killings should all be charged as manslaughter in order to emphasise their seriousness.

There are several reasons for resisting such calls and for retaining the separate vehicular homicide offences. Most important, there are fair labelling and cultural reasons to suggest that the context in which such killings take place is of sufficient moral significance to condemn these deaths differently. The use of motor-vehicles, despite their inherent dangers, is so widespread and accepted that we assign responsibility to (even bad) drivers differently to those who cause deaths in different contexts. Their wrong is "situationally relevant" (Lloyd-Bostock, 1979) to ourselves. We can identify with the actions more than in other cases of manslaughter. Drivers do not have harm to victims as part of their reason for acting and, accordingly, such cases can be regarded as belonging to a different family of offence from murder and manslaughter. Secondly, although empirically unproven, juries might still be unwilling to convict of manslaughter which could result in these cases simply being charged as dangerous or careless driving (as most already are) which would have the effect of undermining the seriousness of causing death by motor-vehicles. Finally, there can be no sentencing reasons for abolition so that the higher range of sentences for manslaughter can be utilised. Research into 91 reported sentencing appeal cases between 1994 and mid-1999 revealed that even in the very worst cases, a sentence in excess of five years' imprisonment was only confirmed or imposed in five cases, the highest being seven years' imprisonment (Clarkson, 2000).

Indeed, one could go further and argue that the option, in exceptional cases, of motor manslaughter should be abolished. Allowing alternative convictions dependent on the standard of driving simply confuses the law's communicative endeavours. Further, a sentence in excess of the ten year maximum available for the special offences is exceedingly unlikely. For example, in *Sherwood and Button* (1995) seven years' detention was imposed in "almost as bad a case of motor manslaughter as can be envisaged". Of course, manslaughter (or murder) must remain the appropriate offence when the defendant uses a motor-vehicle as a dangerous weapon to attack a victim. There can be no moral distinction between using a car or a gun to attack a victim. Such cases do not involve the normal context of driving offences. These are attacks classically within the family of violence and must be treated as such.

A final homicide offence deserves brief mention. Where a mother kills her own child who is under 12 months of age and at the time of the killing "the balance of her mind was disturbed by reason of not having fully recovered from the effect of giving birth to the child or by reason of the effect of lactation consequent upon the birth of the child" (Infanticide Act 1938, section 1), the mother is guilty of *infanticide* and not murder. This offence carries a maximum penalty of life imprisonment. The rationale of this offence is similar to that of voluntary manslaughter. Such "disturbed" mothers are regarded as having a partial excuse for their actions; their mental imbalance renders them less blameworthy; less punishment is deserved. In practice, a probation order is the normal sentence.

While there is some evidence suggesting a link between childbirth and mental illness (Maier-Katkin and Ogle, 1993), the link is, at best, tenuous (West, 1965). It appears that most of the young babies killed are part of the "battered baby syndrome" whose killers are often suffering from environmental stress, coupled with various personality disorders totally unrelated to the effects of childbirth and lactation. In recognition of this the Law Commission (1989) in the Draft Criminal Code proposed expanding the definition of infanticide to include cases where "the balance of the mother's mind is disturbed by reason of the effect of giving birth or of circumstances consequent upon the birth".

This proposal is somewhat limited. These pressures apply just as strongly to mothers coping with older children and to some fathers—yet no excuse is available in such cases. The provision still requires mental disturbance to be established despite research revealing that roughly half the women convicted of infanticide are not suffering from any identifiable mental disorder at all (d'Orban, 1979).

An alternative proposal would be the abolition of this special offence. Mentally unbalanced mothers (and fathers) would then have to plead diminished responsibility if they killed their children (Butler Committee, 1975). This would ensure that the focus was on the excusing condition (the mental abnormality) rather than on the somewhat fortuitous age of the child and gender of the parent. If such a solution were adopted, one would have to recognise that in many cases there would be insufficient evidence to support a finding of diminished responsibility (Mackay, 1993) and, accordingly, there would be convictions for murder or manslaughter in cases which are now infanticide. Should this be so?

The homicide rate for children under the age of one is almost four times higher than among the general population. Nearly half of these babies are killed by their mothers. (Women only commit about 10 per cent of homicides generally.) In 44 per cent of cases the mother is not even prosecuted (Wilczynski and Morris, 1993) and, as already noted, in almost all successful prosecutions the woman is given a probation order. This supports the view that the criminal justice system "medicalises" women. Mothers are assumed to be "nurturing, caring and altruistic" and therefore must be "mad" to kill their own child (Wilczynski and Morris, 1993). Abolition of the offence would be a step towards treating women as fully responsible for their actions. Having a small baby can cause enormous stresses for both parents—but so can other pressures such as unemployment and homelessness. The law does not provide special defences in these latter cases and in the absence of an abnormality of mind (for diminished responsibility) it is difficult to see why killing one's own baby should be regarded as such a lesser offence.

(iii) Conclusion

The boundary between murder and manslaughter is forever shifting to and fro as the tide of public and judicial opinion ebbs and flows. There are countless killers (and not just the legally famous ones such as Mrs Hyam and Mr Woollin) who, as the law has vacillated, are murderers one year and manslayers the next. In many cases where a murder conviction could probably have been obtained, prosecutors are content to charge with manslaughter, or accept pleas of guilty to manslaughter, secure in the knowledge that a substantial sentence (even life imprisonment) will be imposed. Similarly, juries are often unwilling, except in the worst cases, to convict of murder and thereby tie the judge's hands as to sentence. A manslaughter conviction enables the judge to take account of all the circumstances and context of the killing before imposing an appropriate sentence. The result is that of those indicted for murder in 1999–2000, only 46 per cent were actually convicted of murder (Criminal Statistics, 1999).

As a consequence of this difficulty in distinguishing murder from manslaughter and because, since the abolition of the death penalty, one can receive the same sentence for both crimes, there have been calls for the abolition of both these offences and their replacement by a new single offence of unlawful homicide. The judge would have complete discretion as to sentence and could reflect the exact gravity of the offence in the sentence. Such an approach would have the significant advantage of ensuring that only the "worst" cases received life imprisonment. Such defendants would in fact spend substantial periods of time in prison, thus increasing public confidence in the life sentence rather than the present "devaluation" of the meaning of a life sentence by the release of some such persons after a short period of time—persons who never deserved the label and punishment for murder in the first place. This approach would also put an end to the present plea-bargaining that occurs—but only in some murder cases. And finally, the somewhat odd excuses of provocation, diminished responsibility and suicide pact, which exist primarily to ameliorate the harshness of the mandatory penalty for murder, could possibly be abolished and relegated to being mitigating factors relevant to sentencing.

Such arguments, however, overlook three major objections. First, there is the moral significance and deterrent value attached to the label "murder". It is surely not appropriate to lump together under the morally uninformative title "unlawful homicide" deliberate, cold-blooded killers and "fools" such as the defendant in *Lamb* (1967). One of the functions of having categories of offences is to communicate to the public the differing degrees of rejection or unacceptability of certain conduct. Such symbolic messages would not be conveyed if the distinction between murder and manslaughter were collapsed.

Secondly, such a new single offence would mean that a judge would generally receive no guidance from the jury as to important questions of fact, such as whether the defendant intended death or was provoked. Such matters would only be relevant in determining the appropriate level of sentence and unless there were a *"Newton*-hearing" (special hearing to determine relevant facts before sentencing) this would be left entirely to the judge. Thirdly, and finally, such a new offence would greatly increase the judge's discretionary powers of sentencing. We shall see in the final section of this book that over the past two decades there has been mounting criticism of such discretionary powers and attempts made at curbing them. With this background, proposals to reform the substantive criminal law in a manner that would significantly increase the judge's discretionary sentencing powers must be unacceptable.

With the increased recognition of the importance of fair labelling in criminal law other critics of the present law have accepted the need to distinguish between homicide offences. The crime of murder must be retained; its very label, coupled with the mandatory sentence of life imprisonment, emphasises the special stigma attached to the crime and underlines the "dreadfulness" of the offence. However, many argue that the present murder/manslaughter divide is inadequate to distinguish between the many different types of homicide with sufficient precision. Each offence is simply too broad, encompassing too many different degrees of culpability and ignoring the widely differing contexts in which unlawful killings can take place.

Accordingly, it could be suggested that English law follow the lead set by law in the United States and subdivide both murder and manslaughter into several specific separate offences, each carrying its own penalty. How could this be best achieved?

To date English law has proceeded primarily on the basis that offences should be classified according to the differing mental elements of the defendant. Thus, broadly speaking, murder is distinguished from manslaughter by the presence or absence of an intention to kill or cause grievous bodily harm. Such an approach could be extended. For instance, it is fairly common in the United States for first-degree murder to cover planned, premeditated killings with second-degree murder covering other intentional killings. Manslaughters could be similarly categorised. In New York, for instance, "intent to cause serious physical injury" is first-degree manslaughter while second-degree manslaughter covers "recklessly causing death"—and there is an even lesser offence, criminally negligent homicide, extending to killings with "criminal negligence" (NY Penal Law, sections 125.10–125.20 (McKinney)).

Such proposals are, however, fraught with difficulties and could simply exacerbate the present problem of distinguishing between degrees of *mens rea*. An alternative, bolder approach might be to recognise that offence seriousness need not necessarily be totally dependent on differing mental states. Other factors could be relevant. The prime candidates for capturing the essence of the wrongdoing in cases of unlawful killing (apart from the culpability of the defendant) are the method of the killing (for example, killing with a dangerous weapon, by torture or poison) or the context of the killing (for example, through a business operation, while driving on a road, during the commission of an unlawful act, contract killings or during an act of terrorism). Drawing on the experience of various states in the United States, other possible criteria could relate to the identity of the victim (killing a child or a police officer engaged in the performance of duty) or the identity of the killer (for example, a murderer confined in prison). Such an approach was effectively adopted in England "via the back door" with the Home Secretary openly adopting a policy, approved by the courts, of ensuring that certain categories of murderers (those who have killed police or prison officers, terrorist killings, murder during robbery or the sadistic or sexual murder of children) would not be released on licence until the expiry of at least twenty years (*Re Findlay*, 1984).

There would, however, be major problems involved in creating a myriad of specific offences along such lines in that it could lead to over-specificity: having too many specific offences could simply be morally confusing. Further, it is by no means clear that the various factors employed in the United States to distinguish offences are of sufficient moral significance to warrant separate treatment. For example, with regard to the method of killing, it is difficult to see the moral difference between attacking a victim with a wooden post or with a knife if in both situations there was an intention to kill. Or, to take a further example, why should killing a child be regarded as worse than killing an adult? All human life is equally valuable and the law should reflect this.

Fair labelling involves capturing the essence of particular wrongdoing in its paradigmatic form. Murder is the most serious crime and, particularly as long as the mandatory life sentence is retained, should be restricted to its paradigm: intentional killing. Aggravating factors such as the use of torture can be taken into account at the sentencing stage if the judge stipulates a minimum period to be served or at the executive level when the decision to release on licence is taken. The clear moral message encapsulated in this paradigm of murder should not be muddied by any sub-division of the offence. Further, to limit murder to the "worst" cases, the grievous bodily harm rule should be abolished.

However, when moving on to manslaughter and other unlawful killings, there is a strong argument for some sub-division of the present broad offence. Fair labelling involves not only capturing what is morally significant about the wrongdoing, but also structuring offences to reflect a hierarchy of seriousness. The present offence of manslaughter fails this test. In covering killings that range from just short of murder to little more than accidents, the crime label has become morally uninformative. Further, the relative seriousness of the various killings within this broad category remains unmarked and runs the risk of allowing too much discretionary power to sentencers. This problem is exacerbated by the fact that the offence can be committed in various ways (voluntary manslaughter and the different ways of establishing involuntary manslaughter) and the sentencer will not necessarily know the factual basis of the conviction or the basis upon which the defendant pleaded guilty (for example, provocation or constructive manslaughter).

Given these considerations, there is a clear case for the creation of specific offences covering the present territory of manslaughter and other unlawful killings such as vehicular homicide. In structuring such offences not only the culpability of the defendant but also certain contexts in which the killing occurs could be relevant. On this basis it could be argued (Clarkson, 2000) that involuntary and vehicular homicide could be divided into the following specific offences, each bearing its own label and level of punishment; (i) reckless killing; (ii) killing by attack; (iii) grossly careless or negligent killing; (iv) vehicular killing; (iv) corporate killing. The argument for each of these specific offences has already been canvassed. Additionally, assuming they were all to be retained, there would be further offences (separately labelled and punished) covering what is now voluntary manslaughter and the offence of infanticide. In relation to involuntary manslaughter, a Home Office Consultation Paper (2000) has put forward proposals not dissimilar to these suggestions. Acceptance of either of these proposals would mark a significant step forward towards the rational reconstruction of the English law of homicide.

5. PROPERTY OFFENCES

(i) Introduction

The political and economic structure of our society depends to a very large extent upon the concept of private property. Thus legal rights and interests in property such as ownership and possession are encouraged and protected. Unauthorized interferences with such rights and interests are seen as threatening the socio-economic foundations of the state. To ensure maximum protection of the proprietary system, English law has developed a formidable array of property offences aimed at protecting every conceivable interest in property. To list but some of the better known property offences, one finds: theft, numerous offences involving criminal deception and fraud; taking a motor vehicle or other conveyance without authority; abstracting electricity; blackmail; handling stolen goods; robbery; burglary; forgery; criminal damage—and so on.

The common denominator in these offences is that they involve an interference with the property interests of the victim. Both the victim and the community at large are harmed. The victim is deprived of his or her interest in property—or threatened with such deprivation. Property interests are often referred to as "extensions of the personality". An attack upon a victim's property interests can be seen as analogous to a personal attack: his or her "space" has been invaded; he or she has been rendered impotent by the actions of a dishonest person. Insurance, like a medical operation after a physical attack, might help to "heal the wound" but does not alter the fact that the victim has been directly harmed.

The community at large is also harmed by property offences. Apart from threatening the economic base of the social system and threatening the security interests of society, vast resources are expended on the prevention and apprehension of property offenders. Ultimately, the real cost of property crime is borne by the public or sections thereof. The cost of much shoplifting, employee theft and commercial fraud is simply passed on to the consumer. If these crimes were not committed, goods in stores could be anything up to five per cent cheaper than at present. Also, while insurance companies underwrite much of the economic loss in property offences, they are not charities: the real cost is borne by insured persons in increased premiums.

Despite such common features, however, each of the above listed property offences involves its own distinctive wrong and harm. What each of these wrongs and harms is, and whether such features are sufficiently distinctive to justify the wide proliferation of separate offences, is the subject-matter of the remainder of this chapter.

Before starting this examination, two further points must be made. First, most of the property offences are now statutory, the Theft Act 1968 being the major statute and covering a large number of the offences. It is, however, buttressed by other legislation, notably the Theft Act 1978, the Criminal Damage Act 1971 and the Forgery and Counterfeiting Act 1981. Other important offences are contained in specialist legislation such as the offence of fraudulent trading in section 458 of the Companies Act 1985. Much of the work here then is a matter of statutory interpretation. It is nevertheless an instructive task in helping to inform us as to how our courts have coped with an area of law beginning to approximate a code. Such understanding is particularly important in an era that could culminate in a codification of the whole of the criminal law (Law Commission, 1989).

Secondly, the various property offences involve interference with other persons' *rights or interests in property*. It is always necessary therefore to ascertain whether these other persons actually do have such rights or interests in property. The answer to such questions lies in established areas of the civil law: the law of property, contract and quasi-contract. In one of the leading House of Lords decisions on theft, *Morris* (1984), Lord Roskill deprecated over-reliance on technical civil law concepts. For instance, whether a contract is void or voidable was "so far as possible" not a relevant question in relation to the law of theft. On one hand, this approach is to be applauded. The imposition of criminal liability with its concomitant punishment should depend on fundamental issues—such as blameworthiness and the causing of harm; it should not depend on complex, and sometimes controversial, fine points of civil law relating to the passing of property. On the other hand, however, to commit a property offence, some other person must have some legally recognized interest in that property. If no other person has any such interest in the property no crime can be committed as, generally, an owner is free to use and abuse his or her own property to their heart's content. Therefore, it becomes crucial to establish whether the other person does have a legal interest in the property. How can this question be answered? By the jury, on a "common-sense" basis? Or by judges devising new definitions of established civil law concepts to be utilized in criminal cases? Or by ignoring Lord Roskill's exhortations and utilizing the civil law? It is these questions, and the law's inability to answer them, that have been a dominant feature in the interpretation of the various property offences, to an examination of which we now turn.

(ii) The main offences

Again it will be instructive to concentrate on a few offences, primarily theft. Brief consideration will then be given to the deception offences, robbery, burglary and handling stolen goods.

Dealing first with *theft*, section 1(1) of the Theft Act 1968 provides that a "person is guilty of theft if he dishonestly appropriates property belonging to another with the intention of permanently depriving the other of it".

The offence thus contains five elements: (i) appropriation, (ii) property, (iii) belonging to another (these three constitute the *actus reus*); (iv) dishonesty, (v) intention of permanent deprivation (these two constitute the *mens rea*). Each of these elements is defined (or sometimes merely "illustrated"), to varying extents, by sections 2–6 of the Theft Act 1968.

Section 3(1) defines an *appropriation* as an assumption of the rights of an owner. It is necessary that the defendant treat the goods as his own: he must regard them as his to take away, use or abuse. This test of appropriation is easily satisfied in the paradigmatic theft where the thief surreptitiously takes the property of another. He will deal with the property as he chooses and is thus clearly assuming the rights of an owner.

Problems have however arisen in situations where the defendant has done nothing objectively or observably *wrong* because he has been acting with the owner's consent. This will usually occur in one of two ways. First, the defendant might have consent to deal with the property in a certain way but, in doing this, he forms a secret intention to steal the property. For instance, in *Eddy v. Niman* (1981) the defendant in a supermarket placed goods in the store's wire basket with an intention of stealing them. At this stage he was acting with the store's consent; by placing the goods in the wire basket he was doing precisely what the store expected him to do. However, because of his secret intention, he was, in a sense, assuming the rights of owner: he had decided not to pay for the goods; he was going to make off with them when and how he chose; he was dealing with the goods as if they were his and not the supermarket's property.

The second type of problem situation is where the defendant practices a deception with the result that the victim voluntarily hands over the property, that is, "consents" to part with the property. For example, in the House of Lords case of *Lawrence* (1972) the defendant, a taxi driver, grossly overcharged an Italian who had just arrived in this country. The Italian, on getting into the taxi, had offered the defendant £1. The defendant, stating that this was insufficient, helped himself to a further £6 from the Italian's wallet. The Italian was holding out his wallet and so "consenting" to the removal of the further £6. The correct fare was approximately 50p. The defendant was charged with theft of "the approximate sum of £6".

Until recently the courts adopted an inconsistent approach to such cases. In *Lawrence* (1972) it was held that the taxi-driver appropriated the money when he took it from the wallet and that it was irrelevant whether the owner consented to his taking the property. On the other hand, the House of Lords in *Morris* (1984) ruled that an appropriation must involve the doing of something *objectively inconsistent* with the rights of the owner. An appropriation was "not an act expressly or impliedly authorized by the owner but an act by way of adverse interference with or usurpation of those rights". So there would be an appropriation in a case such as *McPherson* (1973) where the defendant in a supermarket placed two bottles of whisky in her own shopping bag—an act she was not authorized to do—but there would not be (and was not) an appropriation in *Eddy v. Niman* (1981) because the defendant was not doing anything unauthorized. In *Morris* (1984) itself, a dishonest shopper switched the price labels on goods and then placed them in the trolley. The shopper here was doing something he was not supposed to do and was assuming the rights of an owner in respect of the more expensive item—or, at any rate, he was assuming *some* of the rights of the owner. This was held to suffice for an appropriation.

However, in *Gomez* (1993) the House of Lords endorsed *Lawrence* (1972) and held that there could be an appropriation in all the above cases where the victim has consented to the defendant taking the property. In this case the defendant, an assistant manager of a shop, lied to the manager that two cheques were valid with the result that £16,000 worth of goods were supplied to a rogue. Despite the manager's consent to the rogue receiving the property, this was held to be an appropriation. There was no need for the defendant to do anything objectively wrong; there did not have to be an act of "adverse interference" with the rights of the owner. In *Hinks* (2000) this approach was confirmed yet again by the House of Lords and extended to cover situations where a gift is validly made and the donee acquires an indefeasible title to property. The person receiving the gift appropriates it because she will be assuming the rights of owner over it. In this case a woman became friendly with a man of limited intelligence who gave her sums of money amounting to £60,000. It was held that receipt of these gifts amounted to an appropriation, irrespective of the validity of the gifts; it is irrelevant whether the conduct is wrongful under civil law. The only issue for the jury was whether, given the man's limited intelligence, the defendant was dishonest in accepting the gifts (the jury had found she was).

Accordingly, an appropriation is now committed in a wide variety of situations. All that is required is that the defendant assume *any* of the rights of an owner—which amounts to no more than doing *anything* that an owner is entitled to do. Even touching goods in a supermarket can be an appropriation. Offering to sell goods even without touching them can be an appropriation (*Pitham and Hehl*, 1976). The only thing that prevents this and numerous other everyday transactions from being theft is the absence of dishonesty.

This whole approach is open to several objections. First, it effectively reduces theft to a "thought-crime"—an unacceptable notion (see earlier, p. 20). It is highly anomalous that a person who has not yet done anything wrong (as in *Eddy v. Niman*,

1981) is already a thief by virtue of his or her criminal intentions. At such a point he or she has done nothing manifestly criminal; no harm has yet occurred. How can one ever be liable for an attempt to commit theft in such circumstances? Secondly, the idea that receipt of a valid gift amounts to an appropriation almost beggars belief. On the facts of *Hinks* (2000) the woman might only have acquired a voidable title in civil law if there had been undue influence. The court, however, emphasized that the validity of the gift was irrelevant. Assuming the gifts to the woman were valid, she would have acquired an indefeasible title to the property and could have sued the man if he took the property back. It is highly unsatisfactory that there should be criminal liability in situations where no civil wrong has been committed and quite unacceptable to assert, as Lord Steyn did in *Hinks* (2000), that if there is a conflict between the civil and the criminal law, this could be because the civil law is defective. The law of theft is aimed at protecting interests in property. Such interests only exist in civil law. The criminal law should follow the contours of the civil law. Cases such as *Hinks* (2000) demonstrate how *all* the work in theft is being left to the concept of dishonesty, which, as we shall see shortly, is a highly elusive concept.

Thirdly, the defendants in *Lawrence* (1972) and *Gomez* (1993) both practised a deception as a result of which property was obtained. As we shall see, there is a special offence, obtaining property by deception contrary to section 15 of the Theft Act 1968, covering just such situations. The result of *Gomez* (1993) is that there is now an almost complete overlap between these two offences. In all such cases the prosecution has a complete discretion as to which offence to charge. This approach offends the principle of fair labelling whereby offences are labelled differently and punished differently (theft by a maximum of seven years' imprisonment and section 15 by a maximum of 10 years' imprisonment) for symbolic reasons to communicate the differing degrees of rejection or unacceptability of the different types of wrongdoing. Unless we were to collapse the distinction between most property offences (see below, pp. 235–240), these two offences should, as far as possible, remain distinct. The decisions in *Gomez* (1993) and *Hinks* (2000) can only be regarded as unfortunate.

Theft is concerned with the appropriation of property, and "property" is given a wide definition in section 4(1) so as to include "money and all other property, real or personal, including things in action and other tangible property". (A "thing in action" is non-physical property where one's rights can only be enforced by legal action, for example, a debt, copyright or shares in a company.) However, subsections (2)–(4) of section 4 severely limit the circumstances in which land, wild plants and wild creatures may be stolen.

The property must *belong to another*. This does not mean that the property must really belong to another in the sense that that other must own it. The law of theft aims to protect a wider range of interests than mere ownership and section 5 accordingly defines "belonging to another" in a wide and, at times, artificial manner. Property is "regarded as" belonging to any of the following persons: (i) one who has possession or control of the property (section 5(1)); (ii) one who has any proprietary right or interest in the property (section 5(1)); this includes the obvious instance of actually owning the property; (iii) where property is subject to a trust, one who has a right to enforce the trust (section 5(2)); (iv) one who gives property to another, placing the other under a legal obligation to deal with the property or its proceeds in a particular way (section 5(3)); (v) one who parts with property by mistake in circumstances where the recipient is under a legal obligation to make restoration of the property (section 5(4)).

It is in relation to this concept of "belonging to another" that the law has been faced with the necessity of introducing civil law concepts in deciding, for example, whether someone has a "proprietary right or interest" in the property, or whether he or she is owed a "legal obligation" by the defendant in respect of the property. For instance, in *Kaur v. Chief Constable for Hampshire* (1981) the defendant chose a pair of shoes from a rack of shoes marked at £6.99 per pair; one shoe was marked at £6.99 and the other £4.99. Without concealing either label she took the shoes to the cashier hoping to be charged the lower price—which she was. She paid the £4.99, placed the shoes in her shopping bag and left the store. She was charged with theft but her conviction was quashed on appeal. She had appropriated the shoes (under the law as it then stood) when, having paid for them, she placed them in her own shopping bag. But at that point she was not appropriating "property belonging to another": the cashier had authority to charge the price specified on the shoe; the cashier's mistake in charging £4.99 was not so fundamental as to destroy the validity of the contract; the contract was voidable; property passes under voidable contracts. Accordingly, the defendant was appropriating property belonging to herself and so not liable for theft.

One possible advantage to be derived from *Gomez* (1993) (even if the only one) is that by redefining the concept of appropriation such problems will now be reduced. Following *Gomez* (1993), the appropriation in *Kaur* (1981) would now occur when she took the shoes from the rack. At that point they would still clearly belong to the store. However, in other situations, these problems could remain. If one sees incorrectly priced goods in a shop behind the counter which one points out and are then wrapped and handed over by an assistant, the appropriation could be held to occur when the goods are handed over, by which time property would have passed. While in some cases (*Pitham and Hehl*, 1976) it has been held that merely pointing out property amounts to an appropriation, this has been in the context of the pointer having (or, at least claiming) power to deal with the property; the shop situation is somewhat different and it is highly unlikely that merely pointing out goods behind a counter in a store could amount to an appropriation.

In *Williams* (1980) the defendant, an enterprising but dishonest schoolboy, went to Stanley Gibbons and purchased some obsolete Yugoslav dinar for £7. He then went to the *bureau de change* at a department store and cashed in the obsolete dinar for some £107—a quick £100 profit on the transaction. His conviction for theft was upheld: he had appropriated the £107 when he received it from the *bureau de change* and placed it in his pocket. The cashier had made a fundamental mistake in handing over the money; the contract was thus void *ab initio*; property never passed to the defendant who had, accordingly, appropriated property belonging to another, namely, the store.

As already mentioned, Lord Roskill in *Morris* (1984) indicated that questions of civil law, such as whether contracts are void or voidable, should not be injected into the law of theft. But if such issues are excluded, on what basis can one decide whether property does "belong to another" in cases such as *Kaur v. Chief Constable for Hampshire* (1981) and *Williams* (1980)? As indicated earlier, the law of theft exists largely to regulate interests in property. It would be somewhat anomalous to define these interests in one manner for the purposes of the civil law and then to ignore that definition in the criminal law (as happened in *Hinks*, 2000) when one of the main objectives of the criminal law is to safeguard and uphold these same property interests as defined in the civil law. Lord Hobhouse, in a powerful dissenting judgment in *Hinks* (2000) dismissed this whole approach of ignoring the civil law as "simplistic and erroneous". It is interesting that the first reported case after *Morris* (1984) was *Walker* (1984) in which the Court of Appeal held that recourse to the civil law was "inevitable". To decide whether the property in that case "belonged to another", the trial judge should have explained the Sale of Goods Act 1979 to the jury.

What is the requisite degree of blameworthiness required for theft? *Mens rea* generally is taken to refer to intention, foresight, knowledge, etc., in relation to existing circumstances or the consequences of the defendant's actions. Such a typical *mens rea* element is indeed incorporated into theft in that the defendant must intend to deprive his victim permanently of his interest in the property. But, additionally, the defendant's conduct must be blameworthy in that her actions must be *dishonest*. This requirement that dishonesty be established is of central importance. With the wide interpretation of appropriation, many innocent everyday transactions satisfy all the other elements specified for theft. It is the requirement of "dishonesty" that is critical in determining which of these transactions should be regarded as theft.

Dishonesty is a moral concept. The taking of property must be one to which "moral obloquy can reasonably" be attached (*Feely*, 1973). The defendant can be fairly blamed for disregarding the value system inherent in the law of theft—a value system that underwrites the importance of preserving property rights. But how is this dishonesty to be established? Section 2 of the Theft Act 1968 specifies three specific situations which do *not* amount to dishonesty, namely, where the defendant believes: (a) that he has in law the right to deprive the victim of the property; or (b) that the victim would consent to the appropriation if he or she knew of the appropriation and the circumstances of it; or (c) that the person to whom the property belongs cannot be discovered by taking reasonable steps (section 2(1)). Section 2(2) adds that an appropriation may be dishonest notwithstanding that the defendant is willing to pay for the property. Apart from these provisions the concept of dishonesty is left undefined in the Theft Act 1968. In *Feely* (1973) it was held that it should remain undefined and be left entirely to the jury. Whether conduct was dishonest was to be judged by the "current standards of ordinary decent folk"—and who better to assess this than the ordinary decent folk sitting in the jury box who could simply apply their own standards to the everyday concept "dishonesty". The jury had to ascertain the state of the defendant's mind—for example, when he "borrowed" the money, did he know that this was not permitted? Did he believe he could repay it soon?—and so on—and then the jury had to assess, applying their own standards of morality, whether the defendant, with these beliefs, was dishonest.

But what of the defendant whose actions might be regarded as dishonest by the jury applying their standards, but who adamantly maintains (and is believed) that according to *his* system of values, he was acting honestly? For example, in *Gilks* (1972) the defendant claimed that he thought he was honest in keeping money mistakenly paid to him by a bookmaker because he thought bookmakers were "a race apart" and thus fair game. The courts were faced with a quandary here. Acceptance of such pleas would undercut the moral imperative laid down by the criminal law. The criminal law largely reflects (and attempts to uphold) community values. The *Feely* (1973) test allows these community values to be enunciated by a so-called representative section of the community, namely, the jury. If the values of the jury and the community are to be ignored and replaced by the values of the defendant, (who, for example, might endorse the political ideology that "property is theft"), the result would be a complete absence of any objective standard. The door would be open to the "Robin Hood defence". The defendant would effectively become his own judge and jury.

On the other hand, the courts were reluctant to dismiss such pleas totally. The criminal law is based largely on the premise of moral responsibility. We blame those who are morally at fault. If a defendant openly rejects the value system inherent in the law of theft, he can be blamed even if, according to his own values, he thinks his actions are honest. He has knowingly "declared war" on the values of society and can be blamed for doing this. It can never be an excuse in the criminal law that one does not agree with any given law. But what of the defendant who genuinely thinks he is acting honestly according to his values— *and* who really believes that most other people would agree with him as to the morality of his conduct—and can convince a jury of these beliefs? Such a defendant is not openly defying the law; he believes he is upholding the value system inherent in the law of theft. The case for exempting such a defendant from blame becomes strong.

This latter thinking was endorsed in the leading decision of *Ghosh* (1982) which lays down that a defendant acts "dishonestly" if what he does is dishonest according to the ordinary standards of reasonable and honest people (the *Feely*, 1973, test), *and* if he realised that what he was doing was dishonest according to those standards. So, using the examples given in *Ghosh* (1982) itself: Robin Hood or anti-vivisectionists who remove animals from vivisection laboratories are acting dishonestly, even though they may consider themselves to be morally justified in so acting provided that they know that ordinary people would consider such actions to be dishonest.

This test has been subjected to fierce and widespread criticism along the lines that it leads to uncertainty and inconsistency in the application of the law; it tends to increase the number of trials and lengthen and complicate them (by defendants "chancing their arm" and claiming they were honest); unlike any other area of criminal law, fact-finders (juries or magistrates) are required to make a moral judgment: this is "entirely a matter of opinion" (Law Commission, 1999); our society is no longer culturally homogeneous and therefore juries are not able clearly to reflect shared values; with the disappearance of objective standards, "Robin Hood" and other "odd" defendants could (just) escape liability; it could lead to inadequate protection of the property rights of "unpopular classes of owners" such as bookmakers, animal experimenters, multinational corporations, and all those from whom many persons regard theft as a "perk" of their job.

Despite these criticisms, as explained above, *Ghosh* (1982) is capable of defence. The quest throughout the criminal law is for the isolation of the blameworthy. If the jury, reflecting community standards, can attach "moral obloquy" to the defendant's actions and are satisfied that the defendant knows he is acting contrary to the moral standards of ordinary people, a judgment of blameworthiness is truly appropriate. The test has tried to combine the need to preserve objective standards within the criminal law with the need to maintain the importance of moral fault (Wasik, 1979). The Law Commission (1999) has, however, argued that, like other areas of law such as assaults or sexual offences, there should be no specific requirement of morally blameworthy conduct. The element of moral blame will normally be incorporated in the definition of the conduct prohibited and should not be superimposed upon it. This is similar to the view encountered earlier in *Kingston* (1995) that moral blameworthiness is not a prerequisite to the imposition of criminal liability even for serious offences. The argument has already been made (pp. 18–19) that as the criminal law is an institution of blame and punishment there ought to be a clear correlation between blameworthiness and criminal liability for the more serious offences. This argument applies with even greater force to the offence of theft where, as a result of the wide interpretation of appropriation in *Gomez* (1993), the remaining elements of the offence are entirely neutrally defined so that no objective wrongdoing is required and the only thing that distinguishes theft from normal everyday transactions is the requirement of dishonesty involving an assessment of blameworthiness. Even if the other elements of theft were to be redefined so as to necessitate proof of wrongdoing, it is difficult to see how the ambit of criminal liability can be determined without some judgment as to the morality of the defendant's actions—which is exactly what the *Ghosh* (1982) test aims to achieve.

Finally, it must be established that the defendant *intended permanently to deprive* the victim of his interest (whether possession or ownership or whatever) in the property. There is no full definition of "intention of permanently depriving" but section 6 provides "illustrations" of the concept (*Warner*, 1970) and specifies, among other things, that a borrowing or a lending may be theft if "for a period and in circumstances making it equivalent to an outright taking or disposal" (section 6(1)). In *Lloyd, Bhuee and Ali* (1985) it was held that this only applied where there was an intention to return the "thing" in such a changed state that effectively "all its goodness or virtue" had gone. For example, if one "borrowed" a football season ticket and returned the piece of paper at the end of the season, "all its goodness and virtue" would have been destroyed. But if, as in *Lloyd, Bhuee and Ali* (1985), films are taken from a cinema, copied for the purpose of producing pirate videotapes and then returned to the cinema, such films would not have lost "their virtue" and therefore there would be no liability for theft in such a case.

There are two exceptions when temporary removals will be criminal: removal of articles from places open to the public (Theft Act 1968, section 11) and taking a motor vehicle or other conveyance without authority (Theft Act 1968, section 12). Apart from these, however, the criminal law is generally not concerned with temporary deprivations of property, no matter how dishonest. The Law Commission (1999) has argued that temporary deprivations are wrong in principle: the victim has lost the use of the property; she might have lost profit from it; she might have to replace it; the property will usually have lost some value by the time it is returned. On the other hand, it can be argued that the wrongdoing in temporary deprivations is qualitatively different from that in cases of an intention of permanent deprivation. In fair labelling terms, the paradigmatic theft involves the permanent loss of one's property (although the law only requires an *intention* to deprive permanently). If someone wrongfully (without my permission) borrows my book for a week (and I know it will be returned to me), I have lost something: the use of my book. However, unless its usage was critical to me during that week (for example, revising for an exam in which case its taking could come within section 6), I would not think of my book as stolen; it has simply been wrongfully borrowed. It follows that such cases should not be theft and, mindful of the dangers of over-criminalisation and the existence of civil remedies for the return of the property, it is doubtful whether dishonest borrowings should be criminalized at all.

The remaining property offences selected for discussion here can be dealt with more briefly. There are several offences relating to criminal *deception*, each offence specifying a different commodity that is dishonestly obtained by the deception, most notably (i) property (Theft Act 1968, section 15), (ii) a money transfer (Theft Act 1968, section 15A, added by the Theft (Amendment) Act 1996), (iii) pecuniary advantage (Theft Act 1968, section 16(2)(b) and (c)), (iv) the execution of a valuable security (Theft Act 1968, section 20(2)); (v) services (Theft Act 1978, section 1), and (vi) evasion of liability (Theft Act 1978, section 2).

The common feature of the deception offences is that a "deception" must have taken place and this deception must have caused the defendant to obtain the specified commodity. The courts, however, have adopted a somewhat cavalier approach towards the necessity for establishing legal causation. Wanting to punish the blameworthy (dishonest practisers of deceptions), they have seemingly been content to adopt the approach (criticised earlier, p. 152) that if blame is established, along with "but for" causation, then the result cannot be too remote and legal causation can be deemed to be established. For instance, in *Lambie* (1982) the defendant purchased goods from Mothercare and paid by Barclaycard, knowing she was way beyond her credit limit and that Barclays were trying to contact her. The assistant accepted the payment by Barclaycard after checking the defendant's name was not on the current "stop-list'. The House of Lords upheld the defendant's original conviction despite the fact that the assistant had made it clear that she was not interested in the state of the customer's credit. Having checked the "stop-list" and Lambie's signature, she knew that payment was guaranteed by Barclays; that is the whole point of credit cards; she did not care about the relationship between Barclays and the customer. It thus seems somewhat contrived to assert that the assistant was deceived and as a result of the deception was induced to enter into the contract with Lambie. Yet that was precisely what the House of Lords held. Presenting the Barclaycard was an implied representation that the defendant had authority from her bank to enter into a contract (as agent for the bank) with the shop: this representation was untrue and so constituted a deception; this deception was the effective cause of the assistant agreeing to contract with Lambie because *if she had known* that Lambie was acting dishonestly and with no authority to use the card, she would not have entered into the contract. Such reasoning is only explicable on the basis that the House of Lords, concerned by the increasing potential for credit card frauds, was determined to convict a blameworthy credit card-holder—even at the cost of having to deem the victim to have been deceived and thereby induced into accepting a credit card.

In addition to there being a deception, all these offences require proof of dishonesty which has been interpreted the same way as for theft. However, while dishonesty is of critical importance in theft in distinguishing everyday lawful transactions from theft, with the deception offences it fulfils a negative function. People who practice deceptions can normally be taken to be dishonest. However, if a defendant can exceptionally establish a good and acceptable reason why the deception was practiced (for example, in a belief they are legally entitled to the property), there will be an exemption from criminal liability. In short, "dishonesty" in the deception offences "serves *only* to excuse conduct which is prima facie unlawful, as distinct from determining whether conduct is unlawful in the first place [as it does with theft]" (Law Commission, 1999). Accordingly, the Law Commission (1999) has proposed that it is unnecessary to retain dishonesty as a separate element in the deception offences. Instead, there should be a special new defence to cover those who practice deceptions believing they are legally entitled to secure the requisite consequences.

A related offence, but one that does not require any deception, is created by section 3 of the Theft Act 1978, namely, dishonestly *making off without payment* when payment is expected "on the spot" (for example, running out of a restaurant without paying).

The crime of *robbery*, contrary to section 8 of the Theft Act 1968, is committed if a person uses force or threatens force in order to steal. There must be a theft and so any defence to theft will be a defence to robbery. It would appear that any degree of force or threatening force will suffice. In *Dawson* (1976) it was held that a nudge causing the victim to lose his balance was sufficient force; like "dishonesty", "force" is an ordinary word that can be left to juries to interpret, as they see fit.

The crime of *burglary*, contrary to section 9 of the Theft Act 1968, is committed if a person enters a building as a trespasser with the intention of stealing, inflicting grievous bodily harm, raping any person or of doing unlawful damage therein (section 9(1)(a)). (Section 9(1)(b) creates a separate species of burglary where a defendant has entered a building as a trespasser and then steals or attempts to steal therein, or inflicts or attempts to inflict grievous bodily harm on any person therein.) And the more serious crime of *aggravated burglary* is committed if, at the time of the burglary, the defendant has with him any firearm, offensive weapon or explosive.

The crime of burglary is well illustrated by the famous case of *Collins* (1973). The defendant, Collins, was a young man who, feeling particularly lustful one night, went to the house of a girl he knew, determined to have sexual intercourse with her "by force if necessary". He found a stepladder, climbed up and looked into the girl's bedroom. The girl was naked and asleep. Collins descended the ladder and stripped off all his clothes with the exception of his socks. (He claimed that a more rapid escape could be effected in socks. Edmund Davies L.J. found himself unable to express any view on this point!) He then climbed the ladder again and pulled himself on to the window sill with its lattice-type window. He was starting to pull himself in when the girl awoke. The girl saw a blond young male with an erect penis crouched in the open window and assumed it was her boyfriend paying her an ardent nocturnal visit. She pulled him into the room and they had sexual intercourse. However, the length of his hair and his voice as they exchanged "love talk" led her to the conclusion that "somehow there was something different". She turned on the light, saw that her companion was not her boyfriend, slapped and bit him and then went to the bathroom.

The defendant was charged with burglary on the basis that he had entered a building as a trespasser with the intention of raping the girl. A trespasser is one who enters without consent. If Collins had entered the room prior to the girl inviting him in, he would have been guilty of burglary as he would have entered as a trespasser, at that stage with the intention of raping her. But if, when she invited him in, he was still on the outside of the window sill, then when he did enter the building he would not have been entering as a trespasser and therefore could not be liable. The facts were not clear: he was on the window sill; while parts of his body might have been protruding into the room prior to her invitation, the Court of Appeal held that to be liable he needed to have made "an effective and substantial entry" into the bedroom as a trespasser. As the jury had not been invited to consider this issue squarely, the conviction was quashed as being unsafe. So the criminal liability of Collins was made to depend entirely upon the point "as narrow maybe as the window sill" (*Collins*, 1973) of how much of his body had entered the room at the stage she invited him in.

Finally, the crime of *handling stolen goods*, contrary to section 22 of the Theft Act 1968, is committed when a person (otherwise than in the course of stealing), knowing or believing the goods to be stolen, dishonestly: (i) receives the goods (or arranges to receive them), or (ii) undertakes or assists in their retention, removal, disposal or realisation by or for the benefit of another person (or if he arranges to do any of these things).

This offence is extremely wide. One of the most effective ways of combating theft and burglary is to make it difficult and less profitable for thieves and burglars to dispose of the goods they have stolen. Accordingly, to assist in law enforcement in this regard, section 22 casts a wide net over all persons in almost any way associated with dealing with stolen goods. It is interesting to note that one commits the offence simply by *arranging* to handle stolen goods; this is wide enough to cover persons who, without this provision, would not have done enough to be liable even for an attempt. And, of course, the net can be cast even wider in that one can be liable for attempting to handle stolen goods which includes attempting to arrange to handle the goods. Further, one can be liable for handling stolen goods if one simply *assists* in the retention, etc., of the goods. This covers those who would otherwise be liable under the rules of accessorial liability. This means, similarly, that one can be liable under the rules of complicity if one helps or encourages another to assist in the retention, etc., of the goods. Whether such a broadening of the scope of criminal liability is justifiable will be discussed in the next section. The defendant must, of course, be blameworthy. Her actions must be dishonest and she must know or believe that the goods are stolen: a mere suspicion is not enough; she must actually believe the goods to be stolen.

At the time of the handling the goods must still be "stolen". Section 24(4) is important in this regard in providing that goods cease to be stolen if they are restored to lawful possession; this covers cases where the police recover stolen property. This means that if stolen goods are seized by the police who, then acting as "undercover agents" or simple "lookouts", attempt to apprehend receivers of the goods, conviction will be impossible as those receivers will not be handling "stolen" goods—unless it can be established that at some earlier stage when they were still stolen the receivers *arranged* to handle the stolen goods.

(iii) Conclusion

The property offences discussed above are mainly concerned with the protection of a variety of interests in property. It is this interference with property interests that constitutes the primary harm in such offences. This simple proposition, however, raises many questions.

First, what is meant by "interests in property"? As seen in the introduction to this chapter, this ought logically to refer to interests in property defined by the civil law. However, as seen in *Hinks* (2000), the criminal law is prepared to regard a person who acquires an indefeasible title to property as a thief. This is anomalous: if the victim would fail in a civil action to recover the property it is difficult to see why the criminal law should punish the new lawful property owner. The Law Commission (1999) states that "the function of the criminal law of dishonesty is to protect economic interests from improper violation" and that the focus of the law should be on "loss rather than gain". However, the law's focus here has shifted away from loss or financial prejudice to a concentration on the wrongdoing and dishonesty of the defendant. This emphasis on the defendant's wrongdoing is further demonstrated by the inchoate nature of many of the offences. For example, in theft the victim need lose nothing: all that is required is that the defendant intend permanent deprivation. In burglary there need only be an entry as a trespasser with one of the specified intentions; nothing need happen in the building. Of course, it is right that the law protect threats to property interests as well as actual interferences with those interests. However, the absurdly broad judicial interpretation of "appropriation" allows the criminalisation of conduct that hardly constitutes a threat to another's property interests: for example, offering to sell another's property when the defendant is in no real position ever to do so. Again, the real focus is on the defendant's wrongdoing irrespective of any threat of loss. This approach is unfortunate. A tighter definition of "appropriation", bringing it closer to its original intended meaning of "misappropriation", would help shift the emphasis to loss to the victim. The law of attempt exists to protect threats of loss and by its rigorous requirement that the defendant's acts be "more than merely preparatory" it is better positioned to ensure that only realistic threats to property interests are criminalized. A final issue about the meaning of "property interests" is whether they should be limited to existing property interests or whether the law should extend its protection to prospective property interests. For instance, Canadian fraud law extends to criminalizing conduct that impairs the victim's prospects of making a profit (Law Commission, 1999). Bearing in mind that the criminal law should be used as a "tool of last resort", the Law Commission (1999) is surely right that criminalisation is not necessary here. Civil redress is the more appropriate response.

If all the property offences are broadly aimed at protecting other people's interests in property, it could be argued that the myriad of specific offences could be abolished and replaced by a single broad offence of dishonesty or wrongful interference with property rights. This approach would simply be an extension of the present law where the broad interpretation of "appropriation" has resulted in theft potentially subsuming most instances of obtaining property by deception and handling stolen goods. Such a new broad offence would have the advantage of criminalizing dishonest conduct that is not criminal under the existing law, for example, a fiduciary making a secret profit at the expense of the principal. It would also be more conducive to effective prosecutions particularly in large-scale frauds where the essence of the wrongdoing could be accurately represented without having to pigeon-hole the conduct into one of the existing offence categories (Law Commission, 1999).

Such a proposal is, however, seriously misguided. The Law Commission (1999) has recently concluded that a general offence of dishonesty should not be introduced into English law for the following reasons: it would extend the reach of the criminal law too far (for example, criminalising all dishonest breaches of contract); it would place too much reliance on the slippery concept of "dishonesty"; it would confirm the much-criticised case of *Hinks* (2000) where persons are currently guilty of theft of what is, in civil law, their own property; and, finally, such a broad offence would probably fail to satisfy Articles 5 and 7 of the European Convention on Human Rights which have been interpreted as enshrining a principle of certainty: offences should be "formulated with sufficient precision to enable the citizen to regulate his conduct" (*G v. Federal Republic of Germany*, 1989).

Equally importantly, however, such a broad single offence would, in fair labelling terms, be completely morally uninformative. It would, in effect, "be an offence to do anything naughty" (Archibold News, 1999). Most of the various property offences in the Theft Acts and elsewhere each encapsulate distinct wrongs and have a resonance with common understandings of the wrongdoing involved. English law has, rightly, looked beyond the simple primary harm of "interfering with property rights" that is involved in all these offences and, in distinguishing between them, has taken account of the secondary consequences involved. In doing this, the impact (or potential impact) on the victim, the method of committing the crime, and law enforcement considerations have been most important in informing the present structure of property offences. To illustrate this point a few examples will now be considered.

Robbery carries a maximum penalty of life imprisonment compared to the seven-year maximum available for theft. The reasons for this are fairly self-evident with both the level of harm and blame being aggravated. Robbery causes fear and apprehension to the victim. The robber is prepared openly to confront his victim and commit his crime in defiance of that victim. It is almost impossible to protect oneself in advance against robbers threatening violence.

Burglary, which used to carry a maximum penalty of 14 years' imprisonment in all cases, and aggravated burglary, carrying a maximum penalty of life imprisonment, are explicable on similar grounds. While liability for these offences need not involve any actual loss of property, the fact is that the security and sanctity of the home (in many cases) has been violated. This can cause special psychological harm: distress, alarm and the fear of knowing one is not safe even in one's own home. The lives of a large majority of victims of burglary are affected for some weeks after the burglary, and over a quarter of such victims suffer serious shock (Maguire, 1980). These harms are increased when the burglar is armed with an offensive weapon. Here the law is perhaps justified in concentrating on the non-economic impact of the crime on the victim and, indeed, recognising that these psychological harms are felt most acutely in cases of residential, as opposed to commercial, burglary. The Criminal Justice Act 1991 has drawn a distinction between such burglaries. The maximum penalty for burglary of a "dwelling" is still 14 years' imprisonment but in other cases the maximum has been reduced to 10 years' imprisonment.

Theft and handling stolen goods are closely related offences with a considerable overlap between them. In most cases a person who handles stolen goods is "assuming the rights of owner" over the property and is thereby appropriating it, becoming guilty of theft—assuming the other elements of the offence to be present, as they usually will be. Indeed, in many cases defendants are charged with both offences in the alternative in the hope that the jury will convict of one or the other or that the defendant will plead guilty to the lesser offence. (One cannot, however, be convicted of both theft and handling: *Shelton*, 1986). Accordingly, it is possible to suggest that the distinction between handling and theft should no longer be maintained (Smith, ATH, 1994). There are, however, good reasons for retaining handling stolen goods as a distinct form of wrongdoing and not merging it within the offence of theft. First, not every case of handling will amount to theft. Handling also extends to goods obtained by deception or blackmail; if the "stolen" goods have been acquired in this manner a voidable title will have passed to the deceiver or blackmailer; similarly in cases such as *Hinks* (2000) the thief acquires an indefeasible title; in such cases the property "belongs to" the thief, blackmailer or deceiver and there can be no dishonest appropriation in relation to that person. Secondly, criminal offences should accurately describe the prohibited conduct as far as possible. The public perceives a clear distinction between a thief and a handler of stolen property; the law should reflect such understanding. And thirdly, it has been considered necessary to demarcate handling as a special offence subject to a maximum of 14 years' imprisonment (as opposed to seven years for theft) for frankly utilitarian reasons. Handlers of stolen goods provide much of the market for theft; their activities are a significant source of the economic motivation behind much theft. For instance, evidence suggests that those committing burglary for the first time or so who are able to convert the stolen property into cash are more likely to commit further burglaries (Home Office, 1998a). If the law could stamp out "fences" (professional handlers) and other handlers, much of the war against theft and burglary would have been won.

Despite these views and the potential for a higher sentence, most people today regard handling as a lesser offence in terms of moral stigma; defendants will often plead guilty to handling on condition that all charges of theft are dropped. This attitude has come about because of a growing view that handlers and purchasers of stolen goods are "only slightly dishonest people" (Spencer, 1985) who are not as blameworthy as those who actually steal or burgle. Buying and selling stolen goods is the most common offence amongst young offenders (Graham and Bowling, 1995). Theft and burglary create an immediate sense of danger in the community; there must often be a risk of violence with such activities; the thief or burglar is the primary cause of harm, directly invading the rights of the owner of property. In contrast, the criminal receiver, the "fence", is regarded only as a shady, somewhat disreputable character—and the secondary purchaser as simply someone who as succumbed to the "natural temptation" of buying something very cheap.

The law is accordingly faced with a dilemma. On the one hand, it recognises that the punishment of handlers is crucial if theft and burglary is to be reduced but, on the other hand, it is faced by an apathetic public almost prepared to "turn a blind eye" to handling. A possible way out of this dilemma could be to divide the offence of handling stolen goods into degrees. The more serious could be reserved for the professional "fence", the lesser offence covering secondary purchasers. Such a division might be a fairer reflection of the moral stigma felt by most to attach to the two categories of handlers and could have the advantage of underwriting the necessity of enforcement against, and harm caused by, the professional handler. The danger with such an approach, however, could be that even less moral stigma would be attached to secondary purchasers than at present and, after all, it is these purchasers who buy stolen goods from fences who are the "key element in the incentive structure that supports property crime" (*Yale Law Journal*, 1980).

The various offences of deception are, if anything, even more closely related to, and overlap with, theft. The defendants in the earlier discussed theft cases of *Lawrence* (1972), *Morris* (1984), *Gomez* (1993), *Williams* (1980) and, perhaps, *Kaur v. Chief Constable for Hampshire* (1981) could all have been charged with obtaining property by deception contrary to section 15 of the Theft Act 1968. It could thus be argued that one single broad offence such as theft could be made to embrace all "involuntary" transfers of property, thus rendering an offence such as section 15 otiose. Such a single offence would eliminate the need in many cases to draw fine distinctions between closely related forms of misconduct. It could also be argued that prevailing moral standards do not differentiate sharply between the "swindler" and the "thief" (Model Penal Code, 1953). As Glazebrook (1991) has argued: "thief or swindler: who cares?"

On the other hand, it is submitted that English law is wise to separate theft from obtaining property by deception contrary to section 15, especially now that they carry different maximum penalties. An important moral distinction exists between the two offences in the paradigmatic instances of each (even if not in some of the overlap cases). A typical theft involves a surreptitious taking; the owner is totally helpless against such a taking; if the thief is interrupted there is a risk of violence; because of his or her anonymity there is extra difficulty in identifying and apprehending the thief. With the typical obtaining property by deception, however, the victim has also "lost" her property— but she handed it over "voluntarily"; she had an opportunity to resist; with greater alertness she might not have been deceived; the deceiver has not resorted to stealth or force and often will have had to face his victim openly, thereby increasing the chances of subsequent identification and apprehension. In our society, where mutual transactions based on trust are valued and encouraged, the wrong of deceiving another into parting with property is a distinctive wrong that is quite different in quality from the paradigmatic theft. "The thief makes war on a social practice from the outside, the deceiver is the traitor within" (Shute and Horder, 1993). While some of these differences might suggest that section 15 ought to carry a lesser potential punishment than theft, the fact remains that the "big-time con-man" can inflict massive losses upon large numbers of persons simultaneously and so the higher maximum penalty is perhaps necessary to cover such cases.

One other possibility remains. Even if the idea of introducing a single broad offence dealing with dishonest interferences with other people's property is rejected, one could perhaps introduce a handful of broad offences each with a different focus. The best example of this is the proposal to collapse all the various deception offences into a single offence of fraud. However, even this more limited proposal seems misguided and has been rejected by the Law Commission (1999) in that it would be too broad covering, for example, a manufacturer who falsely claims that his products are superior to those of his rivals, who lose sales as a result. While such dishonest conduct might be morally reprehensible, criminalisation hardly seems a necessary or appropriate response. If there are gaps in the law of deception and it is genuinely felt that criminalisation is the best way of dealing with the problem, specific reforms aimed at closing the gaps is more appropriate. For example, to circumvent the problems posed by *Lambie* (1982) the Law Commission (1999) has proposed a new offence aimed largely at covering the misuse of payment cards and, in the light of developments on the internet, an amendment to the law, or the creation of a new offence, dealing with the misuse of a machine to obtain a service.

The argument above is that English law needs to retain its separate property offences and should resist calls for their merger into a single broad offence or a few broad offences. However, the sentencing maxima for the various offences appear rather haphazard. For instance, the various deception offences carry a variety of maximum penalties. While section 15 carries a 10 year maximum penalty, section 16 (obtaining a pecuniary advantage by deception—for example, obtaining an overdraft or employment by deception) carries a maximum penalty of five years' imprisonment. Obtaining services by deception and evasion of liability by deception, contrary to sections 1 and 2 of the Theft Act 1978 respectively, also carry a five-year maximum penalty. On the other hand, making off without payment contrary to section 3 of the Theft Act 1978 only carries a maximum penalty of two years' imprisonment. This last offence is the only one on this list that does not necessitate proof of a deception; it is thus in some ways more akin to theft (punishable by a maximum of seven years' imprisonment) in that the participation of the victim is not necessary for the commission of the offence. Clearly, with these offences there needs to be a more careful consideration of the relative seriousness of each. A more coherent structure is needed which must be related to some clear principle and policy. As with all offences, the different forms of wrongdoing (methods, circum-stances, etc., of the crime) can inform the crime label but the relative seriousness of the offence is best determined by combin-ing the degree of blameworthiness involved with the level of harm (primary and secondary) caused.

In assessing this level of harm, the present English law concentrates entirely on the fact of interference (or threatened interference) with property interests. While it might be import-ant at the sentencing stage, English law does not formally concern itself at the substantive level with the value of the property interest interfered with. However, it is clear that the value of property lost in typical cases has influenced the setting of the maximum penalties for offences. For example, victims can be defrauded of millions of pounds explaining the relatively high maximum penalty of 10 years' imprisonment for obtaining property by deception. On the other hand, the relatively low maximum penalty of two years' imprisonment for making off without payment is probably explicable on the basis that typ-ically this offence is applied to persons who rush out of restaurants, petrol stations or hotels without paying. While, admittedly, bills in certain London restaurants and hotels can be astronomic, they will never be of such a magnitude as to warrant imprisonment for more than two years.

However, within any offence category, no account is taken of the value of the property interfered with. For instance, it is as much theft to steal a tin of beans as to steal £10 million. This can be contrasted with the position in the United States where, in many states, theft offences are graded according to the value of the property stolen. For instance, the Model Penal Code says that theft of property worth less than $50 constitutes a petty misdemeanour; theft of property valued at between $50 and $500 constitutes a misdemeanour; theft of property with a value exceeding $500 constitutes a felony of the third degree (section 223.1(2): there are certain qualifications to this broad structure). Each of these offence categories carries its own range of penalties.

The argument in support of the English approach is that the value of the property is only one way of assessing the extent of the harm and it cannot be made decisive. For instance, the following could be cited as possible indicators of the gravity of an offence: the characteristics of the offender (*e.g.* theft by a person in a position of trust); the characteristics of the victim (*e.g.* theft from the old or disabled; theft from individuals as opposed to theft from companies); the circumstances of the offence (*e.g.* pickpocketing—an "offensive and frightening type of theft"; thefts committed jointly with others); and the non-monetary value of the goods (*e.g.* a key to be used subsequently for a more serious offence; property of purely sentimental value to the victim) (James Committee 1975). There are also problems relating to the blameworthiness of the defendant. What if the pickpocket, hoping to find a few pounds, snatches a wallet containing £1,000?

Despite these objections, it is clear that many property offences could be broadly subdivided so as to separate offences involving minor interferences (in terms of value) with property from the more serious cases. It seems ludicrous that theft of a tin of beans or theft by an employee of a box of paperclips should be placed in the same category as major thefts and frauds involving thousands of pounds. The James Committee (1975) proposed a general £20 monetary limit, beneath which Crown Court trial would be unavailable. Section 22 of the Magistrates' Courts Act 1980, as amended, provides that various offences involving criminal damage shall only be triable summarily if the value of the property does not exceed £5,000. The present Government is committed to extending this provision to include other offences such as theft. It would appear to make good sense to extend such a provision, for many offences, beyond the confines of procedural law and into the substantive law itself. However, this approach should only be applied to those property crimes where the essence of the harm involved relates to loss (or threatened loss) of property such as theft and the deception offences. For those offences where other types of harm are more critical (such as robbery and burglary) the value of the property is of secondary importance to the central harm (for example, threat of violence or invasion of one's home) and there should be no differentiation in offence seriousness based on the value of the property involved.

4

THE FUNCTION OF CRIMINAL LAW IN SOCIETY

1. INTRODUCTION

All law, including the criminal law, is designed as a mechanism for achieving social control. Its purpose is the regulation of conduct and activities within society. The criminal law, however, differs from other branches of law in that a conviction involves censure and it employs stigmatic punishment against those who violate its commands. It attempts to reflect those fundamental social values expressing the way we live and then uses this "big stick" of punishment as a means of reinforcing those values and securing compliance therewith. In this way it seeks to protect not only the individual, but also the very structure and fabric of society.

From this it can be seen that the function of the criminal law is as follows. (i) The criminal law must identify which conduct should be brought within its ambit. If all law is designed as a means of social control, on what basis is the decision made to criminalise wrongdoing, as opposed to leaving it to regulation by other, less harsh, areas of law? (ii) Having decided on the values needing protection, the criminal law must define with some degree of moral clarity the precise circumstances in which criminal liability is warranted and it must, for fair labelling reasons, name and grade the relative seriousness of the various offences within each family of offence. (iii) A critical function of the criminal law—and the reason why conduct is criminalised, labelled and graded—is to uphold the values protected by the criminal law and to reduce crime. To achieve this goal, there must be a certain degree of actual enforcement of the criminal law: a law that was never enforced would soon become a dead letter. (iv) The final function of the criminal law, once a breach of the rules has occurred and liability established, is that of determining how much punishment is appropriate. In doing this, the criminal law is presently facing a critical challenge. If the main task of the criminal law is crime prevention, must decisions as to who to punish and how much to punish be made from a crime prevention perspective? For instance, life imprisonment for parking offences would probably greatly reduce the incidence of such offences, if not eliminate them entirely. On the other hand, while possibly effective, such a punishment would be totally undeserved and unjust. In its role of distributing and measuring punishment, and conversely of structuring criminal offences, the function of the criminal law is one of pinpointing those who deserve punishment and for whom punishment would be just—and of grading the severity of their punishment according to such criteria.

Defining and structuring offences (ii above) has been the object of most of this book to date. It is to an examination of the remaining functions listed above that we now turn.

2. CRIMINALIZING CONDUCT

One does not use a sledgehammer to crack a nut. A criminal conviction involves the shame and censure of public punishment. Criminal processes such as arrest, police custody and interrogation are highly intrusive and in themselves involve stigma and humiliation. Accordingly, one should not use the criminal law to control conduct that can be effectively regulated by other means (such as education, advertising, religion and social convention) or by other areas of law (such as tort, contract or administrative regulation). For instance, it was argued earlier, in relation to strict liability offences (p. 142) that some prohibited conduct could be decriminalised and made subject to regulation by administrative action and remedies. In any society that values liberty, the criminal law ought only to be invoked as a last resort method of social control when absolutely necessary.

To a certain extent this was indeed the approach of the law. In the 1960s, for instance, much debate was devoted to whether certain activities that were then criminal could be decriminalised. This resulted in the Sexual Offences Act 1967 under which various homosexual and prostitution activities ceased to be criminal. Since then, however, the political mood and culture of the country has changed and particularly in the last two decades there has been an alarming tendency to adopt the view: "if there's a problem, lets criminalise it". For example, the (supposed) rise in football hooliganism led to the Football

(Offences) Act 1991 which creates the offences of throwing missiles, indecent or racialist chanting and going on to the playing area at designated football matches. The Sporting Events (Control of Alcohol etc.) Act 1985 creates numerous offences relating to possession, etc., of alcohol at designated sporting events. As a result of several highly publicised cases of fighting dogs seriously injuring persons, the Dangerous Dogs Act 1991 creates various offences relating to breeding, selling or allowing such dogs to be in public places without a muzzle and lead. Other examples of this faith in criminal sanctions being the obvious remedy to social ills include the criminalisation of kerb-crawling (Sexual Offences Act 1985), possession of crossbows by persons under the age of 17 (Crossbows Act 1987), and aggravated trespass (Criminal Justice and Public Order Act 1994).

This proliferation of criminal offences has spread into areas not traditionally associated with the criminal law such as nursing (Nurses, Midwives and Health Visitors Act 1997), architecture (Architects Act 1997), the countryside (Countryside and Rights of Way Act 2000) and royal parks (Royal Parks (Trading) Act 2000). While much of this can be seen as political posturing by successive governments determined to win votes by demonstrating a tough attitude to crime, more carefully reasoned law reform proposals have also become infected with this assumption that criminalisation is the cure to any problem. For example, in proposing reforms to the law of conveyancing recently, the possibility of using criminal sanctions was put forward as a mechanism for ensuring compliance with the law (Lord Chancellor's Department, 1998).

Clearly, particular decisions whether to criminalise do need reference to the social, economic and psychological realities surrounding a given activity. For example, the development of new technologies, such as computers and the internet, and the radical restructuring of certain areas of activities, such as financial services, has led to the creation of many new offences (Computer Misuse Act 1990; Financial Services Act, 1986). However, this begs what ought to be the central question: when is it necessary to criminalise conduct? How does one decide whether certain conduct should be prohibited by the criminal law or not? In order to prevent knee-jerk over-criminalisation there ought to be some underlying principles to guide and influence such decisions. Do such guiding criteria exist? If one were trying to determine whether consensual buggery, possession of narcotic drugs, sado-masochism, trespass or invasion of privacy ought to be criminal, how and on what basis would the decision be made?

Discussion here will start with a brief summary of two highly controversial schools of thought before proceeding to the more familiar territory in which this debate is generally waged.

First, there are the views of a school of thought loosely described as "radical criminology". The criminal law represents nothing more than the vested interests of the powerful. It is an expression of power by an elite that is used as a prop to maintain the present social, economic and class structure. In short, it "keeps the lid on the lower classes" (Carlen, 1980). Only conduct affecting interests regarded as significant by this power-group is criminalised.

Such views are particularly important in understanding the phenomenon of crime (who commits crimes and why) and the enforcement of the criminal law: for example, why social security frauds are prosecuted to a much greater extent than tax frauds. And, indeed, many offences are explicable in terms of such a theory, for example, property offences and the public order offences created in the wake of violence during the 1984–85 miners' strike.

The problem with radical criminology as an explanation of criminalisation, however, is its failure to explain how we identify which interests are sufficiently important to the power-group to warrant criminalisation. Particularly when moving away from economic crimes, how does one identify the vested interests of the power-group? Which of their interests are being challenged by victimless crime? With such crimes, ultimately, the interests of this group are largely synonymous with the interests of most persons in society. For instance, it is difficult to see how adult homosexuality or sado-masochistic beatings threaten the interests of the power-group in society any more than they threaten the interests of all persons. To say that an activity is made criminal when it threatens the interests of society is simply not helpful as the very problem under consideration is one of identifying *when* conduct sufficiently threatens society to justify criminalising it. In other words, with too many of the really controversial issues, radical criminology can provide no real independent explanation and one is forced to try to find answers according to the general criteria shortly to be considered.

The second controversial school of thought is that which endorses an economic theory of the criminal law. This theory has mostly been directed at the individual's decision to commit a crime and at the economics of law enforcement and deterrent punishment. However, attempts have also been made to subject the substantive criminal law and issues of criminalisation to an economic analysis.

According to this school of thought, the object of the criminal law is to discourage "market bypassing", thereby promoting "economically efficient" acts. The market is the most efficient method of allocating resources. Such efficiency must be promoted by discouraging people from bypassing the market. Putting it another way, an individual should not be allowed to seize something that he or she could have bargained for. Conduct is criminalised so that the criminal sanction can operate to induce market behaviour. For example, it is more efficient to force me to buy a car than to allow me to steal it; by stealing, I am taking something that I could have bargained for. This is the rationale of theft and other acquisitive crimes.

Even more controversial is the economic analysis explaining why crimes of passion and violence, such as murder and rape, are criminalised. Posner (1985) suggests several reasons relating to the inefficiency of such actions that involve a bypassing of the market. Markets can be explicit or implicit. In a "market" people are compensated for parting with things of value to them. A mugger is bypassing an explicit market: he or she is deriving satisfaction in a manner that confers no benefit on other people and is obtaining an advantage that has not been bargained for. There are also implicit markets—for example, in friendship, love and respect. By raping a person instead of securing consent to intercourse, the rapist is bypassing such an implicit market in sex/friendship/love.

While economics might be useful in contributing to our understanding of criminal behaviour, optimal enforcement policy and deterrent punishment, its utility for our present purposes is limited. Surely, a deliberate breach of contract is "bypassing the market". From an economic perspective, it is difficult to see any distinction between such conduct and theft (Schulhofer, 1985)—yet nobody seriously advances a claim that all deliberate breaches of contract should be criminalised. Similarly, many torts involve seizing entitlements that could have been bargained for. The economic theory does not help elucidate the distinction between tort and crime. Nor does the theory explain victimless crimes. Trading in narcotic drugs clearly involves bargaining for a voluntary transfer of the drugs. Such activity is economically efficient and its criminalisation cannot be justified in economic terms. Is prostitution or consensual sado-masochism bypassing an implicit market in love and marriage when both parties have chosen to reject such a market?

This economic theory is plainly flawed by its failure to recognise the moral content of the criminal law—the moral assessment of harm and blameworthy conduct (involving notions of responsibility). Economic theory focuses exclusively on the inducement aspect of the criminal law (deterrence). No mention is made of desert and justice. To that extent the analysis fails to deal with the reality of the criminal law. It paints a black-and-white picture of an area of law notorious for its bright colouring.

Most theorists in this field do recognise the importance of the moral content of the criminal law and that conduct should not be criminalised unless it is wrongful (the wrongfulness condition). Such wrongfulness is, however, generally regarded as only a triggering condition. Additionally, there should be an assessment that it is necessary to employ the criminal law to condemn and prevent such conduct (the necessity test). In addressing both these issues, two connected principles are of critical importance. First, as already seen, in the interests of liberty and protecting the individual autonomy of people, the criminal law should only be invoked as a last resort. Ashworth (1999) calls this the principle of minimalism. Secondly, the criminal law must respect and uphold fundamental human rights and civil liberties as protected by the Human Rights Act 1998 which incorporates into English law the European Convention on Human Rights. Let us consider each of these matters in turn.

What makes conduct wrongful? This has long been a controversial matter with some theorists arguing that there should be a clear link between wrongfulness and immorality and that it is justifiable to use the criminal law purely to enforce moral standards. For example, if homosexual activity, albeit consensual, were regarded as immoral, that would be a good enough reason, in itself, for criminalising it. President Nixon (1970) justified strict obscenity laws on the ground that "the pollution of our civilization with smut and filth is as serious a situation . . . as the pollution of our once pure air and water . . . American morality is not to be trifled with".

In a more refined version of this viewpoint, Lord Devlin (1959) argued that a common morality is essential for the preservation of any society. If the moral bonds holding it together are loosened, society will disintegrate. Accordingly, as society must protect itself, it is entitled to legislate against immorality. However, while entitled to do so, there are certain "practical" limits; most notably, there must be toleration of a maximum amount of individual freedom consistent with the integrity of society. But when the "limits of tolerance" have been passed, conduct must be criminalized. Thus a grey area exists where, in the interests of freedom, immoral conduct will be permitted—but when the limits of moral tolerance are passed (the cacophony of "intolerance, indignation, and disgust"), the conduct in question must be made criminal.

Commentators, particularly Hart (1959), have launched a fierce attack upon Devlin's thesis. Is there really a shared morality—a unitary set of moral values—in society? Even if there is, there is no historical or empirical evidence that condonation of immorality will lead to the destruction of society. Surely, the limits of tolerance can change indicating that society is progressing and not being destroyed. Does not the fact that the reasonable person feels "intolerance, indignation and disgust" indicate that the common morality is still intact and society is not disintegrating? Is there not the danger that the limits of tolerance could be determined by pure prejudice and bigotism divorced from a true assessment of morality? Finally, this whole approach would widen the reach of the criminal law breaching the principle of minimalism and would almost certainly clash with some of the rights protected by the European Convention on Human Rights, such as Article 8 which provides a right to respect for private life.

Another school of thought rejects legal moralism but insists that the criminal law adopt a paternalistic stance whereby conduct would be criminalised when it causes harm to others (below, p. 250) or to the actor him or herself. Persons should be protected from harming themselves. For example, if it were established that consuming certain drugs was harmful to the person concerned, the law should criminalise the sale and possession of such drugs. The problem with paternalism is that, taken to its logical conclusion, anything that has the potential for harming a person should be criminalised: smoking, mountaineering, insufficient exercise and so on. This would involve the criminal law turning "us all into super-fit, clean-living 'Spartans' whether we like it or not" (Law Commission, 1995a). Further, too broad an endorsement of paternalism could lead to a breach of the principle of minimalism and the rights protected under the European Convention on Human Rights.

Despite such objections, paternalism has a powerful intuitive attraction and there can be little doubt that it has played a significant role in the creation and retention of many criminal offences over the past century and more. For example, it is employed as a central argument against the decriminalisation of prohibited drugs. The Law Commission (1995a) openly acknowledges the paternalistic thinking underlying its proposals on consent: persons should generally not be permitted to consent to seriously disabling injury (above p. 85).

However, both paternalism and legal moralism are firmly rejected by the liberal school of thought that espouses the harm principle. John Stuart Mill (1859) boldly claimed that "the only purpose for which power can be rightfully exercised over any member of a civilised community, against his will, is to prevent harm to others". A century later the Wolfenden Committee (1957) expressed a similar view that "there must remain a realm of private morality and immorality which is, in brief and crude terms, not the law's business".

Liberalism demands that respect be shown to the autonomy of individuals. People should be permitted maximum freedom to make free choices and the state should only intervene and restrict that autonomy when it is necessary to protect the autonomy of others, that is when it is necessary to prevent harm or serious offence to others. Such a "do your own thing as long as you don't hurt anyone else" philosophy is naturally attractive (at least to anyone of the slightest liberal persuasion) and is more likely than the other approaches to respect the principle of minimalism and the rights protected by the European Convention on Human Rights. However, this approach is in fact unhelpful unless one has a clear definition of the inherently ambiguous concept "harm to others". For instance, the taking of narcotic drugs causes no direct harm to others but the drug-user might become addicted to drugs and unable to maintain his or her family. Arguably, society is "harmed" by having to provide support for such persons and by the creation of drug-cultures that can stimulate other crime. Do such "secondary harms" to others justify the imposition of criminal liability? And what of "harms" that have been consented to? Is a person harmed by a sado-masochistic flogging that he or she requested, or by euthanasia? And how does the harm principle account for the non-criminal classification of deliberate but legitimate business competition which results in bankruptcy and ruin for the unsuccessful competitor, or abandoning one's spouse and children? Further, it is possible to expand one's definition of harm. Gross (1979) defines "harm" as the violation of the interests of another. One has an interest in avoiding unpleasant experiences. Are you then "harmed" if the person sitting opposite you in the train begins to masturbate, or is wearing a T-shirt bearing an offensive racist slogan, or is picking his or her nose? And, finally, as members of society, we are arguably "harmed" by threats upon the structure and foundations of that society. Following Lord Devlin, could one actually be "harmed" by threats upon the common morality?

Problems such as these make it obvious that a simple "harm to others" principle is inadequate unless one's concept of "harm" is closely defined, and even then, some further supplementary criteria might be needed before the criminalisation of conduct can be justified.

One of the most ambitious attempts at such a careful refinement of the harm concept is that of Feinberg (1984). He argues that criminalisation is only justified if it would be effective in preventing or reducing harm to other persons or if it were necessary to prevent serious offence to other persons. "Harm" is defined for these purposes as a "thwarting, setting back, or defeating of an interest" that is a consequence of a wrongful act or omission by another. Risk of harm to such interests can also justify criminalisation: the more serious the threatened harm, the less probable it need be. For example, the blood/alcohol limit for drink/driving offences has been set quite low. In such cases the potential harm (death or serious injury to others) is so great that it is justifiable to criminalise the mere fact of driving while over the limit even though statistically it might not be very probable (depending on the circumstances) that such a consequence will occur.

Such harm or risk of harm must be caused by a *wrongful* act or omission. The assessment of whether an act is "wrongful" or not is made largely on the basis of moral judgments. For instance, justified or excused conduct is not wrongful. So, according to this view, if the victim consents to the risks or injuries he or she has not been wronged and so not harmed. Again, the legitimate businessperson has not wronged the competitor and so cannot have "harmed" him or her.

Feinberg (1985) also argues that one is justified in criminalising conduct if it would probably be an effective way of preventing *serious offence* (and if no other means, such as the civil law, would be equally effective). Again, the criminal law can only be concerned with wrongful offence. Recognising that offence is less serious than harm (and so, at most, should only attract light penalties), criminalisation can be justified only if the offence caused is serious (defined by reference to the extent and duration of the repugnance), could not be reasonably avoided and the victim did not assume the risk of being offended and if these factors are not counterbalanced by the reasonableness of the offending party's conduct (measured by the personal importance of the conduct to the actor, its general social value, the availability of alternative times and places where the conduct would cause less offence, and the extent to which the offence is caused by spiteful motives). Applying these tests to one of Feinberg's own examples, public coprophagia (public eating of faeces) in front of a captive audience (on a moving bus): the conduct causes serious offence; this is not counterbalanced by independent reasonableness. Criminalisation could be justified if that were assessed to be an effective and necessary means of combating such conduct. These two criteria, harm and serious offence, are, to Feinberg, the only grounds for justifiable criminalisation. He rejects legal paternalism, legal moralism and the idea of punishing on the basis of other "free-floating" secondary harms.

This debate, as to how to identify wrongful conduct and whether the criminal law should be utilised to enforce morality or to prevent harm (or deep offence) to others, does not purport to resolve fully the issue as to which conduct should be criminalised. As stated above, most commentators insist that further conditions be satisfied before use of the criminal law is justified. In other words, the identification of conduct as wrongful under any of the approaches discussed above is a *minimal condition*. Without this first hurdle being overcome, criminal liability can never be justified. But it is not a sufficient condition. Further hurdles must be overcome to establish that use of the criminal law is necessary and profitable.

In the interests of liberty all criminal law has to pass the test of *necessity*. Is a criminal law necessary to prevent or control an activity? Other non-legal means of social control should be employed if possible. For instance, education, advertising and taxation are, in the interests of freedom, preferred methods of trying to reduce the smoking of cigarettes in our society. Further, if some form of legal control is to be employed it should be both necessary and profitable to employ the criminal law—as opposed to non-criminal methods of legal regulation such as tort law, licensing and franchising and other administrative law. Overutilisation of the criminal law will lead to a devaluation of its currency.

The use of the criminal law must be *profitable* in the sense that the gains derived from its use outweigh any associated losses. Put another way, the benefits of criminalising conduct must outweigh the costs. What are these "benefits" and "costs" and how are they measured?

The "gains" or "benefits" sought by the criminal law are easily stated, namely, the prevention or reduction of crime. An evaluation of this aim of the criminal law and the difficulty of measuring it forms the main body of the remaining sections of this book. Suffice it to provide here one simple illustration of what is meant by "gains" in this respect. If the law makes failing to wear a seat belt an offence, then there is a "gain" if most people do in fact wear a seat belt. Indeed, there is a "gain" if more people wear a seat belt than before the enactment of that law. However, it is more difficult to establish that this "gain" was secured *by* the criminal law; other factors, such as education by advertising, might have been highly instrumental in securing the "gain". On the other hand, it is clear that little "gain" can be derived from the invocation of a criminal law that cannot be effective. For instance, a law punishing vomiting in public could have no "gain" as, in most cases, vomiting is an involuntary action whose occurrence could not be affected by any law.

"Costs" can be assessed in both economic and non-economic terms. Economically, the costs of any criminal law will depend very largely on the level of enforcement of that law: the costs of preventative action, detection, prosecution and punishment of violators. An assessment of such costing depends, of course, upon the individual crime and the type of preventative or detective measures required, the police manpower involved, and actual extent of enforcement of the law. There is, however, immense difficulty in measuring the costs of any one law or, more importantly, trying to estimate what costs would be saved if a particular crime were decriminalised. For instance, if the offence of gross indecency between men, contrary to section 13 of the Sexual Offences Act 1956, and related offences, were decriminalised, the police would presumably cease the expensive practice of "staking out" public lavatories in order to apprehend criminals. However, the amount of money allocated to police departments is not dependent upon the number of offences on the statute book. Resources saved by the decriminalisation of one offence would be spent on other offences, pushing up their "costs".

The non-economic costs of the criminal law are significant and varied. In the famous words of Jeremy Bentham (1789): "All punishment is mischief: all punishment in itself is evil". Bentham was here referring to a variety of evils: the evil of having liberty restricted (felt by those obeying the law); the evil of fearing punishment and then actually suffering that punishment (felt by those breaking the law); and derivative evils such as the pain of sympathy (felt by those connected to the criminal, such as family). Naturally, the effect on the individual here varies from crime to crime and among individuals. With some crimes—say, buggery with animals—the costs in terms of stigmatisation are immense. Conviction for such an offence can spell ruin for the offender.

Another "cost" to be added to the list is the potential "criminogenic effect" of the criminal law. Put simply, this means that crime can breed crime. This can occur in two ways. First, under the "labelling theory" once a person is labelled a "criminal" he or she will start acting in conformity with that label and will be more easily tempted to commit further crimes. This potential "cost" must clearly be borne in mind before criminalising conduct, especially minor crimes; once labelled a criminal it is a short step from minor to major crime. Secondly, crime can breed crime by creating an environment or circumstances in which the commission of other crimes becomes likely. For instance, the existence of drug offences greatly increases the cost of drugs to consumers. An addict will thus often have to commit other crimes, such as theft, in order to feed his or her dependency. This can lead to association with other criminals, again increasing the likelihood of yet further crime.

Outlawing certain activities, for example drug-trafficking and peddling pornography, leads to the creation of illicit black markets whose products are uncontrolled and untaxed and which create ideal economic conditions for organised crime to operate. The decriminalisation of such activities renders them more easily capable of regulation. Abortion is a good example here. Since the Abortion Act 1967 abortion has been legal in a fairly wide range of circumstances. This has resulted in a "squeezing out" of "back-street abortionists" with resultant higher standards of regulation and safety as abortions are now generally performed by qualified personnel in properly equipped hospitals.

If an activity is made criminal, that law needs to be enforced, at least to some extent. A total lack of enforcement contradicts the moral message communicated by the law and raises "the spectacle of nullification of the legislature's solemn commands" and can breed an attitude of cynicism towards the law (Kadish, 1967). But the "costs" of such enforcement can be great—particularly in relation to certain crimes. Some laws, particularly those involving consensual sexual activities, can only be enforced in a degrading manner usually involving an unacceptable invasion of privacy and consequent breach of the European Convention on Human Rights. When the only way to enforce the law is for policemen to conceal themselves in the ceilings of public lavatories watching the activities below through peepholes, one must surely scrutinise the gains from such debasing conduct most carefully before concluding that they outweigh such a corrupting cost.

Of course, in weighing these costs and benefits several crucial issues must be taken into account such as the magnitude and probability of the harm (or offence). Naturally, the greater the harm and the more likely its occurrence, the less will be the significance attached to the "costs" of such a crime. For instance, the costs of enforcing a law prohibiting the sexual abuse of small children might be high, but the harm involved is so great that the gains to be derived from such a law clearly outweigh such costs. Also important is the social utility and degree of acceptance of the conduct in question. The greater the social utility (for example, the value attached to speedy public transport) and acceptability of the conduct (for example, alcohol consumption), the greater must be the harm and the gains to be derived before criminalisation is justified.

As the above analysis reveals, there is no simple answer determining exactly what conduct ought to be criminalised. There are competing guiding principles and a bewildering array of qualifying conditions. Suffice it to conclude by repeating two points central to the philosophy of this book. The criminal law should never be invoked unless there is no other way of dealing with the problem. Secondly, the criminal law has a clear moral content (which should preferably be expressed in a moral definition of "harm"). While the decision to criminalise must be subject to rigorous scrutiny to ensure that such a law could be effective and that the gains would outweigh the costs, nevertheless, moral values will ultimately tip the scales in any close decision. It is these moral values that inform the distinction between various offences, such as murder and manslaughter. It would indeed be an odd system of criminal law that allowed its basic structure to be governed by moral values yet denied such values a decisive role in the anterior, but fundamental, question of what conduct should be criminalised in the first place.

3. CRIME REDUCTION

Criminalisation is concerned with identifying those values so important to society as to need enshrining in the criminal law. Once that decision has been made, the function of the criminal law becomes one of maintaining, and securing maximum compliance with, those values. When the values are maintained, most people do not contemplate crime. For the remainder, the criminal law uses stigmatic punishment as a mechanism for preventing or minimising the incidence of criminal activity. Either way, the net aim is one of securing a reduction of crime.

(i) Maintaining values

All laws have a symbolic or expressive function. We have laws against race and sex discrimination—not purely to provide a remedy for the victims of such discrimination, but also to convey and underline the important message that such discrimination is *wrong*. Expressing this message through the criminal law, with its potential stigmatic consequences, emphasises the total rejection of the activity in question. (For this reason it can be argued that certain instances of direct discrimination should have been criminalised to make the message stronger.)

Simply declaring an activity to be criminal can, in itself, have a symbolic effect in influencing attitudes and moral beliefs. This point is illustrated by the research of Kaufmann (1970) who asked a group of subjects to evaluate the morality of certain behaviour (failing to rescue a drowning man). Some subjects were told that this behaviour was criminal; others were told that there was no legal duty to rescue. The former group judged the inaction more harshly than the latter group. Breaking the law was in itself viewed as immoral. Similarly, Walker and Marsh (1984) discovered that subjects stated that their disapproval of not wearing a seat belt would increase when this became an offence.

While the mere existence of criminal law has important expressive consequences, it is enforcement of that law and the punishment of offenders that gives the criminal law its real "sting". Through punishment society is emphatically condemning and thereby disavowing the offender's acts. Failure to punish, on the other hand, amounts to an endorsement or approval of such actions. Feinberg (1965) uses a telling example: suppose an aeroplane from nation A shoots down an aeroplane from nation B over international waters. If nation A were to punish its pilot this would amount to a disavowal of the pilot's action: the actions would simply be those of a deranged pilot. But a failure to punish the pilot would amount to an endorsement of his actions. Nation A would effectively be admitting that it was responsible for the act and approved of it.

Such disavowals of criminal acts have an important socialising effect in reinforcing attitudes and social values. They are part of the conditioning process that creates conscious and unconscious inhibitions against committing crime. In this way the criminal law can have the effect of strengthening the public's moral code. Every time a person is punished for, say, theft, our underlying conviction that theft is wrong is reinforced. The aim of punishing drunken drivers is not simply to deter other would-be drunken drivers but to try to induce a social climate in which it is regarded as morally unacceptable to drive after drinking too much alcohol.

Acceptance of these views has important implications for the structuring of substantive criminal offences. If the function of the criminal law and punishment is largely an expressive, symbolic one, it is important that the messages to be communicated be informative. For instance, single broad offences would be morally confusing. The law must state clearly, for example, that both murder and manslaughter are unacceptable wrongs, but it must point out the level of rejection of each activity by different labels and punishment levels. Bearing this expressive function more clearly in mind would also lead to a clearer relationship between different offences, for example, theft, handling stolen goods and fraud. The enquiry would simply be: how crucial are the values embodied in each of these offences, relative to each other? The answer to this question would reveal how necessary it was to disavow deviation from those values; appropriate levels of punishment would emerge.

A lesser, but related, claim is that even if criminal law and punishment does not actually mould morality, it nevertheless induces an automatic, habitual response of obeying the law. A soldier in the army might not believe in the justice or morality of every order he receives, but he has been indoctrinated into a knee-jerk habit of obeying all orders. The criminal law and punishment can induce such law-abiding conduct "purely as a matter of habit, with fear, respect for authority or social imitation as connecting links" (Andenaes, 1952).

Punishment for the purpose of inducing the habit of conformity to the law might be necessary for other psychological reasons. Durkheim (1964) has argued that those who obey the law need support. At a subconscious level there might be a temptation to commit crime. By abstaining therefrom, the conformist has been able to maintain internal control. To sustain this balance within the personality and ensure the dominance of internal control, the conformist needs to be able to identify with the police and the courts; the offender must be made unattractive as a role model. The inhibition of deviant impulses must be made to seem worthwhile. The punishment of offenders reassures the conformist that it was worth obeying the law. His or her morale and habit of not breaking the law are maintained.

(ii) Deterrence

A more traditional explanation of the function of the criminal law is that the threat of punishment for violating that law operates as a deterrent. Unlike the above idea of utilising the criminal law to reaffirm social values (often called "educative deterrence"), the threat of punishment operates here at a conscious level, inducing people to refrain from crime. Deterrent punishment can operate in one of two ways.

With *individual deterrence* the hope is that the offender being punished will find the experience so unpleasant that he or she will not re-offend. It is extremely difficult to test the efficacy of this. Statistics as to the number of offenders not reconvicted (and who might therefore have been deterred as a result of their previous punishment) are of limited utility unless one knows why they did not re-offend (and what percentage did commit further crimes but were not apprehended).

With *general deterrence* the punishment of the offender is aimed at the public at large in the hope that the example and threat of punishment will deter them from crime. This operates in two ways. First, regular and normal levels of punishment keep the constant threat of similar punishment alive. Secondly, in the past courts have occasionally passed "exemplary sentences". These are disproportionately severe penalties usually imposed when a particular type of activity is on the increase. For instance, concern over the rise of football hooliganism led to the exemplary sentence of life imprisonment for riotous assembly outside a football ground in *Whitton* (1985)—a sentence reduced to three years' imprisonment on appeal: *Whitton* (1986).

The theory of general deterrence rests entirely upon one assumption: that people are in fact deterred from committing crime by the threat of punishment. It is crucial therefore that the public knows about punishments being imposed. Such publicity is most easily obtained when exemplary sentences are imposed (but is probably counterbalanced by the extensive coverage given to the occasional "lenient" sentence). News media coverage of "normal" punishments is far more selective and mainly confined to local papers—and even there it is the circumstances of the offence and the identity of the offender that attract most attention (Walker, 1985).

There are several celebrated examples purporting to demonstrate the effectiveness of deterrent sentencing. For instance, in 1919 the police went on strike in Liverpool. With the chances of apprehension significantly reduced, the crime rate (especially looting of shops) escalated sharply. Similar results occurred when the Nazis occupied Denmark in 1944 and arrested the entire police force; the general crime rate rose sharply and immediately.

Much of the research on deterrence has been based on an economic model. The potential criminal is seen as a rational calculator who balances the costs and benefits of his or her possible actions. The "costs" include the probability of apprehension, the severity of punishment, the ease with which the crime can be committed, chances of success, etc., while "benefits" refer to the satisfaction, whether monetary or otherwise, to be derived from the crime. Feeding in other variables such as income, earning potential, environment, taste, employment status and education level, the thesis is that a person will only commit a crime if, according to his or her evaluation, the benefits will outweigh the costs (*i.e.* there is a net utility to be derived), and if this perceived utility exceeds what he or she could derive from alternative, lawful activities.

Becker (1968), in a pioneering article, hypothesised that an offence, O, could be expressed as the function

$$O = O(p, f, u)$$

where p is the probability of conviction, f is the expected punishment and u is a composite variable representing all the other influences. In order for deterrence to be effective and crime to be reduced, the costs must be made to outweigh the benefits. Increasing the probability of conviction or the severity of the punishment would make the prospect of crime less attractive and induce the individual not to commit crimes. As p, f and u are all functions of O, albeit without precise values, it follows that crimes with low detection rates would need correspondingly higher penalties. The importance of the other variables must be forgotten. For instance, if education could be increased and unemployment reduced, the utility to be gained from lawful employment might outweigh that to be derived from crime.

Several empirical studies based on this economic model of crime have been carried out and indicate some support for the thesis. For instance, Ehrlich (1973) found that a one per cent increase in p (probability of conviction) was associated with a crime reduction of 0.99 per cent, and a one per cent increase in f (expected punishment) was associated with a crime reduction of 1.12 per cent.

Such an economic analysis of criminal motivation and the entire theory of general deterrence is based upon an assumption that people are always rational and think before they act. They are "rational utility maximizers", which means that prospective gains and losses are weighed against each other with decisions and choices being based on such a calculus. While this might be true of some individuals and some crimes (for instance, one might rationally calculate the gains and losses in parking on a double-yellow line or in failing to declare some income on one's tax return), it is clearly not true of all individuals and crimes. Many crimes (particularly those involving violence) are often committed by persons in highly emotional states who are acting in an exceedingly irrational manner. The man who, in a fury, beats his wife to death is hardly a "rational utility maximizer"; his motivation is anger, jealousy, love, hate or whatever and he is simply not amenable to deterrence at that point. Similarly, many other persons are not deterrable: the mentally disordered, the intoxicated, the drug user, etc. Wright and Deckner (1994) found that burglars typically "perceived themselves to be in a situation of immediate need" and refused to consider the possibility of getting caught. The criminal law might have some effect with some of such persons in inducing some care in the commission of the crime—for instance, a drug addict might not purchase drugs right in front of a policeman—but it will never deter him or her from committing the crime altogether.

Deterrence can only be effective if people think that there is a reasonable prospect that they will be caught. Current research does suggest a clear correlation between likelihood of conviction and crime rates (von Hirsch *et al.*, 1999). This is particularly true of those who have "higher stakes in conventionality" (Nagin, 1998). To such persons the fear of arrest and attendant publicity and loss of esteem is more important than any ensuing sentence. However, if people think there is a negligible prospect of being caught, they are hardly likely to be deterred. A couple wishing to inflict minor sado-masochistic injuries on each other in their own home are hardly going to be deterred by the threat of imprisonment. They know that they will not be apprehended and so will not be deterred. We shall see later (pp. 269–270) that large numbers of crimes are never reported to the police or recorded by them and that overall only about two per cent of offences committed result in a criminal prosecution. The old adage appears true: crime pays; the criminal's chances of not being caught are far higher than those of being apprehended. Further, if one examines the clear-up rate per offence (again, of those recorded by the police) one discovers that generally the offences for which one is most likely to be apprehended (homicide: 95 per cent; violence against the person: 76 per cent; sexual offences: 75 per cent)) are those that are often committed impulsively or by persons not amenable to deterrence while the clear-up rate for crimes more likely to be committed "rationally" is even lower than the general average (burglary: 20 per cent).

Of course, in assessing the efficacy of deterrent punishment, the actual statistics on clear-up rates are not helpful unless the prospective criminal is aware of them. What matters is the individual's assessment of his or her prospects of apprehension. If he or she thinks there is a 95 per cent chance of being caught if committing robbery, then he or she will probably be deterred and it is irrelevant that the assessment of the risk is hopelessly awry. There are no reliable statistics on this. Willcock and Stokes (1968) discovered that the young persons they surveyed tended to overrate their chances of detection. However, while many persons might be overcautious in their estimate of the risks, it would not be unreasonable to assume that many others will think they are "too smart" to get caught—and once they start committing crimes they will become part of the statistical pattern; their assessment of the risks will become more accurate and, knowing the truth, they will be less likely to be deterred.

It is difficult to obtain clear evidence as to the deterrent effect of sentencing (Beyleveld 1980). One clear point does, however, emerge from the research. While, as seen above, there is evidence that a high risk of apprehension and conviction does have some deterrent effect, current research has failed to establish any such clear link between the severity of sentences and deterrence (von Hirsch *et al.*, 1999). Again, here, what matters is the perception of potential offenders. Greatly increasing the severity of sentences cannot possibly have an increased deterrent effect unless potential offenders are aware of the increase. Research suggests that the public tends to underestimate the severity of sentences. For example, Hough and Roberts (1998) found that 75 per cent of their sample of the public thought (the median estimate) that only 35 per cent of adult muggers are sent to prison when the reality is that 70 per cent are sent to prison. Judges, perhaps in desperation, continue to have faith in the deterrent impact of their sentences. Recent successive governments have been more equivocal in their approach. The Criminal Justice Act 1991 and, particularly, the Government White Paper (1990) preceding it, largely eschewed deterrence as a major goal in sentencing. By 1997 this same Government was reaffirming its belief in general deterrence and enacted the Crime (Sentences) Act 1997 containing mandatory and minimum sentences for certain crimes (below, p. 263). The Labour Government then proceeded to bring much of this Act into force. There is a perception that the (voting) public believes in deterrence and so it is politically expedient for governments, who wish to be seen to be "tough on crime", to keep ringing the deterrence bell. However, the most realistic view is probably that expressed by Walker (1985), who concludes that "*some* people can be deterred in *some* situations from *some* types of conduct by *some* degree of likelihood that they will be penalized in *some* ways."

(iii) Incapacitation

Another commonly stated function of the criminal law is the protection of society by the incapacitation of dangerous offenders. Crime is reduced by restricting the offender's opportunity to commit further crimes.

Most societies allow for some special form of protective sentencing. In England the Criminal Justice Act 1991 broadly endorses the concept that sentences should be proportionate to the seriousness of the crime, but allows longer than normal sentences to be imposed for violent or sexual offences "if it is necessary to protect the public from serious harm from the offender" (section 2(2)(b): now Powers of Criminal Courts (Sentencing) Act 2000, section 80(2)(b)). The Crime (Sentences) Act 1997, drawing inspiration from the "Three Strikes and You're Out" laws in the United States, provides that a person convicted a second time of a defined "serious offence" *must* be sentenced to life imprisonment unless there are "exceptional circumstances" (section 2: now Powers of Criminal Courts (Sentencing) Act 2000, section 109). Also, with the wide array of offences carrying a maximum penalty of life imprisonment (for example, rape, causing grievous bodily harm with intent, aggravated burglary, etc.) the sentencing judge can impose such a maximum penalty upon an offender perceived to be dangerous to society. Finally, it must be remembered that non-custodial protective sentences can be imposed. Disqualifying an offender from driving is regarded as one of the most effective means of protecting road-users from dangerous drivers. Fortunately, other more barbaric forms of incapacitative sentence, such as cutting off limbs, deportation to Australia and capital punishment, are no longer with us today.

Two examples of protective sentencing will help reveal the nature of, and the difficulties with, utilising the criminal law and the process of punishment for this purpose. In *Kelly* (1999) the victim threw stones at a group of boys bullying a girl at a railway station. One of the stones struck the shelter in which the offender was sitting. A fight broke out and the offender punched and kicked the victim in the face causing a fractured cheek bone and the loss of two teeth. The offender was convicted under section 18 of the Offences Against the Person Act 1861. 18 years previously the offender had been convicted of a number of robberies involving firearms. Because he was convicted of a "serious offence" and had a conviction of "another serious offence" an automatic life sentence was imposed under the Crime (Sentences) Act 1997, section 2. The time gap, and the dissimilarity, between the offences were held not to constitute "exceptional circumstances" as they were not "out of the ordinary course, or unusual, or special, or uncommon". The other case is a famous and controversial United States Supreme Court decision, *Rummel v. Estelle* (1980) in which a sentence of life imprisonment for obtaining $120.75 by false pretences was affirmed. The defendant had two previous convictions: fraudulent use of a credit card to obtain $80 worth of goods (nine years previously), and passing a forged cheque of $28.36 (four years previously). He was prosecuted under a Texas recidivist statute making life imprisonment mandatory upon a third felony conviction. A majority in the Supreme Court rejected a claim that life imprisonment was a grossly disproportionate punishment and held that it was legitimate for a state to segregate recidivists from the rest of society "for an extended period of time".

An assessment of these two cases leads us directly to a consideration of two central problems associated with sentencing on such bases. First, how is "dangerousness" to be defined for these purposes? Kelly did at least commit a violent offence which could qualify as "dangerous". The same is plainly not true of Rummel. If protective sentencing is to be employed, it must surely be limited to those who are dangerous in the sense of being likely to cause serious harms. Of course, this approach in itself raises problems. While most would agree that death, serious bodily injury and serious sexual assault clearly qualify as serious harms for this purpose, controversy arises in relation to a host of other harms, for example, "loss or damage to property which results in severe personal hardship" (Floud Committee, 1981). One thing does, however, seem certain. It could not be seriously asserted that the kind of offence Rummel might in future commit could possibly justify the imposition of a sentence of life imprisonment.

The second problem is one of predicting dangerousness. How probable must it be that Kelly or Rummel will offend again before we are justified in imposing an incapacitative sentence? How immediate, how frequent and how specific must the risk be? With no previous convictions for 18 years, how could it possibly be predicted that Kelly was likely to reoffend? Numerous research projects have been undertaken aimed at developing accurate criteria for predicting dangerousness. For instance, Greenwood (1982) developed a seven-factor prediction index (based on previous criminal history, drug use and unemployment) to identify persons likely to commit frequent acts of robbery or other violent crimes in future. The problem with this and many other projects is that research has been based on the admissions of imprisoned offenders only, which has prompted the cynical response that this is "like trying to learn about the smoking habits of smokers generally by studying the smoking activity of residents of a lung cancer ward" (von Hirsch, 1986). Even more serious is the fact that such projects to date have tended to yield rather too many "false positives" (classifications of dangerousness that did not materialise). Research tends to suggest that most predictive methods are only successful in one out of three cases and sometimes even lower (Brady and Tarling, 1981: success rate of only 20 per cent).

This last point is critical. A "false positive" is not just a statistic. It is a human being locked up in prison because society has made a mistake in wrongly predicting him to be dangerous. Accordingly, until such time as more accurate prediction criteria have been developed (if this is ever possible) it must be highly questionable whether punishment for such reasons can be justified. The related question of whether it can *ever* be permissible to punish people on the basis of what they might do in the future will be considered in the final section of this book.

(iv) Rehabilitation

Few would dissent from the proposition that it would be in everyone's interests if offenders could be rehabilitated. If most offenders became reformed individuals who were less inclined to commit further crimes, a huge step towards the overall objective of crime reduction would have been achieved. But, while there is general agreement that rehabilitation is a desirable *by-product* of punishment, controversy arises when it is asserted that rehabilitation is one of the main *purposes* of the institution of punishment.

Over the past century our criminal justice system has become more concerned with the rehabilitation and welfare of convicted offenders. Many reforms to the prison system have been instituted, with increasing emphasis being placed on training and educational programmes within prisons so that employment prospects on release will be enhanced. In recent years various cognitive skills courses (Reasoning and Rehabilitation; Enhanced Thinking Skills) have been introduced in prisons. More significant, however, has been the recognition that imprisonment necessarily involves the isolation of the offender from the realities of social life which can hardly be conducive to the rehabilitation process. Prisoners tend to become institutionalised and dependent on a system that relieves them of the responsibility of having to control their own destiny. If, on the other hand, offenders could be kept in society and forced (with help) to deal with the real world while being encouraged to understand and to assume responsibility, rehabilitation could be more easily achieved. To reflect this latter philosophy various non-custodial sentences have been introduced into English law, particularly probation (renamed "community rehabilitation orders" by the Criminal Justice and Court Services Act 2000, section 43) and community service orders (renamed "community punishment orders" by section 43 of the same Act).

With rehabilitative sentencing emphasis is placed on the offender who is regarded as "sick" and in need of a cure. Like a doctor prescribing medicine, the sentencer must impose that sentence predicted to be most effective in making the offender better. This leads to "individualisation" of sentencing. Punishment is made to fit the offender and not the crime. With less emphasis being placed on the crime committed, the result is that two offenders committing similar crimes can receive very different sentences if their "needs" are not the same.

While such ideas have a certain humanitarian appeal, the fact remains that it is almost impossible to justify rehabilitation as a *purpose* of punishment. There are several reasons for this. First, we know very little of the causes of crime and so have limited knowledge of how to change people's behaviour and eliminate their propensity to commit crime. The result is that efforts to tailor the sentence to fit the offender are almost inevitably doomed to failure. Martinson (1974) concluded that rehabilitative sentencing simply does not work; the type of sentence given to an offender made no difference to the likelihood of his being convicted. While this is now widely recognised as a gross exaggeration (even Martinson [1976] partially retracted his earlier sweeping conclusions), the fact remains that it is extremely difficult to assess accurately the rehabilitative effect of any given sentence and the research to date has been inconclusive as to the efficacy of such sentencing. Despite some research in the United Kingdom claiming success for the new cognitive skills programmes, high reconviction rates for offenders on such programmes fails to support such claims (Fraser, 2000). One thing seems certain: the overall picture painted by penologists is so pessimistic that one could never be justified in claiming that it was legitimate to sentence offenders primarily for the purpose of reforming them.

Rehabilitative sentencing can also be attacked on other grounds. Eliminating a person's propensity to commit crime involves altering his personality so that he no longer wants to commit crime. Is one entitled to use any means to achieve this result—even drugs, aversion and electric shock therapy or psychosurgery? And for how long is one entitled to continue such "treatment"? These questions raise the fundamental human rights issues of whether we have the moral right to change a person's personality without his consent. The commission of a crime does not deprive one of all basic human rights so that one can be treated as an experimental guinea pig. As Morris and Hawkins (1977) have asserted: "we must stay out of the business of forcibly remaking man".

The final nail in the coffin of the rehabilitative ideal occurred when research began to reveal the extent to which rehabilitation was leading to sentencing disparity. People committing broadly similar crimes were receiving vastly different sentences—under the guise of individualised sentencing. In the United States, particularly, concern over the extent of such sentencing disparity, coupled with the publication of research indicating that rehabilitative sentencing was not effective, led to the swift and sudden demise of the rehabilitative ideal and its replacement by the notion that one must sentence people according to what they deserve (see later, pp. 273–282).

For all these reasons it seems clear that one is not justified in punishing in order to accomplish rehabilitative objectives. But that is not to say that rehabilitation is of no consequence. Indeed, one of the dangers of minimising its importance is that it could induce those managing the criminal justice system, particularly those involved in executing sentences such as prison warders, to become more punitive-minded, or even vindictive, in their approach to their work. A civilised and humane society cannot afford to ignore the importance of rehabilitating offenders. What this means is that while one might be punishing for other reasons such as deterrence or incapacitation, rehabilitation must remain a desirable *collateral objective*. When espoused as a *purpose* of punishment, rehabilitation becomes vulnerable and in danger of being jettisoned if found to be ineffective. But if clearly understood as a desirable by-product or collateral purpose, the rehabilitative ideal becomes immune from attack on grounds of inefficacy. Put crudely: it doesn't matter if we are successful in reforming people because that is not the object of the exercise—but in trying to achieve our main objectives we should at least try to rehabilitate offenders (subject to any human rights constraints). This is the humane course of action and any success would be of immense additional advantage.

4. ENFORCEMENT OF THE CRIMINAL LAW

We saw earlier that the mere existence of a particular law can have some symbolic impact. But, for the most part, if the criminal law hopes to be effective in achieving its objectives there must be a certain degree of actual enforcement of the law. The task of defining this necessary degree or level of enforcement, however, raises controversial political issues. These will be sketched briefly in this section.

The costs of crime are incalculable but generally agreed to be enormous. A recent Home Office Research Study (2000) estimates the total cost of crime to England and Wales in 1999–2000 to be around £60 billion. Including the "dark figure" on unreported crime it has been estimated that fraud in the United Kingdom financial community results in losses of up to nearly £14 billion a year. For example, in 1998 fraud linked to plastic payment cards amounted to £135 million (Digest 4, 1999) and the Benefits Agency lost £1.4 billion in income support frauds (Law Commission, 1999). Opportunity costs to victims (time spent assisting the police or receiving treatment for injuries together with loss of income) are incalculable. Non-economic costs must also be considered: for instance, fear of violence on the streets in urban areas can cause intense anxiety and restrict the social activities of persons, diminishing the quality of their lives (Maxfield, 1984).

However, on the other side of the balance sheet, the costs of enforcing the criminal law are similarly astronomic. In 1999–2000 the criminal justice system cost £12 billion, 63 per cent of which was spent on the police and the remainder on the CPS, prisons, the probation service, the courts and criminal legal aid. In 1998–99 the Home Office spent about £12.6 million on crime prevention (for example, crime prevention publicity and safer cities programmes) and the private retail sector (in 1997–98) spent £550 million on security (burglar alarms, security transport, etc.) (Digest 4, 1999). In total, over £5 billion was spent in costs in anticipation of crime, mostly on security expenditure (Home Office Research Study, 2000).

Despite this enormous investment, we have already seen that most crimes are never "cleared up" (a crime is "cleared up" when there is sufficient evidence to charge a person) with the result that only some two per cent of offences committed result in a criminal conviction. Why is this?

While in some cases the police act proactively and discover crimes themselves, for example, drug raids or drink-driving campaigns (Ashworth, 1994), more typically their role is reactive. It is members of the public and victims in particular who bring crime to the attention of the police. It has been estimated that crimes are only reported to the police in 41 per cent of cases. For certain crimes, such as vandalism, common assault and robbery, about 70 per cent are unreported (British Crime Survey, 2000). There are several reasons why victims do not report crimes to the police. In many situations the crime might be regarded as too trivial or the victim might feel that as there is no prospect of identifying the offender reporting is pointless. (This latter consideration will not apply in burglaries and car crimes where reporting is more common for insurance purposes.) However, even in cases of serious personal injury where the assailant can be identified, there is still some reluctance to report. Many victims of violence are somewhat marginalised persons such as the unemployed, the homeless and those who spend much of their lives on the street, often under the influence of drink or drugs; such persons recognise that "their damaged status renders them of little value in the currency of the courts" (Clarkson *et al.*, 1994). Other victims might be reluctant to have their own conduct subjected to too much scrutiny. Their own criminality and/or hostile attitude to the police might make them less likely to report. Over 33 per cent of assault victims know their assailants well and in such cases there are immense personal costs involved in reporting a crime. Where the victim and the assailant have an on-going relationship, fear of reprisals or of disruption of that relationship can prevent reporting. Where victims feel that neither the police nor the courts will be able to prevent further violence, there is little incentive to report (Clarkson *et al.*, 1994).

It was stated earlier that crime is widely regarded as an "offence against the state" (p. 2). Accordingly, one might have expected that if a crime had been reported, the police, as agents of the state, would record the crime, conduct an investigation and, if the offender were discovered, apprehend him or her and pass the file on to the CPS who, in turn, would initiate a prosecution. Such an assumption would, however, be naïve. A significant proportion of reported crimes are never *recorded* by the police meaning that overall only 23 per cent of crime is reported and recorded by the police (British Crime Survey, 2000) and even in these cases there will not necessarily be an investigation with the result that only 29 per cent of recorded offences are "cleared up" by the police (Criminal Statistics, 1998). Both the police and the CPS are invested with vast discretionary powers and a wide variety of factors influence their decisions whether to proceed. For example, research into assault cases has revealed that in most cases, rather than acting as independent agents of the state in investigating and prosecuting crime, the police tend to respond to the wishes of the victim. Only if he or she is committed to, and presses for, a prosecution will the police pursue the matter with any enthusiasm. Some of the reasons for this approach are obvious. Unless the victim is prepared to testify in court and is perceived as a reliable witness a prosecution in many cases would be pointless. Such research tends to shatter the traditional "crime against the state" model of criminal justice that is normally projected (Cretney *et al.*, 1994). Of course, there are also other factors that influence police decision-making here: for example, the seriousness of the injury; whether the police construct the incident as having been essentially "private" as occurs with some cases of "domestic violence" (with decreasing frequency) and with fights between young men who know each other; and the character, attitude and criminal record of both the assailant and victim.

Further, even if the matter has been investigated and the file passed on, the CPS will not necessarily prosecute. It will only do so if there is a "realistic prospect of conviction", meaning it is more likely than not that there will be a conviction. Further, prosecution must be in the "public interest" making the prosecution of the elderly and mentally ill, for example, unlikely. The Code for Crown Prosecutors attempts to structure this discretion and stipulates that prosecutors should consider factors such as the likely sentence. If a defendant elects for trial in the Crown Court where proceedings are more expensive than in the magistrates' court and if it is felt that only a light sentence will be imposed, the CPS might well abandon the case. Particularly problematic areas in deciding whether a prosecution will be in the public interest are "political" crimes, offences by soldiers in Northern Ireland and crimes committed by police officers (Greer, 1994). While one might have expected most of these cases to be weeded out or cautioned, by the police, the CPS nevertheless discontinued the prosecution in about 12 per cent of all cases in 1999–2000. (CPS Annual Report, 1999–2000) and, of course, in many cases will reduce the charge either in response to a plea-bargain or to save costs and guarantee a conviction. For example, research in Bristol has revealed that in cases of domestic violence the CPS invariably prefers to charge common assault even though the level of injury would merit a more serious charge. The main reason for this is that the case will then have to be heard in the magistrates' court; this will be quicker and cheaper and less onerous for the victim or witness (Cretney and Davis, 1997). Such discontinuances and lowering of charges has led to a good deal of ill-feeling between the police and the CPS.

Clearly full enforcement of the criminal law is out of the question. The economic costs would be unthinkable and so also would be the social costs of living in a police state with a concomitant erosion of civil liberties and individual rights. The problem of shaping penal policy thus becomes the political one of determining the extent to which resources should be allocated to enforcement of the criminal law (as compared to the entire economy). The answer to this is necessarily shaped by other political considerations. For instance, those who see a clear link between crime and unemployment, inner-city decay and deprivation will obviously favour greater investment in tackling these social problems which will necessarily involve less direct expenditure on criminal law enforcement. Yet this is not the only resource allocation decision that needs to be made. Of the criminal justice allocation, how much should be spent on the police, how much on the courts, on prisons, etc.? And within each component—say, the police—how much should be devoted to each of the numerous branches or departments thereof?

During the 1960s in Britain a certain degree of consensus existed on many fronts. There was a belief in the rehabilitative ideal and in the welfare state: greater expenditure on the latter would tackle the underlying causes of crime and thereby reduce the incidence of crime.

The 1970s and 1980s, however, saw a sharp polarisation of political opinion with the emergence of a "law and order" lobby who, impatient with perceived "softness" towards criminals, began demanding increased police powers and tougher sentences for criminals. The Conservative Party embraced many of these ideas and won the 1979 election with an election manifesto placing "law and order" high on its lists of priorities. The adoption of such a platform was hardly surprising given the Conservative Government's overall policy of returning to "traditional values" which included a great emphasis on discipline and individual responsibility and increasing scepticism of the welfare state. According to this view offenders cannot hide behind the "excuse" of social deprivation but must bear full responsibility for their actions which necessarily means they must be caught and then punished.

In pursuing these objectives the Conservative Government passed the Criminal Justice Act 1982 (attempting to deal more firmly with young offenders in particular) and increased sentences for certain crimes (attempted rape and trafficking in Class A drugs). Further "law and order" statutes such as the Public Order Act 1986 and the Drug Trafficking Offences Act 1986 soon followed. Other legislation aimed at expanding the reach of the criminal law, tightening up sentencing and increasing the powers of the police include the Criminal Justice Acts of 1988 and 1993, the Bail (Amendment) Act 1993 and the Criminal Justice and Public Order Act 1994. (The Criminal Justice Act 1991 was in a somewhat different category and regarded by many as representing progressive thinking. Many of its reforms, however, have been eroded by subsequent legislation). Equally significant has been the government's endorsement of the status and powers of the police. Determined to strengthen the image and moral authority of the police who are at the "cutting edge" of the criminal justice system, the government awarded substantial pay increases to them (greatly in excess of those awarded to other public servants) and enacted the Police and Criminal Evidence Act 1984 clarifying and strengthening police powers significantly. In terms of the punishment of offenders, the "law and order" policy can be seen in the investment of large sums in new building programmes for prisons (Morgan, 1983). The Labour Government, elected on a manifesto pledge to be "tough on crime", has continued such policies in much the same vein, for example, bringing into force mandatory sentences for repeat drug traffickers and burglars of domestic premises along with a range of measures and proposals aimed at curtailing youth offending.

However, despite this greater commitment to enforcement of the criminal law, no measurable reduction in crime has ensued. In fact, the opposite is true. The number of recorded crimes nearly doubled between 1981 and 1998 while even under the British Crime Survey assessment the number of crimes rose by about 30 per cent over this period although there has been a clear drop in the overall number of offences committed between 1997 and 1999 (British Crime Survey, 2000). It thus seems that there is little prospect of further investment in the police and prisons, etc., having any effect on the crime rate. Accordingly, it might be better to channel any extra resources into tackling the causes of crime—homelessness, drug-addiction, inner-city deprivation and so on—and to adopt more realistic goals in terms of the role of the criminal justice system in achieving crime reduction. If the role of the criminal law were seen from this perspective more attention could be devoted to ensuring that it was applied in a fair and just manner—rather than in trying to achieve crime reduction. Over the past two decades this has become a matter of utmost concern to those involved in the criminal law and its application—and it is to this final topic that we now turn.

5. JUSTICE AND DESERT

The function of the criminal law is to identify that conduct which ought to be criminalised and to try to reduce the incidence of such activity. However, there are severe restrictions on the way in which the law can attempt to achieve this objective.

First, in a civilised society cruel or barbaric punishment must be impermissible. Even if it could be scientifically proven that the incidence of theft would be reduced by cutting off the hands of thieves, such an option would simply be unacceptable. The same is true of corporal and capital punishment. A society resorting to controlled, explicit violence against its offenders reduces itself to their level. The hypocrisy of claiming that murder, for instance, is wrong while indulging in ritualised killing is manifest and robs the criminal law of its claim to moral authority. It simply becomes an assertion of power. The Human Rights Act 1998, which incorporates Protocol 6 outlawing capital punishment in the United Kingdom, hopefully means that the role of such punishments in Britain can be assigned to the history books.

A second and more problematic issue relates to the distribution of punishment. Who can be punished and to what extent can they be punished in order to seek a reduction of crime? For instance, could one impose a sentence of life imprisonment for minor theft? Could one punish the children of an offender if this were felt to be an effective deterrent? If we punished someone (anyone!) every time a burglary were committed, the level of such criminal activity would almost surely be reduced by knowledge of such a "100 per cent clear-up rate". But would such sentences be justifiable?

In discharging its functions the criminal law must be structured and applied in a just and fair manner that is capable of commanding general respect. This means that the type of conduct made criminal, the structure and definitions of the criminal law and the extent of punishment must be accepted by the bulk of society. It is thus crucial that the criminal law reflects everyday values: the way we live our lives and treat each other. Integral to these values is the notion of *desert*. Think of the everyday responses: "She deserved to pass her exams"; "The way they played, they deserved to lose the cricket match". What people deserve depends on the extent to which we praise or blame them for their actions and the results of their actions. We praise an actor's performance in the cinema and say, "He deserves an Oscar"; we blame the football team that plays poorly and without spirit all season and say, "They deserve to be relegated to the bottom division".

We have seen throughout this book that generally the criminal law is structured so as to reflect these fundamental values. When a blameworthy actor causes a harm (in an area appropriately criminalised) punishment is deserved. We have similarly seen that there are degrees of blame and different levels of harm. Causing death is "worse" than causing bodily harm. Intentionally causing death is "worse" than recklessly causing it. It follows that the amount of punishment deserved varies with the degree of blame and harm. In other words, the entire structure of the criminal law, with related punishment levels, depends on this notion of desert. It would make no sense to construct an entire system on the premise of desert and then, when it came to punishment, to jettison all such reasoning and resort to pure crime prevention tactics. It is thus clear in principle: no punishment can be imposed unless it is deserved. Life imprisonment for minor theft is not deserved; the children of an offender and other innocent persons do not deserve punishment so that others may be deterred.

Some writers have pushed this idea of desert further and have asserted that the *purpose* of the whole institution of punishment is to give offenders their just deserts. By committing a crime they have gained an unfair advantage over other members of society who have exercised restraint. They must be punished in order to eliminate that advantage and restore social equilibrium. This seems a rather metaphysical justification for the infliction of suffering upon others. There must surely be some greater purpose to the criminal law. It must be permissible at least to strive for some concrete benefit such as crime reduction. But in this quest it is crucial to recognise that the law must be subject to the *constraints of just desert* so that if one fails in one's objectives, at least it would not be a failure involving injustice (cynically called a "failure model" of the criminal law by Rothman, 1981). Put another way, the function of the criminal law and punishment is to reduce crime—but one is only justified in punishing any given offender to the extent that he or she deserves punishment.

This way of thinking might seem uncontroversial when applied to the extreme examples earlier in this section. But that logic must be capable of general application. This means that many offenders who are given automatic life sentences on conviction for a second serious offence and longer than normal sentences for violent or sexual offences to protect the public from serious harm (p. 262) are being punished more than they deserve. They are being sentenced primarily on the basis of what they might do in the future—unless it can be argued that they deserve more punishment because of their persistent violation of the law. Similar reasoning can be applied to exemplary sentences, such as the one imposed on the football hooligan in *Whitton* (1985) (see p. 259). He was being used as a means to some greater end, the deterrence of others; he did not deserve the penalty of life imprisonment initially imposed on him. Excessive rehabilitative sentencing can be similarly condemned. In *Greedy* (1964) a sentence was increased from three to five years' imprisonment "to give time for treatment to be effective". Assuming that three years was the "deserved sentence", this defendant was sentenced to two years' undeserved imprisonment.

While the concept of just desert is by no means new, it is only in the last few decades that it has begun to assume a position of critical importance in criminal law thinking. Until then, belief in the possibility of crime reduction and enchantment with the rehabilitative ideal had held sway for much of this century. The "just deserts" movement began in the 1970s in the United States and was primarily the result of two related factors. First, there was the demise of the rehabilitative ideal (pp. 266–267) and mounting scepticism as to the efficacy of sentencing for deterrent purposes (pp. 261–262) and, secondly, there was growing concern at the extent of sentencing disparity. The injustice of imposing hugely different sentences upon offenders convicted of similar crimes began to be stressed. Whether this was the result of "individualisation" of sentencing or, more likely, judges simply being inconsistent and perhaps even idiosyncratic in their approach did not really matter. The result was the same. Justice demands equality of treatment. There is no justice when persons guilty of crimes of comparable seriousness receive vastly different punishments. The best way to eliminate such inequality is to limit judicial discretion in the sentencing decision, ensuring that the decision is the same irrespective of the judge.

A majority of states in the United States have attempted to give effect to such ideas by developing "guideline models" of sentencing. The best known of these is the Minnesota Sentencing Guidelines Grid that operates as follows. All offences are ranked in a hierarchy of seriousness and are assigned an appropriate level of severity. Similarly, the offender is allocated a criminal history score by scoring points for each previous conviction (the value of these points varies depending on the seriousness of the prior convictions). The offence level and criminal history score are then arranged in the vertical and horizontal columns respectively of a grid. For every level of offence combined with a particular criminal history score there is a cell containing a presumptive penalty. Variation from this presumptive penalty is permitted if mitigating or aggravating circumstances are found to exist—but this only occurs in some 16 per cent of cases (Frase, 1995). For instance, if a defendant with a criminal history score of three points commits aggravated robbery in Minnesota he or she will normally be sentenced to 78 months' imprisonment unless aggravating or mitigating circumstances are found to exist. Parole is abolished, thus eliminating discretion at the stage of release from prison ("good time" reductions still exist but can be accurately computed in advance). Under such a scheme comparable offenders (in the sense of their criminal record) committing the same crime will receive similar sentences.

There are very real problems with such guideline models of sentencing. First, most offences are defined in fairly broad bands, each encompassing a wide range of factual and moral distinctions. For instance, two defendants with identical criminal records might both commit the (English) crime of robbery. The first defendant, motivated by a desperate family financial situation, threatens the victim with a walking stick and makes off with £10. The second defendant holds up a security van with a sawn-off shotgun and steals £100,000. It seems nonsense to assert that these two should obtain the same or even similar sentences. While this problem is less acute in the United States as offences are there generally more closely defined than in Britain (for example, degrees of robbery exist in many states), it has nevertheless been recognised that the guideline method of sentencing ought to involve a more precise breakdown and subcategorisation of offences. We have seen at various stages of this book that there might be real advantages in such an approach but, if judicial discretion is to be tightly controlled, each category of offence would need to be fairly closely defined, which could involve "hammering out a definition of robbery in the 68th degree" (Executive Advisory Committee on Sentencing in New York, 1979). Such an exercise would not only be impracticable but also totally confusing in terms of the law's moral and communicative role.

A second objection to these United States developments is that while they might succeed in controlling judicial discretion, they ignore the fact that the criminal justice system is riddled with discretion at every stage. Why attack judicial discretion when police and prosecutors have enormous discretionary powers as to whether to arrest and as to the actual offence charged. Indeed, abolishing judicial discretion could simply result in an increased shift of discretionary power to other officials, notably the prosecutor. Principles of equality of treatment and notions of receiving one's just deserts not only come into operation in the courtroom, but also have to be applied throughout the whole system. These points have now been recognised in England and some attempts have been made to control prosecutorial discretion, for example, the Code for Crown Prosecutors and Offences Against the Person: Charging Standard. Under the Charging Standard levels of injury are listed giving the police and the CPS guidance as to the appropriate charge. For example, a black eye should result in a common assault charge while loss or breaking of teeth should result in a section 47 charge (see p. 179). While this is an important step forward one must not overlook the even greater (and completely uncontrolled) discretion exercised by the police as to whether to record and then investigate a crime.

Finally, such a sentencing model has clear dangers. The idea of relatively fixed sentences which a guideline model effectively endorses has long appealed to the "law and order brigade" as their response to a perceived ever-increasing crime rate. Such a sentencing model could then be used as a means of imposing stiffer prison sentences on more persons, resulting in a huge increase in the prison population. It ought to be stressed at this stage that the revived just deserts movement in the United States was not the brain-child of "law and order" thinking. It was first articulated by liberal thinkers concerned with injustice in the system and equally concerned to lower prison sentences. For instance, the Minnesota Sentencing Guideline Commission in developing its guidelines deliberately and overtly adopted a policy of prison population constraint (Minnesota Guidelines Report, 1980). One of the most influential early reports advocating the just deserts approach was the von Hirsch Committee (1976) which proposed that the highest penalty for any offence (save murder) should be five years' imprisonment—with sparing use made of sentences of imprisonment in excess of three years. However, the real reason behind the phenomenal success of the just deserts movement in the United States is the fact that this intellectually respectable theoretical framework provided by the liberals is politically convenient to the conservative law and order camp which is concerned at "undue leniency". The lesson is clear. The success of any guideline model of sentencing depends on the political composition of those drafting the guidelines and fixing the levels of sentence and those charged with maintaining the guidelines.

In England there has also been growing concern at the extent of sentencing disparity. Neither informed commentators nor the general public are any longer prepared to sweep such disparity under the carpet of "individualised sentencing". Whether it be a sudden outrageous sentence such as life imprisonment for a football hooligan (*Whitton*, 1985) or probation for a rapist, there is an increasing tendency for such cases to make front-page news and arouse concern. This is supported by a growing body of research clearly demonstrating that great sentencing disparity exists among the 30,000 magistrates handling 95 per cent of all criminal cases. While one can appeal against sentences from the magistrates' court and from the Crown Court, thus eliminating gross discrepancies in sentencing, the fact remains that appeals from magistrates' courts are not common and appeals from the Crown Court require the leave of the Court of Appeal (Criminal Division).

The English response to this problem has been as follows. First, the Criminal Justice Act 1991 firmly endorsed the concept of just desert in declaring that sentences must generally be proportionate to the seriousness of the offence. Secondly, sentencing guidelines for magistrates' courts have been drawn up by the Magistrates' Association. These guidelines are entirely voluntary and research suggests they are being followed in some 75 per cent of cases. However, they are fairly broadly drafted and it is clear that two magistrates using the same guidelines could come up with very different results. The final English response has been that the Court of Appeal (Criminal Division) now issues guideline judgments in which judicial sentencing guidelines are laid down for particular offences, the idea being that a common law of sentencing will emerge. These judgments consider a wide variety of circumstances in laying down appropriate levels of sentence and also specify what is to be regarded as aggravating or mitigating factors. To assist it in this task a Sentencing Advisory Panel was created and began work in 1999. Its task is to provide views to the Court of Appeal to help the Court in framing sentencing guidelines and thereby to promote fairness and consistency in sentencing. The impact that the Sentencing Advisory Panel will have depends largely on the extent to which the Court of Appeal accepts the advice of the Panel. In this regard, it is unfortunate that in the first such case the Court of Appeal concluded that it could not frame guidelines (*Milford Haven Port Authority*, 2000) and effectively treated the Panel's advice "rather like a brief from an interest group" (Editorial, Criminal Law Review, 2000).

The obvious advantage of such judicial guidelines is their flexibility in comparison with legislatively endorsed guidelines as in the United States. But, from another perspective, this is also their weakness. Descriptive guidelines are necessarily broad and generalised and allow for a great deal of discretion by the sentencing judge. Indeed, the existence of sentencing guidelines for football hooligans (*Wood*, 1984—admittedly even more limited and generalised than usual) did not prevent the initial sentence of life imprisonment being imposed on the defendant in *Whitton* (1985).

Perhaps the best way forward is to construct a guideline model of sentencing that combines the best features of both the above systems and reflects a realistic philosophy of the criminal law and punishment. The problem with the models developed in the United States is that they are too committed to an exclusive endorsement of the just deserts doctrine. While the presumptive sentences can be departed from, there is a tendency not to do so except in exceptional circumstances. The Federal Guidelines, for instance, are almost regarded as mandatory and never to be departed from (Doob, 1995). The result is inflexibility. While the role of just deserts is critical in the criminal law and its construction, this does not mean that it is the only consideration. One can never be justified in punishing a person more than he or she deserves. Rights to freedom can only be forfeited to an extent that is deserved. But the fact that one is justified in punishing a person does not mean that one *must* actually impose that punishment. For instance, my student might *deserve* to be reported to the police and prosecuted for stealing a library book but I might recognise that the humiliation of being caught and exposed to others in our institution will have a sufficient deterrent effect on him and others. Nothing would be achieved by reporting the matter to the police. I can afford mercy. There ought to be a good reason for inflicting suffering on other human beings and such reasons are best found in the utilitarian soil of deterrence, incapacitation and rehabilitation. Put simply, a person may have committed a certain crime meaning that he or she deserves three years' imprisonment. We therefore cannot sentence him or her to more than three years' imprisonment because we adjudge him or her to be dangerous or because we feel that an exemplary sentence might be effective in clamping down on the particular criminal activity. Three years' imprisonment is the maximum possible punishment. But that does not mean that he or she must receive the full deserved sentence. Whether we impose the maximum or something less depends on what we hope to achieve thereby. If he or she has been adjudged not to be dangerous or in need of rehabilitation and a punishment was being imposed primarily to uphold moral standards in society (educative deterrence), we might be able to impose a sentence of less than three years' imprisonment.

However, the demands of justice and equal treatment must be borne firmly in mind. It is important that if another student of mine is caught stealing a library book he or she be treated the same as the first student. It would simply not be just to make a sacrificial lamb out of the second student having treated the first so differently. However, there must be room for some flexibility here—but that flexibility must be controlled. All the circumstances affecting a crime cannot be anticipated in advance and spelled out in a list of aggravating or mitigating circumstances. Accordingly, there must be scope for some discretion. But clear guidance needs to be provided as to the type and level of sentence that is appropriate in a given situation. Present offences are too broad, and judicial guidelines too generalised, for adequate control of judicial discretion.

What is needed is a guideline model for each family of offences—say, one for property offences and another for offences against the person and so on. How thereafter to control judicial discretion while admitting some flexibility is the central problem. It must be remembered that while justice demands like cases be treated alike, it also requires that unlike cases be treated differently. There are various possible compromise models that could be adopted here. For instance, one could have a legislatively fixed maximum sentence within each cell of the grid, with judicial guidelines indicating what the appropriate level of actual punishment in the circumstances should be. Alternatively, one could have a legislatively fixed presumptive penalty or range within each cell. Under either scheme any departure from the judicial guidelines or the presumptive penalty or range would need to be expressly justified by the sentencing judge and there would have to be a right of appeal in such cases.

Certain key issues would need resolving whichever model we adopted. Which aggravating and mitigating circumstances should be built into the substantive definitions of criminal offences? Which should be incorporated into the offence level of the grid? And which should be left to the sentencing judge to influence his or her decision whether to depart from the penalty within the grid? Should previous convictions be the only factors to be incorporated into the offender score—and if so, what weight should be attributed to such factors? This last question can only be answered by determining *why* previous convictions are relevant in the first place. Is it because an offender with previous convictions deserves more punishment because of the failure to learn from the experience of past punishment? Or is it because the guideline model represents a compromise between the just deserts philosophy and the desire to incapacitate perceived dangerous offenders?

These are difficult questions. Answers have not yet clearly emerged but it is in this field that the debate in criminal law will be waged. The days of the old-fashioned "substantive criminal lawyer" who regarded punishment and sentencing as matters purely for penologists and philosophers are gone. The substantive rules of the criminal law and the punishment of offenders are too closely related for any step to be taken on one without considering the implications for the other. Whichever solution to the current sentencing debate ultimately prevails in Britain, it will have a profound effect on the structure and substance of the rules of the criminal law.

BIBLIOGRAPHY

Andenaes, J. (1952), "General Prevention", 43 *Journal of Criminal Law*, C & PS 176

Archbold News (1999), "Comment: Fraud and Deception", *Archbold News*, Issue 5, June 9, 4

Ashworth, A. (1991), *Principles of Criminal Law*, Oxford: Clarendon Press

Ashworth, A. (1994), *The Criminal Process: An Evaluative Study*, Oxford: Clarendon Press

Ashworth, A. (1999), *Principles of Criminal Law* (3rd ed.), Oxford: Oxford University Press

Ashworth, A. (2000a), "Is the Criminal Law a Lost Cause?" 116 *Law Quarterly Review* 225

Ashworth, A. (2000b), "The Human Rights Act and the Substantive Criminal Law: A Non-Minimalist View", *Criminal Law Review* 564

Ashworth, A. and Blake, M. (1996),"The Presumption of Innocence in English Criminal Law", *Criminal Law Review* 306

Baker, E. (1994), "Human Rights, M'Naghten and the 1991 Act", *Criminal Law Review* 84

Barclay, G. C. (1993), The Criminal Justice System in England and Wales, London: Home Office

Beale, J. H. Jr. (1903), "Retreat from a Murderous Assault", 16 *Harvard Law Review* 567

Becker, G. S. (1968), "Crime and Punishment: an Economic Approach", 76 *Journal of Political Economy* 169

Bentham, J. (1789), *An Introduction to the Principles of Morals and Legislation*, reprinted 1982 (J. H. Burns and H. L. A. Hart, (eds.)), London: Methuen

Bergman, D. (2000), *The Case for Corporate Responsibility: Corporate Violence and the Criminal Justice System*, London: Disaster Action

Beyleveld, D. (1980), *A Bibliography on General Deterrence Research*, London: Saxon House

Bibbings, L. and Alldridge, P. (1993), "Sexual Expression, Body Alteration, and the Defence of Consent", 20 *Journal of Law and Society* 356

Blackspot Construction (1988), Health and Safety Executive, *Blackspot Construction*, London: HMSO

Blom-Cooper, L. and Morris, T. (1999), "'Life' Until Death: Interpretation of Section 1(1) of the Murder (Abolition of the Death Penalty) Act 1965", *Criminal Law Review* 899

Brady, S. R. and Tarling, R. (1981), *Taking Offenders Out of Circulation*, Home Office Research Study No. 64, London: HMSO

Brennan, F. (1999), "Racially Motivated Crime: the Response of the Criminal Justice System", *Criminal Law Review* 17

Brett, P. (1963), *An Inquiry into Criminal Guilt*, London: Sweet & Maxwell

British Crime Survey (2000), Kershaw, C. *et al.*, *The 2000 British Crime Survey: England and Wales*, London: Home Office

British Medical Journal (2000), "News: Surgeon Amputated Healthy Legs" *British Medical Journal*, 320:332 (February 5)

Buchanan, A. and Virgo, G. (1999), "Duress and Mental Abnormality", *Criminal Law Review* 517

Butler Committee (1975), *Report of the Committee on Mentally Abnormal Offenders*, Cmnd 6244, London: HMSO

Buxton, R. (2000), "The Human Rights Act and the Substantive Criminal Law", *Criminal Law Review* 331

Carlen, P. (1980), "Radical Criminology, Penal Politics and the Rule of Law" in P. Carlen and M. Collison (eds.), *Radical Issues in Criminology*, New Jersey: Barnes & Noble

Chamallas, M. (1988), "Consent, Equality and the Legal Control of Sexual Conduct", 61 *South California Law Review* 777

Clarkson, C. M. V. (2000), "Context and Culpability in Involuntary Manslaughter: Principle or Instinct?" in A. Ashworth and B. Mitchell (eds.), *Rethinking English Homicide Law*, Oxford: Oxford University Press

Clarkson, C. M. V. *et al.* (1994), Clarkson, C. M. V., Cretney, A., Davis, G. and Shepherd, J., "Assaults: The Relationship between Seriousness, Criminalisation and Punishment", *Criminal Law Review* 4

Coffee, J. C. Jr.(1981), "'No Soul to Damn: No Body to Kick': An Unscandalized Inquiry into the Problems of Corporate Punishment", 79 *Michigan Law Review* 397

Cretney, A. *et al.*, (1994), Cretney, A., Davis, G., Clarkson, C. M. V. and Shepherd, J., "Criminalizing Assault: The Failure of the 'Offence against Society' Model", 34 *British Journal of Criminology* 15

Cretney, A. and Davis, G. (1995), *Punishing Violence*, London: Routledge

Cretney, A. and Davis, G. (1997), "The Significance of Compellability in the Prosecution of Domestic Assault", 37 *British Journal of Criminology* 75

Criminal Statistics (1998), *Criminal Statistics: England and Wales 1998* (1999)

Criminal Statistics (1999), *Criminal Statistics: England and Wales 1999* (2000), London: HMSO

Crown Prosecution Service (2000), *Annual Report 1999–2000*, London: The Stationery Office

Crown Prosecution Service (1996), *Offences Against the Person Charging Standard: Agreed by the Police and The Crown Prosecution Service*, London: CPS

Dell, S. (1984), *Murder into Manslaughter*, London: Institute of Psychiatry

Devlin, P. (1959), "Morals and the Criminal Law", 45 *Proceedings of the British Academy* 136, reprinted in P. Devlin, *The Enforcement of Morals*, 1965, Oxford University Press

Diamond, A. S. (1950), *Primitive Law*, 2nd ed., London: Longman

Digest 4 (1999), Barclay, G. C. and C. Tavares, *Information on the Criminal Justice System in England and Wales: Digest 4*. London: Home Office

Doegar, R. C. (1998), "Strict Liability in Criminal Law and Larsonneur Reassessed", *Criminal Law Review* 791

Doob, A. (1995), "The United States Sentencing Commission Guidelines: If you don't know where you are going, you might not get there", in C. M. V. Clarkson and R. Morgan (eds.), *The Politics of Sentencing Reform*, Oxford: Oxford University Press

d'Orbán, P. T, (1979), "Women Who Kill Their Children", 134 *British Journal of Psychiatry* 560

Dressler, J. (1999), "Battered Women Who Kill Their Sleeping Tormenters" in S. Shute and A.P. Simester, *Criminal Law: The General Part*, Oxford: Oxford University Press (forthcoming)

Dripps, D. A. (1992), "Beyond Rape: An Essay on the Difference Between the Presence of Force and the Absence of Consent", 92 *Columbia Law Review* 1780

Duff, R. A. (1980), "Recklessness", *Criminal Law Review* 282

Duff, R. A. (1990), *Intention, Agency and Criminal Liability*, Oxford: Basil Blackwell

Duff, R. A. (1996), *Criminal Attempts*, Oxford: Clarendon Press

Duff, R. A. (1998), "Law, Language and Community: Some Preconditions of Criminal Liability" 18 *Oxford Journal of Legal Studies* 189

Dunford, L and Ridley, A (1996), "No Soul to be Damned, No Body to be Kicked: Responsibility, Blame and Corporate Punishment" 24 *International Journal of Society and Law* 1

Durkheim, E. (1964), *The Division of Labour in Society*, New York: Free Press

Editorial, *Criminal Law Review* (2000), *Criminal Law Review* 629

Ehrlich, I. (1973), "Participation in Illegitimate Activities: a Theoretical and Empirical Investigation", 81 *Journal of Political Economy* 521

Emmerson, B. and Ashworth, A. (1999), *Human Rights in Criminal Proceedings*, London: Sweet and Maxwell

Executive Advisory Committee on Sentencing in New York (1979), *Crime and Punishment in New York: An Inquiry into Sentencing and the Criminal Justice System*, Report to Governor Hugh L. Carey

Feinberg, J. (1965), "The Expressive Function of Punishment", 49 *The Monist* 397

Feinberg, J. (1984), *Harm to Others* (*The Moral Limits of the Criminal Law*, vol.1), New York: Oxford University Press

Feinberg, J. (1985), *Offense to Others* (*The Moral Limits of the Criminal Law*, vol.2), New York: Oxford University Press

Fletcher, G. P. (1978), *Rethinking Criminal Law*, Boston: Little, Brown & Co.

Fletcher, G. P. (1998), *Basic Concepts of Criminal Law*, Oxford: Oxford University Press

Floud Committee (1981), *Dangerousness and Criminal Justice*, London: Heinemann

Foster, Sir M. (1762), *Crown Law*, Reprinted 1982, Oxford: Professional Books

Frase, R. (1995), "Sentencing Guidelines in Minnesota and Other American States: A Progress Report", in C. M. V. Clarkson and R. Morgan (eds), *The Politics of Sentencing Reform*, Oxford: Oxford University Press

Fraser, D. (2000), "A Critique of Research Related to 'What Works' in Reducing Offending", 164 *Justice of the Peace* 356

Gardner, J. (1994), "Rationality and the Rule of Law in Offences against the Person" *Cambridge Law Journal* 502

Gardner, J. (1998), "On the General Part of the Criminal Law", in A. Duff (ed.), *Philosophy and the Criminal Law: Principles and Critique*, Cambridge: Cambridge University Press

Gardner, J. and Shute, S. (2000), "The Wrongness of Rape" in J.Horder (ed.), *Oxford Essays in Jurisprudence*, 4th Series, Oxford: Oxford University Press

Genders, E. (1999), "Reform of the Offences Against the Person Act: Lessons from the Law in Action", *Criminal Law Review* 689

Glazebrook, P. R. (1991), "Thief or Swindler: Who Cares?" *Cambridge Law Journal* 389

Gordon, G. H. (1978), *Criminal Law*, 2nd ed., Edinburgh: W. Green

Grace, S., Lloyd, C. and Smith, L. (1992), *Rape: From Recording to Conviction*, Home Office Research and Planning Unit Paper 71, London: HMSO

Graham, J. and Bowling, B. (1995), *Young People and Crime*, Home Office Research Study No. 145, London: Home Office

Greenwood, P. W. (1982), *Selective Incapacitation*, Santa Monica, CA.: Rand Corporation

Greer, S. (1994), "Miscarriages of Criminal Justice Reconsidered", 57 *Modern Law Review* 58

Gross, H. (1979), *A Theory of Criminal Justice*, New York: Oxford University Press

Guardian (1993), *The Guardian*, August 28, 1993

Gunningham, N. (1987), "Negotiated Non-Compliance: A Case Study of Regulatory Failure", 9 *Law and Policy* 69

Hart, H. L. A. (1959), "Immorality and Treason" 62 *Listener* 162

Hart, H. L. A. (1968), *Punishment and Responsibility*, Oxford: Oxford University Press

Hart, H. L. A. and Honoré, T. (1985), *Causation in the Law*, 2nd ed., Oxford: Oxford University Press

Health and Safety Commission (1998), *Health and Safety Statistics 1997/98*, Norwich: HSE Books

Henderson, L. (1992), "Rape and Responsibility", 11 *Law and Philosophy* 127

Hobbes, T. (1651), *Leviathan*, London: Andrew Crooks (Republished: *Leviathan/Thomas Hobbes*; edited with an introduction by C.B. Macpherson, Hammondsworth: Penguin Books (1968)

Holmes, O. W. (1881), *The Common Law*, Boston: Little, Brown & Co.

Home Office (1998a), *Violence: Reforming the Offences against the Person Act 1961*, Consultation Document, London: Home Office

Home Office (1998b), Sutton M., *Handling Stolen Goods and Theft: A Market Reduction Approach*, Home Office Research Study No.178, London: Home Office

Home Office (2000), *Reforming the Law on Involuntary Manslaughter: The Government's Proposals*, London: Home Office

Home Office White Paper (1900), *Crime, Justice and Protecting the Public* Cm.965, London: Home Office

Home Office Research Study (2000), *Economic and Social Costs of Crime*, No. 217, London: Home Office

Horder, J. (1994a), "Occupying the Moral High Ground? The Law Commission on Duress", *Criminal Law Review* 334

Horder, J. (1994b), "Rethinking Non-Fatal Offences against the Person" 14 *Oxford Journal of Legal Studies* 335

Horder, J. (1995), "A Critique of the Correspondence Principle in Criminal Law" *Criminal Law Review* 759

Horder, J. (1996), "Crimes of Ulterior Intent", in A. P. Simester and A. T. H. Smith (eds.), *Harm and Culpability*, Oxford: Clarendon Press

Horder, J. (1998), "Self-Defence, Necessity and Duress: Understanding the Relationship", XI *The Canadian Journal of Law and Jurisprudence* 143

Hough, M. and Roberts, J. (1998), *Attitudes to Punishment: Findings from the British Crime Survey*, Home Office Research Study No.179, London: Home Office

House of Lords (1989) Report of the Select Committee, *Murder and Life Imprisonment* (1988–89, HL Paper 78) London: HMSO

Husak, D. (1998), "Does Criminal Liability Require an Act?" in A. Duff (ed.), *Philosophy and the Criminal Law: Principles and Critique*, Cambridge: Cambridge University Press

Independent (1994), *Independent*, December 9, 1994

Jacobs, J. and Potter, K. (1998), *Hate Crimes: Criminal Law and Identity Politics*, Oxford: Oxford University Press

James Committee (1975), *Report of the Committee on the Distribution of Criminal Business Between the Crown Court and Magistrates' Courts*, Cmnd 6323, London: HMSO

Justice (1980), *Breaking the Rules*, London: Justice

Kadish, S. (1967), "The Crisis of Overcriminalisation", 374 *Annals* 157

Kadish, S. (1976), "Respect for Life and Regard for Rights in the Criminal Law", 64 *California Law Review* 871

Kaufmann, H. (1970), "Legality and Harmfulness of a Bystander's Failure to Intervene as Determinants of Moral Judgment", in J. Macaulay and L. Berkowitz (eds.), *Altruism and Helping Behaviour: Social Psychological Studies of Some Antecedents and Consequences*, London: Academic Press

Lacey, N. (2000), "Partial Defences to Homicide: Question of Power and Principle in Imperfect and Less Perfect Worlds ...", in A. Ashworth and B. Mitchell (eds.), *Rethinking English Homicide Law*, Oxford: Oxford University Press

LaFave. W. R. and Scott, A. W. (1986), *Criminal Law*, 2nd ed., New York: West Publishing Co

Lanham, D. (1976), "Larsonneur Revisited", *Criminal Law Review* 276

Lanham, D. (1999), "Danger Down Under", *Criminal Law Review* 960

Law Commission (1973), Law Commission Working Paper No.50, *Inchoate Offences: Conspiracy, Attempt and Incitement*, London: HMSO

Law Commission (1980), Law Commission Working Paper No.102, *Attempt, and Impossibility in Relation to Attempt, Conspiracy and Incitement*, London: HMSO

Law Commission (1989), *A Criminal Code for England and Wales*, Law Commission No. 177, London: HMSO

Law Commission (1993a), Law Commission Consultation Paper No. 131, *Assisting and Encouraging Crime*, London: HMSO

Law Commission (1993b), Law Commission No. 218, *Offences against the Person and General Principles*, London: HMSO

Law Commission (1993c), Law Commission Consultation Paper No. 127, *Intoxication and Criminal Liability*, London: HMSO

Law Commission (1994), Law Commission Consultation Paper No. 135, *Involuntary Manslaughter*, London: HMSO

Law Commission (1995), Law Commission No. 229, *Intoxication and Criminal Liability*, London: HMSO

Law Commission (1995), *Consent in the Criminal Law*, Consultation Paper No.139, London: HMSO

Law Commission (1996), *Legislating the Criminal Code: Involuntary Manslaughter*, Report No.237, London: HMSO

Law Commission (1999), *Fraud and Deception*, Consultation Paper No.155, London: HMSO

Leigh, L. H. (1982), *Strict and Vicarious Liability*, London: Sweet and Maxwell

Lord Chancellor's Department (1998), Lord Chancellor's Department (DTI and DETR), *The Key to Easier Home Buying and Selling, Consultation Paper*, London: HMSO

Lloyd-Bostock, S. (1979), "The Ordinary Man and the Psychology of Attributing Causes and Responsibility" 42 *Modern Law Review* 143

McColgan, A. (1993), "In Defence of Battered Women Who Kill", 13 *Oxford Journal of Legal Studies* 508

Mackay, R. D. (1993), "The Consequences of Killing Very Young Children", *Criminal Law Review* 21

Mackay, R. D. and Kearns, G. (1999), "More Fact(s) about the Insanity Defence", *Criminal Law Review* 714

Mackay, R. D. (2000), "Diminished Responsibility and Mentally Disordered Killers" in A. Ashworth and B. Mitchell (eds.), *Rethinking English Homicide Law*, Oxford: Oxford University Press

MacKinnon , C. (1989), *Towards a Feminist Theory of the State*, Cambridge: Harvard University Press

Maguire, M. (1980), "The Impact of Burglary upon Victims", 20 *British Journal of Criminology* 261

Maier-Katkin, D. and Ogle, R. (1993), "A Rationale for Infanticide Laws", *Criminal Law Review* 903

Martinson, R. (1974), "What Works? Questions and Answers about Prison Reform", 22 *Public Interest*, Spring

Martinson, R. (1976), *Rehabilitation, Recidivism and Research*, London: National Council on Crime and Delinquency

Maxfield, M. (1984), "Fear of Crime in England and Wales", Home Office Research Study No.78, London: HMSO

Mill, J. S. (1859), *On Liberty*, reprinted in J. Gray, *On Liberty and other Essays*, 1991, Oxford: University Press

Minnesota Guidelines Report (1980), Minnesota Sentencing Guidelines Commission, *Report to the Legislature*, 2–3 (January 1)

Model Penal Code (1953), American Law Institute, *Model Penal Code, Proposed Official Draft*

Moore, M. (1985), "Causation and Excuses", *California Law Review* 1091

Moore, M. S. (1993), *Act and Crime: The Philosophy of Action and its Implications for the Criminal Law*, Oxford: Clarendon Press

Morgan, N. (1983), "Non-custodial Penal Sanctions in England and Wales: a New Utopia?" 22 *Howard Journal* 148

Morris, N. (1982), *Madness and the Criminal Law*, Chicago: University of Chicago Press

Morris, N. and Hawkins, G. (1977), *Letter to the President on Crime Control*, Chicago: University of Chicago Press

Nagin, D. S. (1998), "Criminal Deterrence Research at the Outset of the Twenty-first Century", 23 *Crime and Justice: A Review of Research* 51–91

Nixon, R. (1970), *New York Times*, 25 October, s.1, p.71

Norrie, A. (1993), *Crime, Reason and History*, London: Weidenfeld & Nicolson

Norrie, A. (1999), "After *Woollin*", *Criminal Law Review* 532

O'Donovan, K. (1991), "Defences for Battered Women who Kill", 18 *Journal of Law and Society* 219

Posner, R. A. (1985), "An Economic Theory of the Criminal Law", 85 *Columbia Law Review* 1193

Queen's Bench Foundation (1976), *Rape—Prevention and Resistance*, San Francisco

Richardson, G. (1987), "Strict Liability for Regulatory Crime: The Empirical Research", *Criminal Law Review* 295

Robinson, P. (1982), "Criminal Law Defences: as Systematic Analysis", 82 *Columbia Law Review* 199

Robinson, P. (1997), *Structure and Function in Criminal Law*, Oxford: Clarendon Press

Robinson, P.H. and Darley, J.M. (1998), "Objectivist Versus Subjectivist Views of Criminality: A Study in the Role of Social Science in Criminal Law Theory", *Oxford Journal of Legal Studies* 409

Rothman, D. (1981), "Doing time: Days, Months and Years in the Criminal Justice System" in H. Gross and A. von Hirsch (eds.), *Sentencing*, New York: Oxford University Press

Royal Commission on Capital Punishment (1953), *Report of the Royal Commission on Capital Punishment*, Cmd 8932, London: HMSO

Rumney, P. (1999), "When Rape Isn't Rape: Court of Appeal Sentencing Practice in Cases of Marital and Relationship Rape", 19 *Oxford Journal of Legal Studies* 243

Sayre, F. B. (1932), "Mens Rea", 45 *Harvard Law Review* 974

Schulhofer, S. J. (1974), "Harm and Punishment: a Critique of Emphasis on Results of Conduct in the Criminal Law", 122 *University of Pennsylvania Law Review* 1497

Schulhofer, S. J. (1985), "Is There an Economic Theory of Crime?", *Nomos XXVII: Criminal Justice*, Part IV

Sentencing Advisory Panel (2000), sentencing-advisory-panel.gov.uk/info.htm

Sexual Offences Review (2000), *Setting the Boundaries: Reforming the Law on Sex Offences*, London: Home Office

Sheen Report (1988), Department of Transport, *The Merchant Shipping Act 1894, M.V. Herald of Free Enterprise*, Report of Court No. 8074, London: HMSO

Shute, S. and Horder, J. (1993), "Thieving and Deceiving: What is the Difference?", 56 *Modern Law Review* 548

Simester A.P, (1998), "On the So-Called Requirement of Voluntary Action", (1998) 1 *Buffalo Criminal Law Review* 403

Smart, C. (1989), *Feminism and the Power of Law*, London and New York: Routledge

Smith, A. T. H. (1994), *Property Offences*, London: Sweet and Maxwell

Smith, J.C. (1981), Comment to *R. v. Caldwell*, *Criminal Law Review* 393

Smith, J. C. (1983), Comment to *R. v. Sullivan*, *Criminal Law Review* 257

Smith, (1998), Comment on *R. v. Powell and Daniels; English Criminal Law Review* 49

Smith, K. J. M. (1999), "Duress and Steadfastness: In Pursuit of the Unintelligible", *Criminal Law Review* 363

Snyman, C.R. (1995) *Criminal Law*, 3rd ed., Durban: Butterworths

Spencer , J. R. (1985), "Handling, Theft and the *Mala Fide* Purchaser", *Criminal Law Review* 92

Sullivan, G. R. (1996), "Making Excuses", in A. P. Simester and A. T. H. Smith (eds.), *Harm and Culpability*, Oxford: Clarendon Press

Sutherland, P. J. and Gearty, C. A. (1992), "Insanity and the European Court of Human Rights", *Criminal Law Review* 418

Tempkin, J. (2000), "Literature Review of Research into Rape and Sexual Assault", in Home Office, *Setting the Boundaries: Reforming the Law on Sexual Offences,* vol.2, Supporting Evidence, London: Home Office Communication Directorate

Tjaden et al., (1998): Tjaden, P. and Thoennes, N., "Stalking in America: Findings from the National Violence Against Women Survey", Washington DC: U.S. Department of Justice, National Institute of Justice Centers for Disease Control and Prevention, 1998, cited in F. Farnham, D. James and P. Cattrell, "Association Between Violence, Psychosis and Relationship to Victim in Stalkers", 355 *The Lancet* January 15, 2000

Twentieth Century Fund Task Force (1976), *Fair and Certain Punishment*, New York: McGraw-Hill Book Company

von Hirsch, A. (1976), *Doing Justice, The Choice of Punishments* (Report of the Committee for the Study of Incarceration), New York: Hill & Wang von Hirsch, A. (1986), "Deservedness and Dangerousness in Sentencing Policy", *Criminal Law Review* 79

von Hirsch, A. (1996), "Extending the Harm Principle: 'Remote' Harm and Fair Imputation", in A. P. Simester and A. T. H. Smith (eds.), *Harm and Culpability*, Oxford: Clarendon Press

von Hirsch, A. and Jareborg, N. (1991), "Gauging Criminal Harm: A Living-Standard Analysis", 11 *Oxford Journal of Legal Studies* 1

von Hirsch, A. et al.(1999), von Hirsch, A., Bottoms, A. E., Burney, E., Wikstrom, P-O., *Criminal Deterrence and Sentence Severity: An Analysis of Recent Research*, Oxford: Hart Publishing

Walker, N. (1968), *Crime and Insanity in England, Vol. 1: The Historical Perspective*, Edinburgh: Edinburgh University Press

Walker, N. (1985), *Sentencing Theory, Law and Practice*, London: Butterworths

Walker, N. and C. Marsh (1984), "Do Sentences Affect Public Disapproval?" 24 *British Journal of Criminology* 27

Wasik, M. (1979), "*Mens Rea*, Motive and the Problem of "Dishonesty" in the Law of Theft", *Criminal Law Review* 543

Wells, C. (1989), "Manslaughter and Corporate Crime" 139 *New Law Journal* 931

West, D. J. (1965), *Murder Followed by Suicide*, London: Heinemann

Wilczynski, A. and Morris, A. (1993), "Parents Who Kill Their Children", *Criminal Law Review* 31

Will, G. F. (1985), "Let Us Now Praise Anger", *Newsweek*, 14 January

Willcock, H. D. and J. Stokes (1968), *Deterrents to Crime among Youths of 15 to 21*, London: Government Social Survey Report, No.SS 356

Williams, G. (1978), *Textbook of Criminal Law*, 1st ed., London: Stevens & Sons

Williams, G. (1981), "Recklessness Redefined", *Cambridge Law Journal* 252

Williams, G. (1983), *Textbook of Criminal Law*, 2nd ed., London: Stevens & Sons

Wilson, (1999), "Doctrinal Rationality after *Woollin*", 62 *Modern Law Review* 448

Wolfenden Committee (1957), *Report of the Committee on Homosexual Offences and Prostitution*, Cmd 247, London: HMSO

Wright, R. T. and S. H. Deckner (1994), *Burglars on the Job: Streetlife and Residential Break-ins*, Boston, Mass.: Northwestern University Press

Yale Law Journal (1980), Note, "Property Theft Enforcement and the Criminal Secondary Purchaser of Stolen Goods", 89 *Yale Law Journal* 1225

Yeo, (2000), "Killing in Defence of Property" 150 *New Law Journal* 730

TABLE OF CASES

TABLE OF STATUTES

INDEX